BELOW THE RADAR

How Silence Can Save Civil Rights

ALISON L. GASH

OXFORD
UNIVERSITY PRESS

OXFORD
UNIVERSITY PRESS

Oxford University Press is a department of the University of
Oxford. It furthers the University's objective of excellence in research,
scholarship, and education by publishing worldwide.

Oxford   New York

Auckland   Cape Town   Dar es Salaam   Hong Kong   Karachi
Kuala Lumpur   Madrid   Melbourne   Mexico City   Nairobi
New Delhi   Shanghai   Taipei   Toronto

With offices in

Argentina   Austria   Brazil   Chile   Czech Republic   France   Greece
Guatemala   Hungary   Italy   Japan   Poland   Portugal   Singapore
South Korea   Switzerland   Thailand   Turkey   Ukraine   Vietnam

Oxford is a registered trademark of Oxford University Press
in the UK and certain other countries.

Published in the United States of America by
Oxford University Press
198 Madison Avenue, New York, NY 10016

Library of Congress Cataloging-in-Publication Data
Gash, Alison L., author.
Below the radar : how silence can save civil rights / Alison L. Gash.
p. cm.
Includes bibliographical references.
ISBN 978–0–19–020115–9 (hardback : alk. paper)   1. Parent and child—United States.
2. Gay parents—Legal status, laws, etc.—United States.   3. Custody of children—United States.
4. Group homes for people with mental disabilities—United States.   5. People with mental
disabilities—Housing—United States.   6. Civil rights—United States.   I. Title.
KF547.G39 2015
323.0973—dc23
2014032885

1 3 5 7 9 8 6 4 2
Printed in the United States of America
on acid-free paper

For Pop-Pop: "We did it."

Contents

List of Figures

List of Tables

List of Cases

Adar v. Smith, 639 F.3d 146 (5ᵗʰ Cir. 2011)
Baehr v. Lewin, 74 Haw. 530 (1993)
Baker v. Nelson, 291 Minn. 310 (1971)
Baker v. Vermont, 744 A.2d 864 (Vt. 1999)
Baxter v. City of Belleville 720 F. Supp. 720 (S.D. Ill. 1989)
Boseman v. Jarrell, 704 S.E.2d 494 (N.C. 2010)
Bottoms v. Bottoms, No. 2157-96-2 (Va. Ct. App. July 29, 1997).
Bowers v. Hardwick, 478 U.S. 186 (1986)
Brown v. Board of Education, 347 U.S. 483 (1954)
Chambers v. Chambers, 2002 WL 1940145, No. CN00-09493. (Del. Fam. Ct., February 5, 2002)
City of Cleburne v. Cleburne Living Center, 473 US 432 (1985)
City of Edmonds v. Oxford House, Inc., 514 US 725 (1995)
Civil Rights Cases, 109 U.S. 3 (1883).
Cole v. Arkansas, 380 S.W. 3d. 429 (2011)
Commonwealth ex rel and Bachman v. Bradley, 171 Pa. Super. 587 (1952).
Conaway v. Deane, No. 44 (Court of Appeals of Maryland, September 18, 2007)
DeBoer v. Snyder Civil Action No. 12-cv-10285, U.S. District Court, Eastern District of Michigan, July 1, 2013
Downey v. Muffley, 767 N.E.2d 1014 (Ind. Ct. App. 2002)
Dr. Gertrude A. Barber Center, Inc. v. Peters Township, 273 F. Supp. 2nd 643 (2003).
Edmonds v. Washington State Building Code Council, 18 F. 3d 802 (1994)
Elisa B. v. Superior Court, 33 Cal.Rptr.3d 46 (2005)
Elliott v. City of Athens 960 F. 2d 975 (1992)
Embry v. Ryan 11 So. 3d. 408 (2009)
E.N.O. v. L.M.M., 429 Mass. 824, 711 N.E.2d 886, cert. denied, 528 U.S. 1005 (1999)

Acknowledgments

THIS BOOK IS about subterranean advocacy—the below-the-radar, behind-the-scene efforts that have (by design) gone unnoticed and unsung but yet are a critical component of the civil rights landscape. As with any research on stealth advocacy, this book would not exist were it not for the trust and generosity of the tireless individuals and organizations who work on behalf of disenfranchised communities—in this case to help them keep their families and their homes. Without their willingness to share their insights and experiences, I would still be sorting through colorful guesses and suppositions. Thank you so much for taking a leap of faith and confiding in me. Neither would this book have the richness of detail were it not for the invaluable contributions of the many other advocates, activists, and consultants who helped me capture the broader backdrop of high-visibility advocacy and opposition politics. I am grateful for your time and your efforts to set me straight.

For those in particular who work to advance LGBT rights, when I started this book there was no such thing as same-sex marriage. As I write these acknowledgments it is a foregone conclusion. Your work has transformed our lives.

Of course, without the dogged support and critical eye of colleagues and mentors, this book would consist of little more than a set of loosely organized (albeit compelling) facts, figures, and anecdotes. Paul Pierson, Robert Kagan, and Gordon Silverstein each championed and challenged my interest in backlash and pushed me to probe the use of low-visibility advocacy. They supplied me with the intellectual space to explore low-visibility advocacy efforts and the critical feedback to keep me on track. Nelson Polsby provided me respite from my own anxieties. With "toadstools," tall tales, and tea he lifted my spirits, cleared my head, and sent me back to work. Daniel Tichenor provided line-by-line advice and day-by-day support. He has been equal parts coach, agent, and friend. Most of the breakthroughs for the book—both substantive and otherwise—came on the heels of strategy sessions either devised or attended by Dan. Gerald Berk kept my eyes on the forest when I was stuck in the trees. His wisdom (and humor) helped me overcome those treacherous moments of doubt and deviation. Joe Lowndes, Priscilla Yamin, Daniel HoSang, and David Steinberg listened to my ruminations and offered an unbiased eye when my own had failed. Melissa Michaux and David Gutterman sat through multiple presentations on various chapters and offered invaluable tips for refining and framing many of the book's more critical empirical contributions. Out of sheer kindness and generosity Lawrence Baum, Steve Wasby, Michael Klarman, and Shep Melnick read versions of the chapters (some in their infancy), offered crucial feedback, and introduced me to other scholars who share my interests in backlash. I also want to extend my gratitude to John Relman for showing me the ropes of fair housing litigation early on in my career and igniting my interest in the group home debate. His interest in my work and willingness to introduce me to other practitioners in the field paved the way for my case study on group home siting battles.

They say it takes a village to raise a child—the same holds true for a book. Sometimes the best thinking comes from the combined talent and expertise of scholars. Not many of us have the chance to collect our idols in one room and have them focus on our work, but thanks to Daniel Tichenor's facilitation and Priscilla Southwell's support, I had the chance to pick the brains of some of the stars in my field. Jeb Barnes, Shep Melnick, and Carolyn Nestor Long each took a full day out of their busy schedules to travel to Eugene and workshop the manuscript. In addition to reading a complete draft of the manuscript, they provided me with detailed verbal and written feedback in the context of a book scrub. From big-picture changes to empirical alterations, their combined feedback—along with the insights of other faculty in attendance—launched a pivotal turning point in the manuscript's evolution. I owe them a debt of gratitude.

My students have always been a source of inspiration and motivation. At least two of my courses have been fashioned off of topics explored in the manuscript. I have been lucky enough to have students in these courses who were intellectually curious and creative. Their keen observations and probing questions forced me to refine my own assumptions about low-visibility advocacy. I am particularly thankful for the handful of students who went the extra mile, either as research assistants or as interested observers, and helped me edit chapter drafts, compile interview data, and collect sources. Lisa Beard, Joshua Ripley, Jessica McGrath, Meian Chen, and Michael Weinerman, thank you so much for your commitment and contribution. And a special thanks to Carl Windrup, who has become a valued colleague and friend. Carl took time away from his studies at graduate school to provide a last-minute but exhaustive read of my manuscript in the weeks before production. If the manuscript is typo-free it is largely because of Carl's efforts.

My deepest gratitude goes to Steve Teles and David McBride, They each saw the project's potential early on and went far beyond the duties of most editors. Well before the book project was completed Steve helped me make the transition from research project to manuscript and, finally, to a published book. It is not easy to write a compelling or accessible narrative while advancing intellectual innovations. If I have achieved this, it is because Steve's early, ongoing, and direct feedback provided me with exactly the right tools to articulate my vision. But Steve's support went well beyond editing and feedback. He worked behind the scenes to introduce me to others in the field whose interests dovetailed with my own and to journalists and magazine editors who had an interest in featuring my work on low-visibility advocacy.

It is through Steve that I met Paul Glastris and the staff at *Washington Monthly*. Paul and his staff provided a forum for me to present my findings and spent far too many hours than they had available helping me market the story to a popular audience.

I would also like to thank the several copy editors who reviewed each word, comma, and hyphen to make my arguments shine and the reviewers who were commissioned by Oxford University Press to evaluate and determine the fate of the manuscript. Their thoughtful and critical remarks prompted another significant shift in its framing. They recognized the book's contribution and helped me to see it to completion.

On a personal note, I want to thank my family and friends for keeping me calm when things were at their most chaotic. David Hopkins, Darshan Goux, and Angelo Gonzales were my collective voices of reason. They each read far too many early and ugly drafts, fielded my obsessions, provided sustenance for long writing binges, and still saw fit to be my friends. Brian Gross was my statistics guru and coffee mate. He operated as my empirical sounding board, even when he had far more important things to do, and shared my preference for late-night study sessions. Luke Harris provided the first crucial ingredient to any rising scholar—the passion for learning. I am so glad to have your friendship and to call you family. Your mentorship and guidance helped me find my voice. Raizie and Michael Axman are in-laws and grandparents extraordinaire. You clocked in far too many Bubbie and Zaida hours while I slogged through drafts of the manuscript, feeding my stomach and my ego during particularly hectic moments. Thank you seems insufficient to express how grateful I am for your help and support. To my parents Susan and John Schmehl—you pushed me to be my own person and humored my rants. Thank you so much for your unbridled encouragement and love and your steadfast belief (despite indications to the contrary) that I would achieve my dreams. Let this book serve as testament to your laudable parenting skills (especially during the middle school years). To Stephanie—you accommodated my long hours and dark moods with humor and sensitivity and, for some reason, you are still here to share in this accomplishment. I am not sure if that makes you a saint or a glutton for punishment but in either case I am so thankful for your patience and willingness to see this through and cheer me on. And, last, to my children, Eliza and Matias—you are my gifts, my miracles, and my inspiration.

I

Introduction

"WE WERE JUST two guys in love who wanted to get married," recalls Joseph Melillo of his attempt to obtain a wedding license in 1991 from a county clerk in Hawaii. "It's unfortunate it's all gotten so political."[1] But intentions aside, Melillo's grievance provoked a hailstorm of opposition toward and public debate about legalizing same-sex unions. When Melillo, his partner, and two other same-sex couples—each of whom had been denied wedding licenses by state clerks—petitioned Hawaii's highest court for redress, they provided an already brewing anti-gay movement with a rallying point. Where previous courts had been unwilling to consider arguments advanced by gays and lesbians (since the early 1970s) that marriage should be extended to same-sex couples, the Hawaii Supreme Court validated their claims. It seemed that Hawaii was on the verge of becoming the first state to permit same-sex couples to marry.

By the time the court handed down its 1993 decision in *Baehr v. Lewin*, arguing that the Hawaii constitution's equal protection clause included protections for gays and lesbians to marry, conservatives stood at the ready to launch a movement to limit marriage to heterosexual couples. In 1994 Hawaii's governor signed into law a bill outlawing same-sex marriage and criticizing the court for attempting to "encroach upon the legislature's law-making function."[2] By 1995 legislators in Utah, Alaska, and South Dakota had introduced measures to ban same-sex marriage—arguing that it would violate "what has been the sanctity of families for the last 100 years."[3] The following year, at least thirty states were considering similar legislation and Congress introduced, passed, and received presidential approval (with unprecedented speed) for the Defense of Marriage Act (DOMA)—barring same-sex marriage at the federal level and granting states the ability to pass state-level bans. Supporters of DOMA claimed that nothing less than our foundations of democracy and family were at stake if "a single judge in Hawaii [could] redefine the scope of legislation throughout the other forty-nine states."[4] Argued Gary Bauer:

> We are being asked to pretend that somehow two men could replace a mother in a child's life or that two women could take the place of a father and that it won't make any difference to children.[5]

Buttressed by federal support, backlash to marriage equality gained momentum. By 1998, just five short years after the Hawaii Supreme Court ventured toward legalizing marriage equality for same-sex couples, twenty-nine states had implemented statutory or constitutional bans on same-sex marriage.[6] The fate of marriage equality had become one of the most hotly contested issues of the early twenty-first century—capturing the attention of school boards, church groups, commentators, Hollywood writers, Oval Office contenders, sitting presidents, and the Supreme Court. And although we know the story will likely have a happy ending—marriage equality has gained an unbeatable momentum—the journey there has been dominated by hostile protests and potshots from scores of demagogues, "average Joes," and political novices hoping to make a name for themselves.

In many ways this backlash was predictable: a minority group receives help from the courts, and the majority fights back with swift recriminations. Yet consider the similarly groundbreaking, but much more quietly received, decisions supporting same-sex parenting issued during the same year. Amidst the fury over Hawaii's movement toward marriage equality, judges in Vermont and Massachusetts issued two equally significant—but much less publicly contested—decisions validating same-sex families, dealing another blow to right-wing conceptions of family values. In what had become almost routine in some jurisdictions, a lesbian couple in each state asked a judge to allow one woman in the couple to adopt her partner's biological child, without requiring, as with traditional adoptions, the biological mother to relinquish her rights. In other words, they were asking the courts to accept the notion that one child could be jointly raised by two mothers (or two fathers). Although these couples were not entitled to the spousal exception inherent in most adoption statutes, which would have waived any biological parent stipulation, judges argued that requiring the birth parent in these couples to terminate her rights was "irrational, unreasonable, [and] absurd" and did not serve the "best interests of the child."[7] By validating these unorthodox adoptions, judges and advocates were more directly challenging values at the heart of the anti-gay rights movement—that children require both a mother and a father.

To be sure, not all courts at this time were amenable to gays and lesbians raising children or willing to use their discretion to grant second-parent adoptions. In the same year as the landmark decisions in Hawaii, Vermont, and Massachusetts, a judge in Virginia removed a child from his mother's home and awarded custody to the child's grandmother because of his mother's sexual orientation. The judge argued that her "immoral" and "illegal" conduct rendered her unfit to raise her two-year-old.[8] An Iowa court argued similarly, in the midst of determining custody, that a mother's lesbian relationship "was disruptive to the continued good relationship between the two children and both parents."[9] In 1994, when faced with a set of facts paralleling those presented in Vermont and Massachusetts, the Wisconsin Supreme Court declined to grant a lesbian couple co-parent status.[10]

However, despite widespread opposition to same-sex families, the parenting cases in Vermont and Massachusetts (and the many that followed them) inspired little public acrimony. While the country feuded over the merits and pitfalls of legalizing same-sex unions and members of Congress referred to President Clinton's choice for assistant secretary of HUD, Roberta Achtenberg, as "a damn lesbian," the co-parenting cases went relatively unnoticed.[11] Few journalists picked up on the courts' decisions. There was little statewide action. And Congress remained silent on the issue. In fact the pro-same-sex parenting court decisions issued since the mid-1980s and through the present day in more than half of the states have remained relatively uncontested in the public realm, despite massive resistance to the concept of gay or lesbian couples raising children.

How can we explain these two contemporaneous and yet divergent responses to same-sex family litigation? Conventional wisdom suggests that civil rights advocates who use the courts will see their efforts stymied by backlash. Scholars and pundits alike warn judges and advocates against pursuing court decisions that buck majority will or ignore "the brutal realities of American politics."[12] As the *Los Angeles Times* suggested, "the probable backlash" from Supreme Court intervention into marriage equality litigation "would be substantial and might well do more damage than good to the future of gay rights and other important causes."[13] From white backlash to *Roe* rage, American history is replete with stories of unpopular minorities attempting to secure rights—especially through the courts—and opponents rising up to impede these rights. Court orders to end racial segregation in public schools were met with resistance, political unrest, and often violence against those who were simply exercising their lawful rights. Efforts by disabled individuals to implement their court-declared rights to establish group homes have been thwarted by irate homeowners, zoning officials, and local politicos attempting to secure their seats. And of course, *Roe v. Wade*'s "clash of absolutes"[14] produced, as David Brooks describes, "a cycle of political viciousness and counter-viciousness that has poisoned public life ever since."[15] From this perspective, then, same-sex parenting litigation may be just an aberration or, perhaps, simply an indication that the public actually supported the idea of same-sex parenting during its heyday in the courts.

I offer a different interpretation. Although the threat of backlash is real, its consequences significant, and its effect on judicial actors and outcomes considerable, it is neither inevitable nor invulnerable. Minority rights court victories are not always at the mercy of opposition efforts. Nor are the exceptions mere happenstance. In sharp contrast to supporters of same-sex marriage, same-sex parenting advocates were able to minimize backlash and opposition by capitalizing on a range of low-visibility techniques that rendered the copious litigation in this field virtually invisible to even the staunchest gay rights opponents. Instead of focusing on strategies that would either deliberately or unintentionally catapult the issue of same-sex parenting into the limelight, advocates deployed methods to shield their clients (and their wins) from public scrutiny.

The use of low-visibility court-centered tactics to advance civil rights claims is not unique to same-sex parenting advocacy. Individuals with disabilities and their supporters also recognize the merits of low-profile advocacy in their attempts to secure group homes in single-family neighborhoods. Although, on the whole, the group homes issue is not as *nationally* contested as gay rights, group home residents have long been the subjects and victims of intense local public opposition. When those who are battling mental illness, contending with physical disabilities, or recovering from substance abuse explore group living as a viable housing alternative, many single-family homeowners bristle and fight back. In their efforts to secure housing in single-family neighborhoods, group home residents risk having to confront property owners who will go to great lengths to bar them from their neighborhoods. During zoning board hearings, city council meetings, or less formal community gatherings, proposals for group homes are often defeated by the anxious cries of middle-class families—"We don't want that! I've got to think of my child. I do not want them on my property."[16]

From professors to preachers, opponents come from all walks of life and will consider a wide range of strategies to keep their neighborhoods group-home free. While most will simply air their grievances in hearings or letters, others will resort to intimidation, slander, or even coercion or arson to block group homes from setting up shop. Some group home advocates attempt to mollify "NIMBY" (Not in my Backyard) sentiments by courting communities and public officials early in the group home siting process. Others adopt an approach similar to same-sex parenting advocates. Rather than encouraging public debate about group homes, these advocates remain below the radar about their housing intentions in order to minimize the duration, severity, and damage of their opposition.

The following chapters explore in detail the use of both high- and low-visibility legal strategies in same-sex family (Chapters 3 and 4) and group home (Chapters 5 and 6) advocacy in order to understand how legal advocates minimize or mitigate against opposition efforts. Exploring issue areas that have been at times highly visible and at other junctures have gone unnoticed serves several purposes that have both substantive and scholarly implications. First, in many ways the high-visibility narratives provide a glimpse of the expected outcome in each case study. In these instances members of a disenfranchised community (same-sex couples or individuals with disabilities) engaged in advocacy strategies that attracted significant attention and scrutiny and, inevitably, contended with or succumbed to backlash efforts. These stories, then, illustrate the climate of opposition surrounding all advocacy efforts within these policy domains. Same-sex parenting advocates feared that the same tactics used to bar marriage equality would be used to thwart parenting gains. Low-visibility group home advocates understood the costs and risks of transparency and sought to diminish these costs by delaying notification. The low-visibility case studies illustrate advocacy strategies developed to compensate and accommodate for this potential for backlash. In so doing, they challenge commonly held assumptions that civil rights legal advocacy is always vulnerable to significant opposition and backlash when the causes or beneficiaries are unpopular. They suggest that advocates have more attractive choices than helplessly walking into the backlash abattoir or abandoning litigation entirely.

The low-visibility cases also confirm and enhance a growing body of research pointing to subterranean governance as a potent source of policy change. According to these narratives, policymakers can, and do, hide policy initiatives from the public, often through artful modifications to the tax code or administrative rules. However, in general, these accounts suggest that the subterranean state is accessible only to elites in their attempts to decrease social, or increase corporate, welfare. Low-visibility legal advocacy, while similar in concept to its legislative or administrative counterparts, utilizes different tools and produces distinct outcomes. On the whole, then, examining these lesser-known, yet extremely significant, instances of low-visibility civil rights advocacy will expand our understanding of the promise and the pitfalls of both litigation and below-the-radar policy development.

In order to understand why some court-centered civil rights efforts become mired in opposition, while others elicit a more temperate response or remain unscathed, it is important to examine theories on backlash, opposition, and movement-countermovement dynamics. My analysis takes seriously the notion that advocates often contend with opposition or backlash in ways that undermine the ultimate success of their policy campaigns. I am also compelled by arguments suggesting that legal action, compared to other forms of civil rights advocacy, may be more vulnerable to backlash. However, when we move beyond instances of high-impact and high-visibility litigation, the politics surrounding civil rights legal advocacy begin to shift or wane—and a new set of outcomes emerges. Unlike common perceptions of civil rights battles, where advocates are powerless to anticipate or prepare for opposition efforts, these accounts suggest that civil rights advocates can and do shape both the incidence and influence of backlash.

This study of below-the-radar approaches is informed by a number of traditions within political science, sociology, and public law. Borrowing from current research on low-visibility policymaking, I focus on the capacity of legal advocates to choose, from among a range of options, strategies that not only maximize wins in court, but also promote policy longevity. In so doing I draw from theories that explore the application and implications of various policy mechanisms; among them, the most critical are theories of framing, venue-shopping, and choice of legal doctrine or authority. At the same time, this study speaks to those who suggest that the range of policy tools available to legal advocates is often contingent upon the characteristics of the issue, the risks at stake, and the population featured in the policy debate. Finally, my analysis is deeply informed by debates about the benefits and drawbacks of public deliberation and transparency in the policy process. As the next chapter illuminates, these frameworks and perspectives are critical to examining both why and how legal advocates develop low-visibility tactics and the degree to which these tactics, in turn, play a role in promoting or discouraging the incidence and potency of opposition efforts.

The case studies discussed over the following chapters offer detailed accounts of high- and low-profile advocacy initiated on behalf of same-sex families (through marriage and parenting litigation) and group home residents. Through extensive interviews with advocates and opposition elites and current legal and media analyses, I explore why specific strategies were chosen and the outcomes that emanated.[17] I also analyze public attitudes in each policy domain as a way of underscoring the potential for backlash that advocates faced.

The case study on same-sex marriage offers a sense of the degree and scope of backlash feared by parenting advocates, and, more generally, an example of a predictable majoritarian response to high-visibility minority rights advocacy. Although recent victories suggest that same-sex marriage is on its way to widespread legalization, the politics of marriage equality can best be characterized as a stormy tango between courts and voters. During the period between 1996 and 2006—in response to only a handful of court decisions validating marriage equality—more than forty states had instituted same-sex marriage bans. Despite the fact that these cases were based on interpretations of state constitutions, many feared that other states would be constitutionally required to recognize these marriages through the full faith and credit clause. The majority of the bans remained in place up until the fall of 2014—when the Supreme Court let stand several appellate decisions rulings that overturned state bans, increasing the total number of marriage equality states to 30 plus the District of Columbia.[18] In addition to electoral battles (and likely in response to rapid progress on the marriage equality front) the LGBT community saw a concomitant increase in the number of hate groups targeting its members and a persistent (and in some areas increasing) trend in the incidence of hate crimes against LGBT individuals—especially in states that had legalized same-sex marriage.[19]

The topic of same-sex marriage has enjoyed a high profile since that fateful 1993 Hawaii decision. Local and national media outlets devote significant time and space to debating the merits and costs of marriage equality. Public officials at all levels of government, from local school boards to the US president, have weighed in on the issue. In public debates, hearings, and campaign advertisements, supporters and opponents pit equality and justice against children's welfare and religious freedom. It is, therefore, not surprising that the pattern of backlash exhibited in the aftermath of state court decisions validating marriage equality—particularly between 1996 and 2006—is similar to that of *Brown v. Board of Education (1954)* and *Roe v. Wade (1973)*. It follows the familiar pattern of majoritarian backlash against a controversial court decision. The courts advanced an unpopular cause and opponents quickly expressed their disapproval, consistent with our conventional understanding of courts and social change. Significantly, it also underscores the puzzle as to why same-sex parenting cases—which involve similar stakes—have yet to provoke a full-scale assault.

From the perspective of the LGBT community (and its opposition), "adoption rights is one of the most threatening policy agendas pursued by the movement."[20] And yet, despite this threat, the multitude of court rulings validating same-sex couples and gays or lesbians as parents have yet to trigger the kind or degree of opposition witnessed on the marriage front. By 2006—when the country was awash in same-sex marriage bans—co-parenting lesbians and gays in at least twenty-five states had the option of being jointly and legally recognized as parents to their children.[21] Only eight states had either legislatively or judicially imposed restrictions on same-sex parenting—ranging from full adoption bans to limitations on second parent adoptions. In the aftermath of the 2003 Massachusetts court decision in *Goodridge v. Dept. of Public Health*, gay adoption and parenting advocates geared up for the battle to protect the gains they had made through the courts. In 2006 in particular, sixteen states were in play to restrict same-sex parenting rights through legislation or initiatives. However, this battle never came to fruition, in part, I argue, because of the reliance on below-the-radar tactics. As one scholar remarked, "Given how significantly the welfare of children figures in the same-sex marriage debates, it is curious that the adoption, custody, and visitation rights of LGBT parents have not become a bigger political issue in their own right."[22] This project directly addresses why the politics of same-sex marriage and parenting played out so differently.

As we shall see in Chapter 4, based on interviews with advocates, experts, and opponents of parenting rights (and other evidence), same-sex parental rights advocates maintained a low profile in order to minimize the *incidence* of opposition. By eschewing high-profile legal strategies and, instead, locating their arguments within the technicalities of family law and precedence established in heterosexual parenting cases, they diluted one key ingredient to a successful counter-campaign—public awareness or interest. Similarly, they opted for a legal frame that focused on children's rights rather than gay rights in order to promote commonality across all family structures, gain powerful political allies, and avoid the hot button topic of homosexuality. To date, despite significantly more widespread court approval (relative to marriage) for same-sex parenting, the topic has received far less public or right-wing attention.

But some legal advocates may not always be in a position to minimize the incidence of backlash—even when they pursue low-visibility tactics. That does not mean, however, that they are doomed for smiting at the altar of the opposition. Instead, these advocates minimize visibility in order to reduce the influence or potency of backlash efforts. Where backlash is a near certainty, secrecy can significantly diminish the challenge posed by a determined opposition. The case studies on group home advocacy, discussed in Chapters 5 and 6, provide this narrative. In contrast to same-sex parenting, these accounts highlight how low-profile strategies are used to lessen the *sting* of backlash— even when its incidence is rampant.

Despite the passage, in the late 1980s and early 1990s, of the Fair Housing Amendments Act (FHAA) and the Americans with Disabilities Act (ADA), both of which require landlords and municipalities to make reasonable housing accommodations for mentally and physically disabled individuals, group home operators serving disabled clients face significant barriers when trying to establish their homes in single-family neighborhoods. Across neighborhoods and communities of all varieties of partisan and ideological stripes, group home operators have come to expect unbridled NIMBYism when trying to identify housing opportunities that will benefit their clients. As one operator of a group home for the developmentally disabled stated, after "twenty-five years . . . I'm still fighting the same battle. It saddens me."[23] In its final report, President Bush's New Freedom Commission on Mental Health attributed many of the housing obstacles encountered by those who suffer from mental illness or other disabilities to the "too many communities" who were "unwilling to have supportive housing programs in their neighborhoods."[24] The struggle has always found its way to the courts, and in the vast majority of cases since the passage of these statutes, courts have ruled in favor of the group homes. However, municipalities and organized property owners continue to block group homes from locating in their neighborhoods. Property owners use their electoral strength to discourage public officials from supporting group home requests, provide financial incentives to sellers and landlords to withdraw offers to group home operators, or simply resort to legal or personal intimidation or brute force.

In an attempt to manage backlash, advocates have differed in the approaches they use to protect the housing rights of their clients. Some prioritize transparency and promote visibility in their dealings with potential neighbors and zoning officials. Prior to obtaining housing, these operators notify potential neighbors, petition zoning boards, or hold public hearings to gain permission to live in single-family neighborhoods. These providers feel that early and frequent communication offers the best salve to temper an impassioned opposition. If the petition is denied—most often due to public opposition—they either sue the municipality or find an alternate location.

Others opt for a low-visibility approach and obtain their property without notifying neighbors and petitioning zoning boards. Similar to same-sex parenting advocates, group home operators who sought to keep their housing intentions below the radar until after housing was acquired, did so with opposition in mind—in this instance, though, using secrecy to blunt the sting of opposition. That is, group home operators who elected to find and move into homes in residential neighborhoods without first requesting variances from zoning boards or conducting outreach to community members, deliberately chose this method in order to minimize the impact of backlash from neighbors that would result in the loss of the proposed group home property. These accounts, then, counter increasingly popular assumptions about the benefits of public deliberation and notification, which equate communication with conciliation. Instead these operators reasoned that, even if they were ultimately victorious, without proprietary rights, any outreach carried the risk of homelessness or housing insecurity. Public opposition could lead to protracted litigation or endless bureaucratic deliberation—each of which could compel even the most well-meaning sellers or landlords to offer their properties to other interested parties.

Combined, these case studies offer examples of both the prophylactic and palliative uses of low-visibility advocacy. Where same-sex parenting advocates limit visibility in order to minimize opposition outbreaks, group home advocates go below the radar to soothe their effects. These examples challenge theories about the relationship between courts and countermovements and rebut assertions that deliberation is essential to maintaining democratic values. Low-visibility same-sex parenting and group home advocates were able to minimize the incidence and influence of opposition, securing the rights of their clients. Their strategies suggest that, at least where unpopular minority rights are concerned, calls for public debate may be hasty or, in some cases, ill-advised. That said, these case studies do not imply that there is one elixir for social change, or one definitive diagnosis of the benefits and risks of below-the-radar policymaking. As with any policy strategy, there are tradeoffs to pursuing low-visibility policy change. Hiding same-sex parenting victories from public view likely stymied public debate about the capacity of gays and lesbians to parent effectively. By delaying rather than preventing backlash, low-visibility group home advocacy may have even fueled the incidence and intensity of opposition. Instead, these discussions are meant to enrich or update current narratives about policy change and the politics of dissent in order to encourage further research in low-visibility advocacy.

To that end, this project opens the door to several underexplored areas of inquiry. For one, the case studies explored in the book offer a range of insights into the nature of low-visibility legal advocacy and its relationship with opposition politics. However, as the inquiry is limited to questions of civil rights, one obvious path of research would be to explore in greater detail how below-the-radar legal advocacy translates to issue areas beyond civil rights. Second, although the findings shed new light on the relationship between legal advocacy and backlash, they also introduce new costs. These case studies, then, should enhance or invigorate, rather than inhibit, current debates on the low-visibility state and the transformative potential of legal advocacy. As one lawyer explained of low-visibility parenting advocacy in her state, "There was absolutely a sense that this was groundbreaking work. Most people thought it just couldn't be done . . . I think thirty years from now we will look back on this the way we look at *Brown*."[25]

2

Below-the-Radar Advocacy

The brutality with which officials would have quelled the black individual became impotent when it could not be pursued with stealth and remain unobserved. It was caught—as a fugitive from a penitentiary is often caught—in gigantic circling spotlights. It was imprisoned in a luminous glare revealing the naked truth to the whole world.

DR. MARTIN LUTHER KING, Jr.

One man's transparency is another's humiliation.

GERRY ADAMS

IT SHOULD COME as no surprise to students of American government that policy advocates often have a choice of strategies for achieving policy goals. Institutional pluralism is at the heart of our system of shared powers among separate branches and spheres of government. Depending on the policy goal, some institutions, procedures, or tactics may be more appealing to policy advocates in their efforts to achieve discrete objectives. If legal, rather than legislative, precedent appears to favor a particular policy perspective, for instance, advocates may privilege litigation over legislation in their pursuit of policy innovation. Where a position enjoys popular support, groups can take their cause directly to the voters. For those hoping to catalyze public participation, strategies that focus on soliciting or encouraging media attention will pack the biggest strategic punch. And for activists advancing complicated policy initiatives, a more targeted, incremental, or restrained approach will, likely, prove essential. Considerations of policy objectives and procedures go hand in hand. In simple terms, "strategy is how we turn what we have into what we need to get what we want."[1]

Advancing policy goals within a representative democracy, particularly those involving majority/minority tradeoffs, presents a distinct set of challenges for policy advocates and requires specific tactical calculations—namely, how to balance deliberation and representation. On its face the two operate in tandem. A policy process is not truly deliberative if it privileges the input of the few over the voices of the many. Deliberation requires a consensus or, at minimum, some contemplation of public views and, therefore, at least a modicum of citizen engagement. However, as Shapiro points out, "there is no particular reason to think deliberation will bring people together, even if they hope it will and want it to."[2] In fact, there are times when democracy necessitates exclusivity. Both Madison and Hamilton warned against the majority's "temporary errors or delusions," preferring instead "opportunit[ies] for more cool and sedate reflection."[3] Where decision making entails a more judicious analysis of policy options, policymakers may favor expert over popular consensus and, therefore, opt for strategies that diminish rather than promote public awareness.[4] In so doing, deliberation will contravene rather than complement democratic pursuits.

This quest to find a point of equilibrium of public and professional input privileges neither transparency nor secrecy. Policy entrepreneurs may at times choose tactics that prioritize elite deliberation over mass decision making and at others prefer openness rather than obfuscation. That said, it is the latter that has curried favor among proponents of good government.

Policy transparency and public debate are often regarded as the hallmarks of a functioning democracy.[5] Visibility promotes good citizenship, compels participation, and prevents distrust. For some, policy visibility is tantamount to policy viability; the more the public is informed or consulted, the more they can be mobilized to support a cause and the greater the likelihood of its success. Public hearings, town hall meetings, or more informal information-sharing mechanisms help foster mutual respect and, ideally, produce a reasoned and acceptable policy solution.[6] Even the transfer of information, either through news media or other outlets or by word of mouth, is viewed as a fundamental component of policymaking in a free society. In the words of James Madison, "a popular government, without popular information, or the means of acquiring it, is but a prologue to a farce or a tragedy; or, perhaps both."[7]

Many of our history's most contentious social debates have been catalyzed by publicizing significant policy moments. During the Civil Rights Movement, television broadcasts of the brutality of white police officers toward young African American and white protesters provided the movement with a national stage upon which to showcase the atrocities of Jim Crow.[8] "The whole world watch[ed]" the, often violent, skirmishes between

Chicago police and young protestors at the 1968 Democratic convention.[9] News footage of police brutality catalyzed a range of reforms that changed the face of presidential politics. The protests at Tiananmen Square gained worldwide attention and significance as CNN captured on film one of the most memorable images of the twentieth century, that of a single man blocking the path of four military tanks.

These represent only a handful of the countless political or social debates that were transformed by public scrutiny. Visibility can help plant an issue firmly on the legislative agenda or open windows for a policy dialogue among parties who would otherwise remain disinterested or uninvolved.[10] It can lend a human face to an issue or population plagued by stereotypes and misperceptions.[11] Issue awareness may also assure that policy outcomes benefit the public rather than a privileged few.[12]

But what if there are instances where visibility hinders progress? What if constraining, rather than expanding, the scope of conflict promotes policy innovation?[13] After all, policies are not developed in a vacuum of like-minded individuals. Instead, they are pursued in a marketplace of bombarding and conflicting ideas, strategies, and objectives. While one set of advocates works tirelessly to advance their initiatives, others are equally committed to undermining these goals. Consequently, those interested in policy development must simultaneously energize supporters while minimizing opposition efforts. Within this context, then, expanding policy participation or presentation may impair, rather than bolster, policy pursuits. As Soss and Schram argue, a policy's visibility can significantly alter the degree of unfettered autonomy that policymakers have over their policy pursuits. Under certain conditions, they argue, visibility will only amplify, rather than dispel, dissent.[14]

Furthermore, some policy advocates and social groups will be unfairly disadvantaged within this policy marketplace.[15] Regardless of the strength of their arguments, some groups or causes are consistently downgraded in the eyes of the public. Social, economic, or political factors may serve to maintain a group's second-class standing, making it impossible for them to be treated as equals in the deliberative process. For these groups no amount of reason or adherence to the principles of public debate will save their cause.[16] These groups, then, have two choices: either sacrifice their substantive goals for the ideals of a functioning democracy or reject public engagement for tangible gains. Of course, these pursuits need not be perceived as producing mutually exclusive tradeoffs. By addressing material or structural inequalities, bypassing debate may actually support democracy in the long term. Where prescriptions for public engagement prematurely force disenfranchised groups to make their appeals in arenas that presume mutual respect yet preserve power imbalances, altering these disparities first, without public input, can produce the conditions required for future deliberation.[17]

Growing evidence suggests that low-profile tactics are both more common and more potent than we might think. However, these accounts often focus on backroom ploys to use the tax code or rely on legislative inertia to advance the "haves" at the expense of the "have-nots."[18] Less explored but equally significant is their use by disenfranchised communities as a tool for dampening the incidence or influence of an impassioned opposition.[19] This project focuses on instances where, instead of advancing the privileged, low-visibility tactics are used to promote reform efforts on behalf of disenfranchised communities that are among the most vulnerable to majority reprisals.

Legal Advocacy

In reality, few who hope to transform policy ideals into tangible gains are immune from considering the benefits and risks of seeking public input. Although advocates who are aligned with venues that are directly accountable to the public, such as legislatures or local boards, have a clear obligation to contend with public participation in policy debates, those who frequent less democratically charged venues must also consider how best to manage citizen input. On the one hand, there are instances where public involvement is inevitable. Effective implementation may rest on public approval. State policy procedures may prescribe—or the opposition may utilize—mechanisms such as ballot initiatives or public hearings that encourage citizen input. Or an issue may occupy an important position on the public agenda, rendering moot any efforts to diminish public involvement. On the other, however, as the struggles over same-sex parenting and group home advocacy showcased below will demonstrate, there are times when the risks to public involvement far outweigh the payoffs. On these occasions, and where a policy's infrastructure permits, advocates can diminish the scope and severity of public challenges by utilizing more low-profile policy tools.

Policies that rely on legal advocacy present exactly this type of opportunity structure.[20] Although many court decisions attract attention—either by virtue of their constitutional claims (i.e., corporations are people) or their controversial subjects (abortion or sodomy)—most opinions enjoy little public scrutiny. Offers one scholar about the judiciary's influence on the rise of laissez faire economics:

> It was the judiciary . . . that proved to be most assertive, on the one hand, and least visible, on the other . . . Often invisible, rarely noted, even by contemporary observers, the judiciary radically reshaped the legal standing of corporations between Reconstruction and the first decade of the 20th century.[21]

Both the number of courts and the volume of cases that occupy the American legal system make it nearly impossible for all but the most scrupulous followers to track policy changes that occur through judicial fiat. Consequently, depending on the policy, legal advocates may have considerable autonomy in determining when and how much to engage the public.

In addition to having greater leeway, advocates who pursue legal, rather than legislative, solutions may also have a greater incentive to descend below the radar—especially when working on behalf of unpopular minority groups or advancing deeply contested policy initiatives. By their very nature, issues that pit minority needs against majority desires are vulnerable to public condemnation. This is often amplified when courts are involved.

Where the rights and benefits of disenfranchised groups are imperiled, advocates typically look to the courts for protection. Institutionally, courts are governed by principles that invite minority rights claims. Judges often enjoy more distance from majoritarian concerns that contravene minority interests.[22] At the federal level judges are not elected or accountable to the public. Even where elections are the primary engine for judicial selection, as they are in some states, judges often run unopposed or with significant incumbency advantages.[23] This makes courts a natural refuge for disenfranchised groups who are seeking governmental support.[24]

While their isolation from the public provides judges with the flexibility to consider minority rights claims, it also makes judicial proclamations vulnerable to citizen disapproval. For one thing, courts lack resources. Having "no influence over either the sword or the purse," Hamilton observed in Federalist 78, courts have only the power to persuade a skeptical majority to cede their freedoms to minority demands. Courts also carry more baggage than majoritarian institutions when issuing policy commands to the public. Judges who make decisions that counter majority sentiment are often lambasted as judicial activists or charged with "legislating from the bench." Judicial decisions themselves may lack majoritarian buy-in because they are the product of a process that is disengaged from public sentiment. This baggage, in turn, has the potential to increase the incidence and ferocity of opposition or backlash among stakeholders, elites, and the broader public.[25] In the end, if advocates use judges, rather than legislators, to pursue unpopular policy objectives, public discomfort may turn to hostility.[26] Under these circumstances, legal advocates anticipate the risks of public debate and may consider strategies to diminish public awareness in order to delay or minimize the incidence and impact of opposition efforts.

Despite an institutional orientation that facilitates low-visibility advocacy, we know little about the use of low-profile tactics among legal advocates. Low-visibility research tends to focus on legislative and regulatory modifications—leaving underexplored their use within the legal realm. These narratives frequently focus on elite reliance on low-visibility strategies—often to privilege the powerful. Overlooking low-visibility advocacy by civil rights activists skews our impression of subterranean strategies. Below-the-radar approaches may, at times, actually benefit the have-nots as well as the haves. Studying their use in the context of legal advocacy will enhance both our understanding of the mechanics of the subterranean state and its costs and benefits.

Our knowledge or perception of legal advocacy is similarly slanted. Although scholars caution against court interaction, they do so without considering instances where legal advocates delve beneath the radar in order to protect their clients. Instead, they tend to focus on highly salient (often constitutional) cases. Consequently, our understanding of how both low-visibility and legal strategies contribute to public policy debates is incomplete. By limiting the study of courts and social change predominantly to landmark (and well-known) moments of civil rights litigation, we may have prematurely dismissed the capacity for courts to advance the rights of disenfranchised minorities.[27]

I argue that winning in court is not everything. The evidence introduced in the following chapters showcases the power of low-visibility advocacy to facilitate important legal and substantive gains for members of communities who garner significant public opprobrium. Although judicial approval is clearly a top priority for these legal advocates, they are also both aware of and engaged in efforts to shield court victories from political battles that may erode their scope, reach, or meaning.[28] These accounts challenge assumptions that legal advocacy is limited to the altar of the judge and, instead, introduce to readers legal advocates who anticipate both the legal and political fallout. Their efforts take place both *during* the process of seeking court approval and *after* achieving a court victory. For instance, while they are crafting their legal strategies, legal advocates, where possible, will employ frames or rely on arguments that optimize both the legal and political standing of their policy position. After a decision has been issued, advocates will engage in strategies that minimize the traction of counter-mobilizing efforts. In either case, issue visibility can emerge as an important factor in determining the degree to which legal victories can escape the reach of negative political repercussions. Rather than operating in a world that is siphoned off from political considerations, then, these advocates adopt strategies that attempt to maximize both legal and social gains.

The legal advocacy featured in this book showcases two distinct approaches to managing opposition by minimizing visibility. The first, in the case of same-sex parenting, shows the potential for subterranean tactics to minimize backlash attempts. The story is largely intuitive: if likely opponents are unaware of civil rights reform efforts, they can (and will) do little to stand in their way. The group housing case study illustrates the second, and less obvious, use of low-visibility tactics—to diminish the impact of opposition efforts regardless of their frequency. Here, advocates shield their efforts from public view not to prevent but to achieve as many substantive gains before the backlash ensues. In this case low-visibility tactics are employed to minimize destruction.

Opposition Politics

This book starts from the premise that minority rights advocacy, regardless of venue or tactics, is always vulnerable to opposition or backlash.[29] If the majority were amenable to accepting rights-claiming minority groups, there would be little need for concerted advocacy. For most disenfranchised groups seeking rights recognition or validation, opposition is inevitable. The question, then, is not whether advocates can avoid backlash altogether but whether they can manage or contain it in such a way that minimizes either its *incidence* or *impact* on implementation efforts.

Where a fissure between majority wants and minority demands exists, publicizing intentions to override popular preferences could provoke an intense and unyielding opposition.[30] This may be especially true when courts set the bar for minority rights advancement through landmark rulings.[31] For example, when the Court dismantled racial segregation in public schools in *Brown v. Board of Education*, it awakened vocal and widespread opposition. The decision, which not only diminished state authority to maintain racially separate schools, but also relied on social science to do its bidding, incited immediate protest. Shortly after its announcement, critics decried the decision as "a clear abuse of judicial power."[32] Southern opposition was particularly acute. In many ways, it had a lasting effect on the ability of *Brown* to meaningfully alter the landscape of educational opportunity for black students. Today, this backlash has been largely attributed to *Brown*'s "unambiguous, highly salient pronouncement that southern race relations were destined to change."[33] Suggests Klarman, "it could not easily be ignored or discounted as gradual, diffuse and less salient changes could be."[34]

In this sense, then, *Brown* has become "an icon not of judicial success" but of its failure and "relative impotence" in the face of majoritarian pressures.[35] Through this historical lens, some scholars caution against taking civil rights claims to court.[36] Court victories may be susceptible to swift, significant, and enduring reversals or constraints, leaving those who stand to benefit from these decisions with, at most, a superficial or symbolic win. Of course, there are obvious benefits to litigation. In addition to presenting an alternative to majoritarian mandates, court decisions are used by advocacy organizations to leverage support or compliance from other, less cooperative, actors.[37] They also provide a bargaining chip for legal advocates in their negotiations with opposition elites. However, for some legal advocates, the threat of backlash—any instance where those who oppose a policy take action to reverse or limit its reach or implementation—looms large.

First, voters can take action through the ballot box.[38] In states with judicial elections, voters can remove judges from office for decisions that run counter to public approval—just as they can with other elected officials. One need look no further than a 1986 campaign that successfully removed three justices from the California Supreme Court because of their opposition to the death penalty. Same-sex marriage opponents similarly ousted three justices from the bench of the Iowa Supreme Court in retaliation against their decision in *Varnum v. Brien* (2009) to legalize same-sex marriage in the state. Electoral threats against judges "send a message across the country that the power resides with the people. It's we the people, not we the courts."[39] And despite their irrelevance to out-of-state actors, judicial elections can attract significant support and resources from out-of-state and national organizations. In the Iowa election, for instance, a large share of the campaign's proceeds—more than $650,000—came from out-of state conservative or

religious organizations.[40] Judges, then, are answerable not only to their voters, but also to watchdog groups across the country.

Court decisions themselves are also vulnerable to voter backlash. Those
issued in states with active use of ballot initiatives or referenda to reform
policies may fall prey to swift reversal at the polls and may well prompt voters in other states to take action at the ballot box. Same-sex marriage was
merely a possibility in Hawaii, for instance, when voters in more than half of
the states barred marriage equality.[41] As Reed suggests in his study of ballot
box responses to gay rights, if activists ignore the threat of ballot initiatives,
"much political and legal energy may be unwisely spent or misdirected."[42]

Beyond the ballot box, opponents of court decisions can petition their
legislatures, seek a regulatory change, attempt to limit or curb a court's jurisdiction, initiate impeachment proceedings, or simply ignore a ruling. This
opposition need not emanate from organized interests, but rather from
administrators, bureaucrats, or other individuals who are asked to implement a decision that they condemn. For instance, teachers and administrators have continued to permit prayer and Bible study in the classroom despite
a half-century's worth of Supreme Court precedent limiting the relationship
between religion and public education.[43] This is especially acute in the context of same-sex family rights rulings, where registrars and vital records clerks
have autonomy to determine the scope of protections provided by court rulings. For instance, Darlene Smith, a Louisiana registrar, refused to issue a
corrected birth certificate (standard practice in adoption proceedings) listing
two men as the fathers to a child born in the state but adopted in New York.
Although a New York court ruling legalized the adoption, the two fathers
would have no formal proof without the birth certificate. A three-judge
panel in the Fifth Circuit initially overruled Smith's arguments as violating
full faith and credit. However, on appeal, the full court upheld Smith's (and
the state's) position stating that although the validity of the adoption cannot be revisited, "the full faith and credit clause does not oblige Louisiana
to confer particular benefits on unmarried adoptive parents contrary to
its law."[44] Bureaucratic anarchy also exists in states with marriage equality.
Clerks in Iowa, where same-sex marriage has been legal since 2009, refused
to issue either birth or death certificates listing both parents in a legally married same-sex couple. Although Iowa courts did ultimately overrule the vital
records clerks' actions, the state expended significant resources defending
their actions in two separate (and lengthy) court proceedings.[45]

Opponents also fight litigation with litigation. They may find solace in a
state or lower federal court judge who is willing to disagree with or modify

a prior state, appellate, or Supreme Court ruling.[46] Supreme Court justices, too, may depart from their own precedent. Despite the norm of stare decisis, requiring the justices to uphold their past decisions, there is often ample room for justices to differentiate subsequent decisions, even if they are substantively similar, in ways that limit the Court's past rulings.[47] For instance, although the Supreme Court generally upheld a woman's right to choose to have an abortion in *Planned Parenthood v. Casey* (1992), the case circumscribed much of the logic presented in *Roe v. Wade*—the decision that established this right.[48] Consequently, states now have far more latitude to regulate access to abortion services. Between 2011 and 2013, 205 new restrictions on access to abortion services were enacted.[49] Ten states now require a woman to have an ultrasound before receiving an abortion. Multiple states have diminished the pool of physicians who can provide abortion services by requiring both that the procedure take place in a hospital and that the physician have attending privileges at the hospital. The restrictions supplement existing provisions that allow individuals and institutions to opt out of providing abortion services.[50]

More generally, court decisions may incite backlash by further polarizing opponents and supporters, forcing them to pick sides—and diminishing opportunities for a middle-ground debate.[51] In the wake of *Brown*, southern communities and politicians who once embraced incremental movement toward desegregation began to align themselves with staunch segregationists.[52] Judicial involvement may also galvanize the formation of a formidable opposition movement where none previously existed, as was the case in the aftermath of *Roe v. Wade*.[53] Prior to the ruling, although grassroots efforts to relax abortion restrictions were gaining momentum across the states, an organized pro-life campaign had yet to form. *Roe* is often cited as the catalyst for this movement.[54] More than ten years after the landmark decision, the *New Republic* described it as "the worst thing that ever happened to American liberalism" and charged it with helping to "create a mass movement of social conservatives that has grown into one of the most potent forces in our democracy."[55]

These backlash threats are not confined to one policy domain. Particularly where a disadvantaged community is seeking gains along multiple policy fronts, backlash in one area can spread to other similar arenas. For instance, early debates among gay and lesbian organizations about the merits of pursuing marriage equality centered, in part, on concerns about how these efforts would affect other campaigns or influence action in alternate policy arenas.[56] Advocates feared that opposition would not only target same-sex marriage, but could also truncate the progress of a whole host of gay rights initiatives that were gaining ground. More generally, advocates worried that antipathy toward marriage equality would translate into increased aggression toward gays and lesbians. Many had watched as increased gay visibility inspired a paralleled increase in violence against members of the gay and lesbian community.[57]

Nor are these threats confined to one community. The fair housing rights of many disabled individuals seeking communal living, for instance, were imperiled by antipathy toward recovering substance abusers or individuals with mental health issues who sought the benefits of group housing. Although most property owners who oppose group homes harbor little disdain for individuals with physical disabilities or the elderly, they fear the slippery slope. These neighbors actively oppose the group housing rights of "acceptable" populations out of fear that permitting *one* group home to move into the neighborhood would pave the way for *any* group home to set up residence.

By these accounts, when you are working on behalf of minority interests, pursuing court action can be risky. In reality, though, the story is more complicated than these anecdotes would suggest. First, legal reforms offer a range of other benefits that are ignored in these examples.[58] Often, backlash narratives accord too much weight and significance to opposition efforts, ignoring much of the progress that elicited the negative response. In the early years of the marriage equality movement, for instance, only a handful of scholars acknowledged the potential for same-sex marriage litigation to significantly alter the landscape of opportunity for same-sex couples (now considered a fait accompli).[59] Second, there is no reason to believe that legal advocacy suffers from an absolute disadvantage relative to other policymaking mechanisms. There may be instances where the particular characteristics of courts invite strategies that deflect rather than invite backlash or opposition. As stated above, the sheer quantity and diversity of legal venues in the United States makes it nearly impossible for all but the most astute legal experts to recognize changes in legal precedent.[60]

I argue that legal reforms provide a space for both highly visible and low-profile advocacy strategies. Depending on the legal setting, doctrine, or argument, an issue can enjoy widespread publicity or remain entirely off the public radar. By reducing visibility, then, some forms of legal advocacy can hinder opposition efforts. I argue, further, that low-visibility advocacy can work in silent (and often unintended) partnership with highly visible campaigns to produce meaningful social reforms. Although low-visibility advocates may seem to operate in separate spheres from their high-visibility counterparts, in reality the fruits of one camp can be enjoyed by all. Finally, low-visibility tactics create significant "facts on the ground" to challenge opposition claims. As Chapter 4 explains, the fact of increased legal support for same-sex parenting cast significant doubt on state arguments that same-sex marriage bans protected children. As one scholar notes, that lesbian and gay couples were increasingly coming out as parents "made family less metaphorical and more descriptive of the contours of queer life."[61]

However, diminishing visibility—even if it reduces the sting of backlash—has its drawbacks. First, by obscuring policy gains, stealth strategies may harm the communities they are meant to protect. One by-product of advancing civil rights claims through inconspicuous means is that communities who stand to benefit from these public campaigns remain in the dark about policy victories. In so doing, low-visibility tactics can prolong, rather than dispel, oppression. If we believe, as Hamilton suggests, that the judiciary has "neither force nor will, but merely judgment" then court opinions are most potent when they are publicized. When visibly implemented, court opinions provide messages, cues, and a shared language of the promise of state authority and often serve as a game-changing resource in negotiations among and between individuals, interest groups, and state actors.[62] Concealing legal advocacy, then, dilutes both the judiciary's legitimizing capacity and the power of minority groups to denounce majority infringements.

For similar reasons, political participation and empowerment may also be at risk when advocates mask or subvert their intentions and outcomes. Visible court rulings can inspire the formation of political organizations and increase overall political participation and activity among individuals who have previously been unwilling or unable to access the political process. Gay rights litigation sparked greater political participation among gays and lesbians even as it catalyzed opposition.[63] The number of new gay rights organizations as well as membership in previously existing organizations has increased in the aftermath of recent same-sex marriage decisions. With increased presence comes increased political power.[64] I take up these issues below.

The Potential *for Invisibility in Civil Rights Advocacy*

This project asks whether policy actors and advocates can *deliberately* alter the visibility of an issue to decrease either the likelihood or costs of public intervention. The fact is that, despite commitments to open government, a great deal of governance eludes public observation. On the whole, although many significant policy modifications occur through visible expressions of policy change, a host of innovations have blossomed through concerted efforts to advance policy goals below the public's radar.[65] In many instances, policy elites go to great lengths to hide the hand of government. Rather than "governing less," then, policymakers simply "govern less visibly."[66]

The most obvious method for masking policy intentions is to simply withhold information from the public. Policymakers can remain secretive about their policy intentions and goals or rely on informal policy mechanisms to negotiate policy preferences. For example, bureaucrats and interest groups often engage in "ex parte contacts" or "off-the-record" communications to modify rules and regulations without tipping their hand to the public.[67] Presidents may (and frequently do) avoid—or deliberately withhold—taking a policy position, particularly when they are on the fence or when opposing parties have the potential to damage the success of the policy's goals. Civil rights advocates may find it beneficial to diminish media attention toward their clients and the communities they represent. For example, disability rights advocates purposely attempted to minimize media coverage of deliberation over and passage of the Americans with Disabilities Act out of fear that journalists would stereotype individuals with disabilities in ways that would hinder rather than further their cause.[68] Some will delay informing the public of their intentions until after their gains are safeguarded from backlash. Explored in greater detail in the following pages, for example, are instances where group home operators shielded their plans to establish homes in single-family neighborhoods from community members and public officials until after they had secured their desired housing—all to limit the effects of NIMBY protests.

Of course, maintaining a low-visibility profile is not always feasible. Rather, it is contingent upon a number of factors that shape a policy's legal and political environment. These factors influence and constrain both advocate and opposition strategic options. First and foremost, the possibility of low-visibility reform is issue or population dependent. Some issues, regardless of advocacy strategies, occupy an important position on public or opposition agendas.[69] An issue or group may be so hotly contested that any attempt to remove it from the public agenda or maneuver behind closed doors will draw increased attention and polarization. It is far more common, for instance, for group homes of all varieties to generate anxiety among their future neighbors than to be welcomed with open arms. Gays and lesbians are similarly vulnerable to opposition. Suggest Meyer and Staggenborg, "For issues such as abortion and gay liberation, it would seem much more difficult if not impossible to avoid arousing opposition insofar as the behavior in question itself offends the values of existing groups."[70] Opponents to same-sex marriage publicized its possibility (and their deep disapproval) long before marriage equality appeared on the agenda of LGBT advocacy organizations. Once conservative organizations realized the potential to galvanize constituents and voters around same-sex marriage bans, there was little marriage equality advocates could do to dampen public awareness.[71] On other issues public ignorance may pave the way for low profile advocacy. For instance, in the 1990s, although the idea of LGBT individuals raising kids was viewed with either skepticism or disgust, most Americans did not acknowledge that lesbians and gays were already parenting.[72] Even during the recent upswing of same-sex marriage victories (and despite more than thirty years of precedent supporting lesbian and gay headed households), LGBT parenting is still referred to as an "experiment" about which there is little supportive data.[73] This has stemmed in part from the unwillingness of individuals to alter their perception that gay life is intrinsically "associated with sexual abandon and deadly disease."[74] It also relates, however, to the fact that lesbians (the primary engine of LGBT parenthood precedent) "were largely erased from mainstream discourse."[75] Their invisibility permitted pioneering lesbian parents (and parenting advocates) to navigate family courts and establish important precedent with little notice from the public.

In many instances, the viability of low-visibility strategies also depends on the venues and vehicles tied to particular reform efforts. In some cases, policy innovation requires a grand gesture: a clear policy pronouncement or a large-scale policy overhaul. Either because there is no existing policy apparatus to support the reforms or because the policy's success requires broad public buy-in, some policy events rely on public proclamations such as presidential initiatives, sweeping congressional mandates, or multi-state campaigns. Other reform efforts, however, will prosper with the support of less attention-grabbing mechanisms. In order to accomplish these policy goals, advocates may need only lobby executive agency staff to make minor changes to administrative or regulatory rules or seek support from state, county, or municipal rather than federal officials. In these cases the opportunities for stealth advocacy abound.

The same holds true for court-based reform efforts. Legal advocates must consider the jurisdictional and doctrinal boundaries that establish where and on what grounds a claim can be defended. Depending on the policy domain, the specific claim, and the group or individual leading the charge, challenges can be funneled through specialized courts with specific jurisdictions and expert knowledge, or reviewed by state or federal judges. Advocates who can deploy policy innovations in lower or lesser-known legal venues stand a better chance of shielding their victories from the public.

Stealth advocacy is also contingent upon the availability of idiosyncratic rather than large-scale vehicles for policy change. Advocates can diminish visibility by grounding their arguments in statutory, regulatory, or doctrinal language that receives little public notice. Arcane or highly technical policy debates—like those surrounding modifications to the tax code or retirement benefits—produce far less public contestation than large-scale policy initiatives that can be summarized in twenty-second sound bites or even shorter catchphrases.[76] Omnibus or spending bills also subvert public discussion by grouping a number of unrelated policy changes into a hodgepodge of enactments, as was the case in the 1980s with Medicaid expansion.[77] These bills are often a collection of modifications to programs with budgetary implications, making it difficult to track any one initiative. Consequently, they provide an attractive policy alternative for public officials who want to support controversial initiatives without tarnishing their public image. Low-visibility legal advocacy hinges on the availability of applicable statutes, administrative rulings, or common-law precedent—legal authorities that typically ignite less public attention than arguments based on constitutional claims. To a large degree, then, visibility is determined by the ability of advocates to cloak or render mundane the claims of their clients.

Incrementalism is another hallmark of low-visibility advocacy. Low-visibility strategies flourish through the use of marginal, rather than wholesale, policy modifications. Often this means leveraging the subterranean or obscure policy vehicles referenced above to discretely alter a policy provision in a manner that, over time, produces significant gains. Some of the most significant alternations to the American welfare state—both in the form of massive disinvestment and shifts in resource allocation—occurred through modest modifications to policy or regulatory technicalities, rather than wholesale reversals or enactments.[78] Policymakers can phase out programs by neglecting to enact modifications that would reflect higher costs or changing conditions. They can also drastically alter a policy's scope and trajectory through small, but frequent, adjustments to program language.[79] By limiting public awareness and, by extension, opposition, incrementalism may provide a more attractive policy environment to critical stakeholders who would otherwise remain divorced from an issue. For instance, where political parties may disagree about the merits of expanding benefits through large-scale programs, policy elites have found common ground by providing financial support to the working class through a range of tax credits and incentives.

In many ways legal advocacy is by definition incremental. Very rarely does one legal decision resolve a policy debate. Instead, litigation involves repeated, complicated, and often non-linear attempts to articulate the boundaries of a policy or doctrine. Rather than being self-contained, the language from one decision often interacts with other opinions to form the judicial response to an issue—and court interpretation is always subject to change depending on new cases or judges. This constant evolution of judicial doctrine can provide advocates with coverage if they choose to remain off the radar. Often, advocates can further submerge cases by limiting review to lower or specialized courts or resting their claims on regulatory or administrative arguments that either by design or happenstance attract little attention.[80]

Court decisions also play an important behind-the-scenes role when they are used to leverage policy movement in legislative or regulatory arenas.[81] Unlike high profile instances of court reform, which highlight the capacity of judicial actors to issue policy decrees that supplant the positions of other policy actors, here, court action is used more discretely as a bargaining chip. Policies are formed through an exchange of directives among courts, regulatory agencies, and legislative bodies. Through this lens, the marginal policy gains from any individual venue are regarded as instrumental, rather than definitive, policy statements. In many ways court decisions like *Lawrence v. Texas* (2003)—which outlawed anti-sodomy statutes—or *Goodridge v. Dept. of Public Health*, establishing marriage equality for same-sex couples in Massachusetts, are the exception to the rule. While these decisions offered absolute and unambiguous policy statements, most legal advocacy efforts involve piecemeal adjustments to legal precedent. Legal advocates devise incremental (and consequently less visible) approaches in which legal arguments and doctrines are supplemented and revised.

Even within naturally high-profile policy debates, incrementalism can emerge as a promising (and for some a preferred) strategy among policy actors. For instance, in the infancy of modern-day same-sex marriage litigation, the Vermont Supreme Court adopted an incremental approach to extending marriage rights to same-sex couples, focusing on the rights and benefits of marriage instead of the institution itself.[82] Rather than forcing the legislature to legalize same-sex marriage, as the *Goodridge* court would do four years later, the Vermont Supreme Court gave the legislature a choice between legalizing same-sex marriage or creating civil unions.[83] This approach drew praise among those concerned about judicial overreach. As Eskridge advised in an article on the Vermont decision,

> Law cannot liberalize unless public opinion moves, but public attitudes can be influenced by changes in the law. For gay rights, the impasse suggested by this paradox can be ameliorated or broken if the proponents of reform move step-by-step along a continuum of little reforms.[84]

In some ways, this approach was prompted by the advocates themselves, despite their collective disappointment that the state would not be required to provide gay couples with marriage licenses. As Pierceson suggests, "in their brief and during oral arguments the plaintiffs' lawyers played down gender and sexual orientation discrimination arguments, instead relying on a rational basis analysis. Perhaps out of fear of the barriers to breaking new legal ground, advocates shied away from grand claims."[85]

The feasibility of low-visibility advocacy is also contingent upon the availability of "policy paradigms" that can be marshaled to justify or explain proposals. Policy reforms that tap into numerous or varied policy frames can provide advocates with options to camouflage their more polarizing policy goals. Depending on the availability of these frames, advocates can foster relationships with broader coalitions of advocacy communities. These partnerships—particularly if they invite more sympathetic stakeholders to the forefront—can decrease the public's focus on a policy's more controversial subjects. For instance, Beland finds that Social Security reform advocates ushered in significant, yet hardly contested, expansions by focusing on a family benefits frame. As he states, "although the main actors involved in that 'deal' remained quiet about the true scope of the reform they supported, it represented a genuine paradigm shift in Social Security."[86] These "low-profile policy ideas" were hardly challenged.[87]

In the context of legal advocacy, frames and doctrines vary by group, issue, and grievance. Some groups may be limited from accessing specific doctrines because their characteristics disqualify them from taking up particular arguments. Some activities may be, similarly, barred from referencing legal precedent.[88] Some legal questions, however, can be resolved through a broad range of legal frames and doctrines. While there was limited doctrinal space, outside of "rights" precedent, to support marriage equality arguments, parenting cases could access a bounty of family law decisions in which "the best interests of the child," not a parent's traits, determined the outcome of custody or adoption cases.

Finally, low-visibility options depend on the venues and tactics available to reform adversaries. When exploring the possibility for low-visibility strategies, legal advocates consider both where and in what form backlash efforts will emerge. At the same time that legal advocates make calculations about the availability of doctrines, venues, and frames that support their reform efforts, they must also consider whether these mechanisms will place their efforts in the line of fire. For instance, the vast majority of anti-gay advocacy efforts have been formulated by national groups who rely on electoral strategies. Groups like Focus on Family or the Family Research Council have devoted significant resources to mobilizing conservative voters in key states to either dismantle or ward off gay rights advances, forcing gay rights advocates to defend their rights the ballot box. This has served two purposes. First, electoral (especially voter-driven) platforms for policy change presented the best option for limiting gay rights advances. Novkov argues that, particularly during the early years of marriage litigation, state legislatures were especially ripe for gay rights hostilities. Significant "right-wing entrenchment" within the Republican base—and among key officeholders—halted any progress on hate crimes or employment discrimination legislation and created a captive audience for those interested in carrying the torch for traditional marriage.[89] Rampant homophobia within the party made it easy for opponents to mobilize against the interests of same-sex couples. Second, Republican-induced pressures to mount defensive and costly electoral campaigns forced LGBT advocates to divert their limited resources away from complementary policy campaigns and more hospitable venues.[90] Until 2012 anti-gay advocates had successfully corralled state-level publics to legalize statutory or constitutional bans, or pressure legislators into sponsoring anti-gay rights bills. Any effective low-visibility approach for LGBT advocates during this time, then, would have had to minimize the potential for conservatives to mobilize their voting base.

Group home advocates contend with a far different environment for political opposition. Those who actively oppose group home sitings— often referred to as NIMBYs—are typically neighbors who come together to seek out any feasible strategy for denying group home operators access to single-family neighborhoods. Relative to anti-gay efforts, group home opposition is typically far less organized and more ad hoc. In general, rather than establishing permanent structures for imposing widespread obstacles on group home sitings, protestors will, most often, come together as needed to address individual incursions by group homes. Opposition goals also differ. Where anti-gay rights opponents focused their efforts on amending state constitutions or enacting legislation to limit marriage to heterosexual couples (and stymie court behavior),[91] group home opponents have one simple charge: to block the group home from moving into their neighborhood. In order to accomplish this narrow task, NIMBY forces explore a wide variety of political and legal (and not so legal) strategies. Zoning boards, landlords, sellers, or the group home operators and residents themselves—each are potential targets for group home opposition campaigns. Their primary goal is to convince as many individuals or entities to deny or withdraw their support for the group home's housing plans (and make it impossible for them to move forward with renting, purchasing, or developing the proposed property). Group home operators, then, face an opposition environment comprised of a small, but intense, group of adversaries who, once informed, will use any tactic at their disposal to block group housing rights.

Individuals and advocates confront a range of different political and legal opportunity structures in their attempts to pursue or counteract policy reforms. Policy venues and doctrines set the stage for the advocacy options. Frames or narratives provide the language or imagery of reform. Veto points mark the fault lines. Together these define the contours of any policy environment—and the potential to employ the low-visibility tactics described in the pages that follow.

Below-the-Radar Tactics

The cases analyzed in this project introduce readers to several different techniques devised by civil rights advocates to minimize either the *frequency* or *potency* of backlash by diminishing issue visibility. Advocates leveraged various aspects of their policy's political and legal opportunity structures to reduce opposition attention. For same-sex parenting advocates—who hoped to limit the incidence or frequency of backlash attempts—this included seeking rulings from specialized or lower-level courts and resting their legal claims on technical or lesser-known statutory, administrative, or common-law, rather than constitutional, precedent. They also utilized policy narratives that would both distract the public from focusing on their policy proposals' more controversial elements and allow them to expand their network of allies to include organizations with broad-based appeal.

Group home advocates attempting to reduce the sting of backlash efforts (despite their frequency) manipulate visibility by avoiding the most likely (and most volatile) locations of public contestation. The group home advocates featured below understood both the culture of noncompliance that typifies group home siting requests and the shortcomings of existing enforcement mechanisms to help group homes carry out fair housing decrees. Low-visibility group home advocates thwarted opposition efforts by sidestepping formal requirements and informal norms of public deliberation until after their housing options were secured. To be sure, once the opponents found out about these efforts, they moved quickly to block their progress. However, because of the delayed notification, NIMBY forces often mobilized too late to significantly derail group housing plans.

Legal Vehicles and Venues

In the legal realm, significant constitutional rulings on controversial topics, such as *Brown, Roe*, and *Goodridge*, are highly visible and may incite equally high profile doctrinal or institutional attacks. [92] Claims that do not rely on constitutional principles, conversely, are often less visible (a fact highlighted by relatively low levels of scholarship devoted to instances of statutory, rather than constitutional, civil rights advocacy.) For instance, during the course of Vermont's marriage equality litigation, notes Pierceson, in order to minimize public outcry a group of "prominent law professors supportive of same-sex marriage claims argued" in an amicus brief "that statutory interpretation alone justified same-sex marriage." They "avoided constitutional arguments altogether."[93] Although *Roe, Brown*, and the same-sex marriage cases are important examples of the courts' foray into civil rights, they are by no means representative. Nor are they, necessarily, the most significant.

In the wake of the Civil Rights Act of 1964 and other civil rights statutes, much of the federal courts' pro–civil rights docket has taken the form of protecting statutory gains made by minority groups. Yet, as with general studies of American policy formation, scholars have paid considerably less attention to these lower visibility court cases and their effect on minority populations.[94] Take the Court's decision in *Olmstead v. LC and EW* (1999), which relies on statutory authority to protect the rights of mentally disabled patients to live independently (when they are deemed ready) in smaller community-based settings. Despite its status as a landmark civil rights victory, known among disability rights advocates as their *Brown*, it has yet to receive significant scholarly attention.[95] Similarly, although regarded by many in the legal community as a landmark case, the Court's decision in *Griggs v. Duke Power* (1971), which argues that racially neutral promotion standards such as intelligence tests or high school diplomas violate the Civil Rights Act of 1964, has received scant coverage in political science.[96] This attention imbalance is even more remarkable in light of the increase in statutory advances in civil rights, both at the state and federal level, and the concomitant wealth of litigation expanding the reach of these statutes. Below-the-radar advocates leverage this inattention and rely on these more obscure legal authorities in order to indemnify court victories against backlash.

Reliance on statutory, administrative, or common law also provides groups with tested and validated precedent to reference in their legal arguments. Rather than resting a legal theory on constitutional language—which in the realm of civil rights can often be interpreted as asking the courts to recognize a "new right" or an additional category of protection—using statutes or administrative law only requires courts to expand an existing legal franchise to additional groups. For instance, one of the common questions addressed by courts early in the same-sex marriage movement was whether or not gay rights advocates were seeking to establish a new right or simply access an existing right in their attempts to secure marriage licenses. In *Singer v. Hara* (1974), a Washington State appellate court rejected a same-sex couple's reliance on the Court's precedent in *Loving v. Virginia* (1967) that marriage is a fundamental right.

> [Appellants] argue that at the time *Loving* and *Perez* were decided, marriage by definition barred interracial marriages and that the *Loving* and *Perez* courts changed that definition through their interpretation of the Fourteenth Amendment ... We disagree. The *Loving* and *Perez* courts did not change the basic definition of marriage as the legal union of one man and one woman; rather, they merely held that the race of the man or woman desiring to enter that relationship could not be considered by the state in granting the marriage license ... In other words, contrary to appellants' contention, the Fourteenth Amendment did not require any change in the definition of marriage.[97]

A Maryland court argued similarly that, although there is a fundamental right to marriage, there was no fundamental right to same-sex marriage. In other words, the court refuted appellants' arguments that they were seeking an extension of the traditional institution of marriage to same-sex couples.[98]

Not surprisingly, early on in the marriage equality movement, in the instances where courts viewed the issue of marriage equality as one involving a new right, it was more difficult for gay and lesbian couples to prevail. Even where courts were willing to acknowledge the logic of extending rights protections to new issues or groups, the specter of backlash, and the baggage of judicial activism, gave some advocates pause about these goals.[99] Pressures to practice restraint and respect for distinctively legislative powers can compel courts to limit intervention to those issues or groups that are supported by existing legal precedent.

Couching legal innovations, where possible, within a statutory or administrative framework, offers judges a less risky (and less controversial) option for crafting legal innovations. As Melnick describes of court-based AFDC reforms, pro-expansion judges "considered it prudent to package innovation as statutory and thus reversible by Congress—rather than as set in constitutional stone."[100] This is because, in addition to being more obscure, precedent based on this language is perceived by the public as being both narrowly applicable and more easily reversible.[101]

In practice, however, checking judicial discretion may be no easy feat. Vague or convoluted statutory provisions are often the result of deadlocked or polarized legislatures unable to reach consensus on legislative details. In the event that a court "misinterprets" this language, the same obstacles that prevented a legislature from initially producing clear legislative mandates will likely hinder the legislature from taking corrective action to limit and prevent future judicial expansions. Furthermore, court validation of one particular legislative perspective gives those who share the court's views leverage and incentive to maintain this language.[102] (Of course, we know that, in practice, constitutional rulings, at least those at the state level, are no more immutable than statutory decisions. In a post-*Baehr* and *Goodridge* world, any state constitutional civil rights victory has the potential to be swiftly dismantled at the ballot box.)

Looking outside the Constitution for legal support, then, serves two goals. First, it provides judges with leeway to expand significant rights, privileges, or services to unpopular minorities while sidestepping larger constitutional landmines. Second, it allows these court decisions to be validated through more technical and banal legal doctrines. It is for this reason that many of the parenting advocates discussed in Chapter 4 deliberately chose to support their arguments using heterosexual family law precedent.

The decision of which legal authority to use is often tethered to advocate preferences about which court to petition. As an increasing number of civil rights arguments extends into areas of law considered mundane—custody, divorce, adoption, zoning—the locus of social change has also expanded to include lower courts or administrative bodies at the state and local level. Those who want to stay below the radar will develop legal arguments within the substantive jurisdiction of less conspicuous venues. In the realm of same-sex parenting, for instance, this meant keeping most early advocacy confined to family and lower courts. These advocates often consulted lower courts and resisted taking their claims to higher, and more visible, judicial venues. Lower court rulings, then, established critical data points. The existence of a growing population of LGBT-headed families, legitimized by courts, directly challenged anti-marriage and parenting campaigns that characterized same-sex couples as either unlikely or unacceptable parents. The increasing prevalence of gay couples raising kids also elevated advocate appeals about the welfare costs and rights impingements for children if LGBT parenting or marriage opponents prevailed.

That said, some venues of limited *national* public significance—such as zoning or licensing boards—still impose visibility risks for legal advocates. In group home advocacy, for instance, most of the contentious battles occur in the midst of zoning board or licensing hearings. Decisions to stay off the public radar, for these advocates, center on whether or when to alert zoning officials of their intention to establish a group home.

Reform Paradigms

Frames or narratives help individuals to conceptualize issues and provide, as Gamson et al. suggest, "a central organizing principle that holds together and gives coherence and meaning to a diverse array of symbols."[103] In many ways, considerations of framing and issue salience go hand in hand; a strong frame can capture the attention of the media and shape public perceptions.[104] Since most policies are multidimensional, a policy's frame can take on many different forms depending on the audience, the source of the frame, the political context, and the policy's purpose.[105] While some frames may be used to promote a shared understanding or inspire collective action and civic responsibility, others may fuel opposition or countermovements.[106]

Framing does not occur in a vacuum, nor can it be completely controlled. Policy elites, on a variety of fronts, develop and alter frames in response to, and in anticipation of, opposition narratives. The rhetoric adopted by advocates will ultimately confront competing imagery in the race for public attention or institutional support.[107] That said, advocates can utilize language that minimizes or distracts public attention. One study found that gays and lesbians interested in diminishing blowback to proposed anti-discrimination legislation in Oregon resisted "identity politics" and instead opted to use more widely inclusive and less polarizing policy paradigms.[108] Similarly, frames can steer individuals toward or away from adopting a "group-centered"—rather than "individualistic"—policy conception. Although individuals tend to develop policy opinions based on their attitudes toward the implicated group, framing determines the degree to which group perceptions dictate public opinion.[109] In other words, framing plays a pivotal role in determining *whether* and *how* individuals think about a policy issue, and it may be the difference between quiet disagreement with a policy position or active opposition.[110]

While many narratives are unique to a given policy domain, policy advocates often borrow, recycle, and reconstitute popular imagery from other policy battles or movements to fast-track buy-in from the public. Advocacy efforts that invoke well-established or broadly supported principles and symbols conjure histories, trigger emotions, and outline an array of policy alternatives for less-informed publics.[111] "Rights" and "equality," for instance, resonate with the public because of their association with numerous civil rights struggles and their connection to the courts.[112] To a large degree the very language of rights has its roots in legal doctrine. We establish rights and use rights-based claims in order to organize human interactions within a framework of rules and obligations. The language of rights plays a particularly important role in checking and challenging majority power. Arguably the most common incidence of rights rhetoric occurs when an institutional mandate attempts to limit the actions of a particular group. In these instances the constrained group will claim that the restrictions burden a behavior, belief, or form of expression that is fundamental to their livelihood and protected by legislation, the Constitution, or some higher authority. African Americans invoked their equal protection rights to dismantle segregation in public schools. They further articulated a right to be free from the influence of racism and discrimination when attempting to access the political process, patronize public facilities, or seek housing and employment. Women sought the right to choose to have an abortion. Gays and lesbians have claimed a right to intimacy. Even corporations have achieved a right to express their political preferences through campaign contributions. The language of rights abounds and in many instances legitimizes policy battles by establishing connections to past civil rights struggles.[113]

However, using a "rights" discourse can also provoke strong public resistance.[114] When rights claims are deployed in ways that contravene public preferences, those opposed often stand poised to malign the intentions of advocates and the communities they represent. Recasting rights narratives as "favoritism" or "special treatment," for instance, has become a potent opposition tool for polarizing minority rights debates. In response to recent attempts to pass anti-bullying legislation, for instance, opponents have, successfully, reframed the debate as offering some students "special rights."[115] Similar arguments have been used to restrict affirmative action programs and dismantle a number of anti-discrimination statutes designed to limit discrimination on the basis of race, sexual orientation, and a range of other categories. Colorado officials argued that a ballot initiative preventing gays and lesbians from pursuing anti-discrimination legislation did "no more than deny homosexuals special rights."[116] Indeed, even early attempts to protect minority groups from discrimination fell prey to the rhetoric of special rights. Concomitant with the passage of the Reconstruction amendments, for instance, Congress passed a number of accompanying statutes designed to further protect former slaves from the "badges and incidents of slavery." In its arguments overturning these statutes, the Supreme Court explained that

> When a man has emerged from slavery, and, by the aid of beneficent legislation, has shaken off the inseparable concomitants of that state, there must be some stage in the progress of his elevation when he takes the rank of a mere citizen and ceases to be the special favorite of the laws, and when his rights as a citizen or a man are to be protected in the ordinary modes by which other men's rights are protected.[117]

Legal advocacy is often a primary target for anti-rights backlash.[118] As guardians of the law, lawyers are the primary champions of what some refer to as the "myth of rights."[119] For reasons outlined above, the demand-driven, highly decentralized nature of American litigation—known as adversarial legalism—makes it easier for courts (and more attractive for advocates) to recognize and validate rights claims relative to their legislative counterparts.[120] In fact, without legal support, rights rhetoric would fall on deaf ears. Argues Epp, "rights revolutions have occurred only where and when and on those issues for which material support for rights litigation—rights advocacy organizations, supportive lawyers, and sources of funding—has developed."[121] Nevertheless, some castigate "rights talk" generally as hindering the mechanics of democracy by limiting the relevance of public opinion when determining policy outcomes.[122] Skeptics argue that legal advocates rely on the myth of rights at the expense of other more effective modes of legal redress.

The decision of whether to use "rights" over other legal, political, or popular frames is also contingent upon both the object of the frame and its beneficiaries. For one thing, although an institution, behavior, or action may be perceived as important, it may not rise to the level of a "right" in the minds of the public. For instance, resources like housing and health care, while critical to a working society, are not considered "rights." There is no constitutional guarantee of shelter, for instance. Although legislation like the Fair Housing Act limits discrimination in the acquisition of housing, there are few statutory obligations for the government to provide affordable quality housing to all of its subjects.[123] Similarly, early on in the push for marriage equality, it was a matter of public debate whether or not same-sex marriage advocates could properly use a "rights" frame in their campaign. While "marriage," in its traditional sense, had been deemed a fundamental right by the Supreme Court, "same-sex marriage" had not. Opponents argued that heterosexuality defined the institution of marriage. Accommodating LGBT demands would necessarily alter the institution beyond recognition. Therefore, any constitutional guarantees that safeguard marriage applied only to opposite-sex couples. In these instances, then, borrowing rights rhetoric from past legal precedent and movements prompted debates that shifted public attention away from the substantive merits of same-sex marriage campaigns to more divisive theoretical debates about the legitimacy of the frame.

Finally, in the court of public opinion, individuals and groups are not on equal footing and are not equally equipped to claim rights narratives as their own. Those in high public standing are more likely to be perceived as sympathetic and, therefore, more worthy recipients of "rights" protections than less well-regarded communities. For instance, Engel argues that making rights claims based on equality "may have a depressive effect on public perception of a range of LGBT rights claims" because the public is especially "uncomfortable with that particular conceptualization" in the context of LGBT policy debates.[124]

In order to diminish public outcry and preempt or combat opposition efforts, some advocates limit or refrain from using rights rhetoric when working on behalf of unpopular groups or controversial policy goals—even if this frame is legally permitted and historically supported. One way to modify a "rights" frame to minimize opposition is to highlight a more sympathetic population who may also benefit from this right—or at least minimize the presence of the unpopular group. For instance, in the 1990s, President Clinton defended Medicaid against budget cuts by highlighting their effect on "mainstream seniors" rather than welfare recipients (the program's more conspicuous beneficiaries).[125] Similarly, the first real federal commitment to AIDS funding, the Ryan White Comprehensive AIDS Resources Emergency (CARE) Act of 1990, focused on the dangers of contracting HIV/AIDs through blood transfusions, as the legislation's namesake had during treatment for hemophilia. Although LGBT activists had been lobbying Congress since the early 1980s, when the AIDS epidemic first hit the gay community, the federal government was loath to publicly support research for a disease that was largely attributed to the "gay lifestyle." When Ryan White, a thirteen-year-old boy, was diagnosed with AIDS and, consequently, prohibited from attending his school, federal officials had their hook. Naming the bill after a child who had contracted AIDS from a medical procedure, effectively "de-gayed" the illness and "assuage[ed] conservatives who feared that supporting an AIDS-related bill would label them pro-gay."[126] Same-sex parenting advocates have relied on similar tactics. Rather than framing limits on same-sex adoption or co-parenting as LGBT rights infringements, advocates have, instead, focused on the rights of children who are raised in same-sex-headed households. To a large degree advocates have attempted to make the sexual orientation of their clients irrelevant to judges and public officials. In the context of marriage equality, one study found that canvassing for support and funding was less lucrative when the individual LGBT campaign staff made personal references about their sexual orientation.[127] Perhaps drawing on this (or similar) data, later campaigns for marriage equality limited explicit references to same-sex couples. For instance, they were noticeably absent in advertisements against California's marriage ban.[128] According to a "No on 8" representative, montages of gay couples "are not the best images to move people."[129] Instead, the ads purposely focused on pleas for equality from heterosexual parents raising LGBT children. One showcased an elderly couple imploring viewers to vote against the initiative, to protect "our gay daughter and thousands of our fellow Californians who will lose the right to marry." Overall, marriage equality supporters made very little mention of the word "gay" or the phrase "gay marriage."[130] Successful, marriage equality campaigns in Washington and Maine utilized similar strategies.

This inclination to de-couple the relationship between sexual orientation and marriage equality is evident in opposition strategies as well. Opponents attempted to limit their discussion of the gay couples they were targeting and instead steered their arguments toward children's welfare, in part to argue that they had no interest in stigmatizing gays and lesbians. Rather, their only motivation was to protect the children.[131]

Advocates can also disguise rights claims by redirecting public attention to the material benefits that extend from these rights. Typically, narratives forge rather than sever connections between rights and benefits. Welfare and disability advocates, for instance, convinced judges to recast statutory benefits providing cash assistance to single mothers and education to disabled children as programmatic rights, rather than discretionary privileges that could not be withdrawn without adequate due process of law.[132] However, where a rights approach proves too risky, advocates may choose to sever this relationship. Instead of focusing on marriage as a fundamental right, for example, in some instances marriage equality advocates stressed the legal and financial costs that stem from marriage bans.

Below-the-Radar Partners

Coalition-building is critical for any reform effort. The more credible the supporters, the more legitimate your cause, at least in the eyes of the public. The presence of allies—especially those of high standing—can provide cues and shortcuts for an ill-informed public, which can often translate into increased policy support. For advocates representing polarizing issues or groups, partnership-building takes on added significance. Advocates will attempt to harness the support of sympathetic advocates or organizations in good public standing in order to raise the reputation of their own clients.

Advocates also develop or downplay partnerships in service of their low-visibility pursuits. When groups like the NAACP, National Organization for Women, or Lambda Legal approve new civil rights claims, they not only legitimize these demands, but they also prime the public to evaluate these efforts through a specific organizational, rhetorical, or historical lens.[133] On many occasions, this support helps advocacy causes—especially when national-level support for an issue is coming from organizations whose substantive interests differ. For instance, both President Obama's announcement supporting marriage equality and the NAACP's concomitant resolution recognizing same-sex marriage as "consistent with equal protection under the law" validated advocacy claims that same-sex marriage is a civil right and its denial is discriminatory—an argument that had previously drawn significant criticism.[134] However, these endorsements can also further polarize a debate—especially when the high-profile organization is associated with the community in question. National organizations such as Lambda Legal or Human Rights Campaign attract attention. Regardless of the nature of their work on a particular issue, their presence in a debate is newsworthy and therefore risky for those who want to minimize the focus on gay rights in order to maintain a low profile..

Low-visibility advocates, then, will establish relationships with communities or organizations that have widespread support in order to mask their more polarizing clients. Same-sex parenting advocates, for instance, focused on building relationships with children's welfare organizations in order to present their struggle as a battle for children's, rather than gay, rights. In many instances this meant camouflaging the presence of gay rights organizations and instead highlighting, in the media and in legal proceedings, the perspectives of children's advocacy groups. The more they could manage to not only use "children's welfare" frames but speak through "children's welfare" spokespeople, the more credible (and less polarizing) their efforts—and the more difficult it would be for opponents to classify these reforms as part of the "gay agenda." Studies performed by neutral and well-respected children's welfare researchers provided a similar benefit—especially as a response to the social science commissioned by anti-marriage equality supporters showing poor outcomes for children raised in same-sex couple households. The supportive findings— that children raised by LGBT parents show no significant developmental deviations from children raised in heterosexual households—were all the more beneficial because they were produced by organizations who have no vested interest in LGBT advocacy. In short, like frames, partnerships with neutral allies helped LGBT advocates remove the stigma of sexuality and sexual orientation from discussions of parenting. Without the controversy of sexual orientation driving advocacy efforts, parenting arguments and cases provoked little public awareness.

Partnerships can also help advocates access local and low-visibility venues. Popular accounts of civil rights advocacy often celebrate the efforts of national civil rights groups and leaders to organize and galvanize local support. In low-visibility legal advocacy, local experts play a starring role. While national involvement may prove too costly, community-based expertise is well suited for low-profile advocacy. In addition to generating less public awareness, local advocates are both familiar with the likes and dislikes of local judges and bureaucrats and sensitive to the frames and arguments that may set off local opposition. They can use this knowledge to advance claims within the comfort zone of local decision makers without inspiring local dissent. They are also often better situated to sense when opposition is inevitable and, therefore, when to postpone advocacy efforts. While national or high-profile groups make significant contributions to low-visibility efforts, their role is often to support or enrich local talent—and where they do play a central role they will typically attempt to downplay or disguise their contributions.

If inattention is the deliberate, rather than unforeseen, product of advocacy strategies, one question emerges: how are these low-visibility strategies coordinated across advocates—especially if they are geographically disperse and more locally active? It stands to reason that in order for advocates to conceal their intentions on a large enough scale to meaningfully diminish public participation or backlash, they would need to be unified in both purpose and process—a condition often lacking in legal campaigns. Even within the context of civil rights battles with strong centralized leadership, there is often dissension among the ranks. For instance, although popular narratives imply a uniformity and clarity of purpose among NAACP officials in pursuit of school desegregation rulings, studies suggest instead that this litigation was, to some degree, ad hoc and the subject of conflict among civil rights leaders.[135] Legal campaigns that rely on local rather than national leadership are likely to be even more vulnerable to internal dissent.

As a general rule, more than other modes of policy development, court-centered campaigns invite renegade advocacy. Where legislative or regulatory approaches offer fewer institutional avenues for policy change, there are numerous opportunities for *judicial* intervention, and the bar for entry is relatively low. These efforts are initiated by hundreds of advocacy groups, thousands of attorneys, and millions of individuals seeking to protect their rights.[136] In many instances they are not working in service of a broader national strategy.[137] Instead, members of disadvantaged minority groups and their advocates often decide to pursue a legal claim of their own volition, without the aid or approval of leading advocacy groups in their community. It is difficult, for instance, to conceive of modern struggles for same-sex family or group housing rights as resulting from an organized movement. Same-sex couples, rather than organizations, initiated much of the early litigation in the modern movement for marriage equality. So, too, did same-sex parenting litigation emerge out of the individual needs of gay and lesbian parents who were struggling to maintain custody of their children. In neither of these cases was litigation developed as part of an elite-driven, proactive strategy. Instead, particularly in the early stages of recent marriage equality efforts, national advocacy groups played catch-up to a legal strategy that was already in motion.

However, strategic cohesion is possible, even where national elite involvement is minimal.[138] If resources and incentives reward coordination, even the most fragmented advocacy network can adopt conforming strategies.

First, litigation campaigns that rely on innovative, yet technical, arguments encourage information-seeking and sharing across advocates. Advocates who use novel approaches to secure positive precedent will often advise others who are hoping to piggyback on these efforts or emulate victories in other jurisdictions. In fact, the more idiosyncratic an approach, the more barriers to entry, and the more concentrated knowledge will be in a handful of legal experts. These experts maintain control by selectively sharing the secrets of their success. For instance, while there are numerous same-sex parenting verdicts, the legal arguments and strategies were formulated and pursued—especially in the early years—by only a few parenting experts in each state. These attorneys are in frequent communication with each other, share information only with attorneys they trust to safeguard precedent, and intervene when inexperienced advocates attempt to enter the fray. Second, even if they do not serve a leadership role, national organizations can convene local experts to facilitate resource and information exchanges.

Furthermore, the degree to which *national* coordination is required to keep the public in the dark depends, to a great extent, on whether the *public* at issue is national or local. Some civil rights struggles are the product of widespread but nevertheless local disputes. Although the battles are being waged across the country, the "publics" involved are discrete communities, neighborhoods, or towns. Group housing advocates focus their efforts on combatting local attempts to derail their clients' housing rights. To that end, their below-the-radar strategies concentrate on minimizing or delaying local, rather than national, awareness of specific activities. Whether another group home advocate in a different state or community chooses to utilize more transparent approaches is often of little immediate concern to their housing efforts.

Avoiding Fault Lines

To some degree, as intimated above, same-sex parenting advocates enjoy more widespread options for low-visibility advocacy than do group home advocates. While conservative organizations have spent excessive resources to fund voter initiatives to bar same-sex couples from seeking marriage licenses, parenting advocates stayed out of the electoral limelight and instead sought co-parenting rulings from family court judges. Group home advocates face a more complicated policy environment—one that, in many ways, advantages group home opponents. Although most courts have fully embraced the right for group homes to operate in single-family neighborhoods, NIMBYism imposes a significant burden on that right. Opponents resort to a range of devices (electoral pressures, bribery, coercion, threats, violence) to prevent group homes from locating in single-family neighborhoods. If opponents can coerce or cajole a landlord or seller against offering their property to a group home operator, or create a sufficiently hostile environment so as to discourage a group home from setting up shop, they will have succeeded—even if their tactics are, later, admonished and sanctioned in court. Group home operators attempting to keep their homes amidst the outlaw justice of their adversaries will reject calls for deliberation and notification in order to protect their clients.

As stated above, proponents of deliberative democracy believe that only through forums of consensual citizen-driven decision making can we assure that policy outcomes reflect public desires. Citizens must be provided with a space to listen, debate, discuss, and, ultimately, determine their policy preferences. By promoting the free exchange of diverse views and experiences, citizens and policymakers can "gain new information, learn of different experiences of their collective problems, or find that their own initial opinions are founded on prejudice or ignorance, or that they have misunderstood the relation of their own interests to others."[139] Agreement and consensus among those affected by policy mandates legitimizes policies and fosters mutual respect among its subjects. It also promotes an environment of cooperation and compliance between winners and losers of policy struggles. Because all sides have been given the full weight of consideration and all parties equal space and time to make their case, the products of deliberative democracy, according to its champions, are less likely to polarize the public or pander to the privileged.

According to this ideal, participants would "regard one another as equals" and would be free to "defend and criticize institutions and programs in terms of considerations that others have reason to accept."[140] This push for greater citizen consensus has resulted in an increased reliance on formal modes of citizen deliberation in the policy process. Particularly at the local level, town hall meetings, zoning hearings, and other forms of citizen engagement attempt to formalize and institutionalize approximations of deliberative democracy into their policymaking processes. Before they can make any decisions, for instance, zoning, school, and licensing boards must often convene a public forum for all who are inclined to air their grievances and defend their preferences.

Critics of deliberative democracy (and these formalized approximations) argue that, although it has its virtues as a democratic ideal, its use as a standard practice in policy debates is problematic. Specifically, these critics question whether the pre-conditions upon which proponents of deliberative democracy base their assertions exist in current deliberative forums. In order for people to engage as equals and dissect each other's preferences through dispassionate reason and logic, each party must be perceived as equals.[141] In reality, however, individuals "encounter one another from very unequal professional, economic, political or cultural positions."[142] Depending on their social status, individuals may not be free to promote their views. Instead, they will be automatically disregarded or downgraded.[143] Rather than providing a space for reason to prevail, these public forums often reify and prolong identity-based hierarchies.[144] They can also devolve into arenas of denigration where individuals use such harsh language as to exact significant harm on its subjects. Even those who enter into citizen negotiations with goodwill and high hopes fall prey to using arguments and narratives that, unbeknownst to them, reflect prejudice rather than fact.

Under these circumstances the costs of public deliberation or notification could prove onerous for already disenfranchised groups. As Fung suggests, only "foolhardy idealists" would "limit themselves solely to persuasive methods of politics."[145] Requirements of public engagement demand that frequently maligned individuals, whose interests are marginalized by more politically dominant groups, subvert their own substantive gains for the virtues of perceived procedural fairness or the trappings of inclusion. This is most obvious in the context of voter-driven policy initiatives. Studies of the ballot initiative process, for instance, have found that subjecting minority rights to a majority vote most often curtails these rights and privileges.[146] This is true in smaller scale venues as well—such as hearings and board meetings. Although these arenas provide opportunities for citizens to air their complaints and register their perspectives, they have the potential to further alienate members of unpopular and unsupported minority groups. At a public hearing in Iowa concerning the state supreme court's decision to validate same-sex marriage, participants expressed dismay that individuals would now be required to view same-sex relations as "normal" and described the court's opinion as "violating the design of the almighty from creation . . . demolishing the very core of our society—the family unit."[147] Similarly, as discussed in Chapters 5 and 6, group housing advocates and residents are often subjected to inflammatory comments when they participate in public hearings to support their bids to establish group homes in single-family neighborhoods. In addition to imposing psychological burdens on minority groups seeking community approval, in many instances hostile hearings pressure elected officials to rule against minority demands—even when doing so violates legal precedent.

Critics assert that under conditions of endemic inequality—where discriminatory motives rather than objective reason drive policy debates—individuals are free to reject requirements of consensus in favor of other less democratically deliberative advocacy strategies.[148] While public notification requirements and town hearings claim to provide a respectable forum for considering and weighing public perspectives, in reality, they can achieve just the opposite. The debates they engender are frequently framed in the same discriminatory rhetoric that greases the wheels of exclusivity that drive American public policymaking. When faced with these barriers, advocates can regard venues of deliberative democracy as misaligned to their own circumstances or needs and sidestep them, as have low-visibility group home advocates, in favor of strategies that will dispel rather than reproduce these inequalities. Instead of alerting zoning boards, homeowners associations, public officials, or neighbors of their plans to move into a single-family neighborhood, some group home advocates secure housing without first notifying the public in the hopes that, when the public is eventually apprised of the group home's existence, opponents will have little substantive influence. By delaying notification until after their housing is secured, these advocates are choosing to engage with their communities from a more equal playing field (as co-equal community members).

The Promise of Invisibility in
Civil Rights Advocacy

Even where structurally feasible, however, low-visibility advocacy is not always advantageous. While certain issues may blossom within the shadows of public scrutiny, others will only wilt or whither. As Schattschneider suggests, those involving "individualism, free private enterprise, localism, privacy, and economy" will benefit from less visibility, while policy agendas concerning equality and civil liberties may thrive in the limelight.[149]

The costs and benefits of low-visibility policy reform are underexplored and mis-estimated. On the one hand, it is undervalued as a source of policy innovation. As one scholar suggests, "government action is sometimes most powerful when it is less visible."[150] Policy advocates may be able to enjoy great and enduring success when they keep their intentions off the public radar. Not only are policy prescriptions more likely to pass, but their outcomes and effects may also be more sustainable over the long term. Low-profile tactics invite less division and often promote collaboration among critical stakeholders. Consequently, this approach may offer more opportunities for policy elites to maneuver through a range of policy solutions and implementation options to reach an acceptable compromise. For instance, maintaining a low profile about positions or intentions, argues Covington, gives policymakers room to make concessions in order to further negotiations and facilitate consensus.[151]

Arguably, decreased or delayed opposition is the most significant benefit to low-visibility advocacy. It stands to reason that "visible" issues—causes that make headlines, or otherwise inspire public debate—have the potential to attract more negative attention and increase active opposition. Attempts to derail a policy's passage or implementation often rely on an organized "public will" to compel policymakers, activists, or administrators to either disregard or overturn legal victories. Visibility, therefore, through the media or other mechanisms (flyers, hearings, word of mouth) provides the first essential ingredient—a narrative for catalyzing a shared reaction among a group of, as-of-yet unrelated, individuals.

We also know that visibility and opposition are mutually reinforcing. Publicity invites opposition and opposition invites publicity. Not only is conflict more newsworthy by its very nature, but the desire to appear balanced and impartial prompts reporters to seek out counterarguments. This, argue Meyer and Staggenborg, "leads to coverage that emphasizes conflict, rather than content, and that often suggests an equivalence between opponents on a particular issue."[152] Early abortion coverage, they argue, illustrates this dynamic. Abortion advocates who wanted to publicize their position on decriminalization were able to gain media interest by offering to publicly debate abortion opponents. By providing this space, Meyer and Staggenborg contend, "media organizations helped to mobilize anti-abortion forces."[153] The desire for balancing provides "an automatic opportunity for countermovement activists, encouraging and magnifying their activity."[154]

That said, low-visibility tactics may prove costly. By minimizing public awareness of judicial victories, low-visibility civil rights legal advocacy withholds from minority groups a rallying point to encourage political engagement. In other words, the very strategies used to prevent counter-mobilization may also cripple minority empowerment. Without political empowerment, there is little opportunity for meaningful policy advancement beyond discrete court judgments. Just as backlash can permeate beyond one policy domain, so, too, can the benefits of public debate. Visibility in one policy arena— even where backlash ensues—can promote progress in other related issues.

Despite constitutional amendments and statutes banning same-sex marriage, for instance, pro-same-sex marriage rulings in Hawaii and Massachusetts helped to usher in increased economic benefits and partnership rights for gay and lesbian couples.[155] Against the backdrop of marriage equality campaigns, domestic partnerships and civil unions, which had previously been dismissed as radical, emerged as a workable compromise. Delay public awareness and you delay progress.

In addition to impeding political participation within disenfranchised communities, low-visibility tactics also diminish opportunities for public input and education, which could obstruct policy longevity. As stated above, public deliberation or stakeholder input is often cited as the key to good policy design. In the views of its proponents, public debate and participation in policy development increases civic engagement, promotes broader tolerance for opposing viewpoints, and bridges different social identities.[156] In most instances, the beneficiaries of policy modifications will, eventually, have to contend with public judgment. Particularly in cases where an unpopular issue or group gains policy traction, public awareness can be, at best, postponed rather than prevented. Promoting rights advancements through back channels may only further enflame public hostility once these policies see the light of day.

Whether backlash poses enough of a risk to forfeit the benefits of public debate varies by issue and advocate and depends largely on the degree of harm that would be incurred by clients, communities, and broader advocacy efforts were the opposition to prevail. If they lost in court or at the ballot box, for instance, gay or lesbian parents risked losing custody of or visitation with their children. On the other hand, in most cases, a loss for same-sex couples seeking the right to marry maintained the status quo, leaving them no worse off—in terms of legal protections and benefits—than they were prior to the enactment of anti-marriage initiatives. This is not meant to minimize the harm imposed on gays and lesbians by efforts to ban same-sex marriage. As I argue in Chapters 3 and 4, exposure to anti-gay rhetoric and the widespread use of legal mechanisms to promote discrimination was detrimental to many members of the LGBT community. The point here, quite simply, is that the status of their relationships, and the benefits provided, did not appreciably shift as a result of anti-marriage policies. For parenting advocacy, however, gays and lesbians could be legally worse off if a court ruled—or a policy required—that they could no longer continue to care for their child.

Even advocates fighting for the exact same policy gains will disagree about the value of inconspicuous advocacy. A combination of risk averseness and differing priorities may compel one set of advocates in a particular field to downplay transparency and others to champion public awareness. Group housing operators, for instance, vary significantly in their evaluations of the merits of visibility. Some will avoid public debate at all costs when attempting to secure housing, believing that the best cure for opposition to group homes is to have one as a neighbor. Others insist that public education is the only panacea for NIMBYism and will go to great lengths to invite public input early in the siting process.

At first blush, variation among advocates would seem to pose a problem for those attempting to maintain a low profile. If one set of actors wants to engage the public, their efforts would hamper below-the-radar tactics. In reality, however, the absence of a singular and widespread commitment to low-visibility advocacy does not always diminish its potency as a policy tool. First, although, there may be disagreement about which strategies to pursue within the same broad community of advocates, smaller or local pockets of legal experts may still work in tandem to shield court victories from the public. This is particularly true where the audience of a specific policy proposal is local, rather than national. In these instances, variation among stakeholders is not as risky—and may be beneficial as a method for adapting to local conditions.[157] Second, variation can sometimes serve complementary rather than conflicting purposes. Low-visibility gains for gay and lesbian parents, for instance, were used to leverage marriage equality victories. In its decision legalizing same-sex marriage, the Massachusetts Supreme Judicial Court relied on earlier, and far less publicized, precedent permitting same-sex couples to co-parent.

Housing and Family Rights

Group housing and same-sex family rights struggles provide us with two ideal platforms to explore the degree to which legal advocates can alter the visibility of issues that are prone to backlash in order to minimize its incidence or influence. For one thing, lesbians and gays and group home residents receive significant opposition simply because of their perceived identity as deviants or social misfits. Second, in each of these narratives these groups are challenging deeply entrenched societal norms and beliefs concerning "family values." For many, the "traditional family," comprised of two married heterosexual parents raising children, provides the foundation for good citizenship.[158] As such, "family" occupies a privileged status in American public policy—inviting both reputational and financial advantages.[159] In their attempts to integrate either physically or socially with "traditional" families—by moving into their neighborhoods or appropriating their institutions and benefits— LGBT parents and group home residents further threaten majority interests and become even more vilified.

Where these advocacy narratives each present policies that confront presumptions about traditional familial privilege, these policy arenas also present two unique examples of how and to what end advocates reduce visibility in order to secure policy gains. Through same-sex family rights advocacy we can see how low-visibility tactics are used as a preventive measure to stave off backlash efforts and prevent their growth. Although history will soon speak of the rapid turnaround in support for same-sex marriage, its polarizing politics served as a reminder to same-sex parents of what they could lose if they engaged the public in their demands for parenting privileges. By determining which legal authority, institutional setting, and frame would attract the least attention, same-sex parenting advocates were able to minimize public scrutiny of their gains in court, despite amassing judicial victories in at least half the states. These advocates located their arguments in statutory, administrative, or common-law doctrine rather than seeking constitutional validation. They avoided, especially in the early years, seeking appellate rulings and elected instead to concentrate on lower or family court victories. They also framed court and media narratives in terms of children's rather than gay or parenting rights.

Group home advocacy explores the prophylactic or soothing effects of low-visibility tactics. Although individual group housing plans do not often attract widespread *national* attention, housing, as a policy subject, holds significant weight for local communities. Group home opposition, in particular, has occupied all levels and segments of government. The potential neighbors of proposed group homes perceive these residences as posing a palpable and immediate threat to their family's quality of life and livelihood. Consequently, group home operators must, in their proposals, account for any opposition to their plans to locate in single-family neighborhoods. Both the high-visibility (collaborative) group home providers and low-profile (stealth) operators featured in the following chapters adopted their chosen strategies in response to the backdrop of opposition that typifies group home sitings. Collaborative providers pursued transparent or high-profile tactics, believing that, if kept in the loop, community members would come to accept their residents and trust the operators. Advocates who adopted a low-visibility approach delayed or sidestepped public notification or zoning requests until after they rented or purchased their property. These advocates determined that informing the public—either through informal communication with community residents or homeowners associations or through formal zoning board hearings—*prior to securing their housing* would only give the opposition ample time to organize and attack before group home operators could claim legal rights over their property. By postponing notification, advocates controlled the timing of, and consequently the damage caused by, public intervention. Although the outbreak of backlash is still significant, its effects are dampened when group home advocates and operators employ low-profile tactics.

Bearing the costs in mind, the low-visibility efforts of both group home and same-sex family advocates are profoundly instructive. They demonstrate the potential for court-based advocacy to successfully protect the rights and privileges of minority groups even in the presence of heavy public opposition. In both cases advocates deliberately chose lower-visibility strategies in order to keep the issue off the radar of public political discourse. The findings offer evidence that, in addition to more traditional avenues of high-impact litigation, low-visibility legal advocacy can be a relevant and viable mechanism of policy protection for those most vulnerable to majoritarian proscriptions.

3

A Public Debate on Same-Sex Marriage

IN 1992 THE issue of same-sex marriage made its first real appearance on the national political stage when Pat Buchanan, former Republican presidential candidate, announced at the Republican National Convention (RNC) that "there is a religious war going on in our country for the soul of America." He urged party leaders to "stand with [President Bush] against the amoral idea that gay and lesbian couples should have the same standing in law as married men and women.[1]" The RNC had recently altered its platform to oppose granting sexual orientation protected class status under civil rights laws and to ban same-sex marriage. During a convention speech Vice President Dan Quayle rejected the idea that "every so-called 'lifestyle alternative' is morally equivalent." When accused of "gaybashing," he appeared on *Good Morning America* to defend his position and explained that, while individuals "have the right to make that choice," most people "think that lifestyle is wrong."[2] Gay and lesbian advocates feared that their community would be used by Republicans to strike terror in the hearts of conservative voters. "Never in the history of American politics have we seen such aggressive anti-gay campaigning," announced a spokesperson from the National Gay and Lesbian Task Force.

> President Bush and Dan Quayle have vilified and demonized gay people as a threat to patriotic, traditional American family values . . . The political establishment doesn't have the communists to kick around anymore. Then it was Willie Horton. That won't work this year, following the Los Angeles riots. That leaves gays and lesbians.[3]

Even though, at that time, no state had validated same-sex marriage, the issue had become an important element of the Religious Right's call-to-arms against gay rights and the "liberal" social agenda.

Not since the Supreme Court's ruling in *Roe v. Wade* had there been such a perfect storm of opportunity for conservative mobilization. In addition to striking a chord with members of the Moral Majority and others harboring discomfort with homosexuality, same-sex marriage ignited a fierce defense of democratic values. Reliance on judicial, rather than legislative, mandates to achieve this policy goal added an extra layer of opposition to an already polarizing issue.[4] Unlikely coalitions of straight Americans united to oppose what were "seen as undemocratic courts and the too costly and illegitimate rights claims of an undeserving minority group."[5]

Just as one's position on abortion has long been the litmus test for commitment to traditional values, so too had one's position on same-sex marriage during this period. As early as 1992, presidential and vice presidential candidates (mostly Republican) sought to publicly affirm their animosity toward the legalization of homosexual unions. Even at the local level, political candidates used same-sex marriage to disparage their opponents. In 1983 a candidate hoping to make a name for himself as the Moral Majority candidate for Virginia State Senate "accused" his incumbent Democratic opponent of supporting same-sex marriage—much to the surprise of his opponent, who had never even considered the issue.[6]

Scholars, pundits, and politicians described initial backlash to same-sex marriage court rulings as further evidence of the courts' inability to advance social change.[7] In the now age-old argument that pits legislative power against judicial review, some cited the early public failure of marriage equality court opinions to dismantle public opposition in any but a few states as evidence of the courts' limited reach on issues that buck majority will. It is now clear that these warnings were premature. By October 2014, battle-fatigued marriage advocates had seen the fruits of their labor. Public opposition had waned. Public officials in both parties had "come out" as marriage supporters. Federal courts in several circuits had overturned numerous state constitutional bans. Even the Vatican had indicated a willingness to show sensitivity towards same-sex families (albeit attracting significant opposition from conservative Catholics worldwide).[8] The "pro-family" movement appeared to have lost traction.

That said, it is also without question that the politics of same-sex marriage have been as volatile as they are visible. This chapter provides a history of the evolution of same-sex marriage in the United States and a discussion of its public prominence. The fight for marriage equality is a prime example of high-visibility civil rights advocacy, having occupied significant public and elite attention over the past twenty years. It provides an especially relevant comparison for analyzing the low-visibility approach adopted by same-sex parenting advocates and detailed in Chapter 4. But same-sex marriage also has substantive significance for same-sex parenting. Parenting advocates devised their strategies against the backdrop of marriage equality (and broader anti-gay) opposition. Marriage equality politics, then, showcases the type of backlash that lay in wait for same-sex parenting advocates—and the context for their low-visibility efforts.

The Evolution of Same-Sex Marriage

As with many court-based movements, the high-profile fight to legalize marriage for same-sex couples was launched from humble beginnings. Although many credit the *Baehr v. Lewin* plaintiffs as the first set of couples to test the limits of heterocentric marriage statutes, attempts to expand marriage to include same-sex couples began in the early 1970s—but with little support from the courts.[9] In 1970 two gay men, Jack Baker and Michael McConnell, asked the city of Minneapolis to validate their relationship with a marriage license. They were denied the license and, ultimately, took their plea to the state supreme court. The court dismissed the couple's statutory and constitutional claims, arguing that procreation and child-rearing were essential elements of marriage and validated their state's prohibitions on same-sex marriage. Childless heterosexual couples, asserted the court, were theoretical imperfections; their existence did not require the court to constitute a ban on same-sex marriage as an equal protection violation.[10] The couple appealed to the US Supreme Court, but the Court showed little interest.

Baker and McConnell, however, were no amateurs to activism and were not easily discouraged. Baker had recently been elected student body president of the University of Minnesota-Twin Cities as a law student, making him the first openly gay individual elected to that position of any major university.[11] While pursuing their Supreme Court appeals, the couple simultaneously researched precedent that would allow Baker to "adopt" McConnell in order to provide McConnell with benefits that could only be conferred upon family members. In August 1971 a Minneapolis court approved the adoption of Jack Baker by Michael McConnell.[12] In 1972 a Methodist minister presided over the couple's wedding. Three years later they received word from the Internal Revenue Service that they had misfiled their '72 and '73 tax returns as joint returns and were owed $309 in tax savings under their readjusted status as two single men. The couple refused the refund and appealed the decision.[13]

On September 20, 1971, Paul Barwick and John Singer, upon learning that Washington State's marriage statute contained no gender-specific language, entered an auditor's office seeking a license to marry. Lloyd Hara, the auditor, contacted a local prosecutor to determine whether he was permitted to grant the couple a license. Although Hara supported the two men's efforts, he was required to deny their request, and was named as the defendant in their case against the state. "As a person of color, I've always been concerned about discrimination against anyone," he stated regretfully, years later. "I thought it was wrong then and I still firmly feel the same way."[14]

Not surprisingly, both the state superior and appellate courts ruled in favor of the state. The court argued that "the term 'marriage' . . . is the legal relationship between one man and one woman" and that the state's statutes "relating to marriage and marital property are clearly founded upon the presumption that marriage, as a legal relationship, may exist only between one man and one woman."[15] The two men chose not to appeal the matter to the Washington Supreme Court, concerned about the implications of bad precedent at such an early stage in the state's marriage equality debate.

Anthony Sullivan and Richard Adams successfully secured a marriage license from a Boulder, Colorado, county clerk in April 1975, after the district attorney's office approved the request. Six other couples had previously received marriage licenses from the same clerk, who later stated in an interview that the matter could be resolved simply by using the term "person" in lieu of any gender pronouns in the statute.[16] Ultimately, it was a representative from the United States Immigration and Nationalization Service who invalidated Sullivan and Adams's license while processing Sullivan's request for a green card. In a letter to the couple, the INS official, rejected their request and stated, "You have failed to establish that a bona fide marital relationship can exist between two faggots."[17] The letter was later rescinded and replaced with the following, less inflammatory, language:

[the male partner in a homosexual relationship] cannot function as a wife by assuming female duties and obligations inherent in the marital relationship. A union of this sort was never intended by Congress to form a basis of a visa petition.[18]

The two men lost their fight in federal court and Sullivan was asked to voluntarily leave the country or face deportation charges.[19] They left the country but returned one year later, without the blessing of U.S. officials and "under the radar of immigration authorities."[20] Adams passed away in 2010, shortly after he and Sullivan had begun talking about traveling to Washington state to legalize their marriage.[21]

While these efforts garnered little mainstream attention, the topic of homosexuality was, more generally, gaining increased interest from mainstream journalists. In the mid- to late 1960s the "homosexual in America" became a topic of popular inquiry through a series of articles published in *Time* magazine. These articles explored society's mixed reactions of "loathing... tolerance [and] empathy"[22] toward a "newly visible"[22] yet "anxiously camouflaged"[23] gay community. Journalists pondered how both societal and gay and lesbian ambivalence about their "position in society" would be resolved. Homosexuality, declared one contributor, "deserves fairness, compassion, understanding and, where possible, treatment. But it deserves no encouragement, no glamorization, no rationalization, no fake status as minority martyrdom."[24]

Their media visibility was amplified as gays and lesbians became the subject of heated political debates. Anita Bryant's "Save Our Children" crusade to strip sexual orientation from recent amendments to local anti-discrimination ordinances garnered national attention—due in part to Bryant's celebrity status as a popular singer and the spokesperson for the Florida Citrus Commission. Although her campaign repealed only four ordinances, her foray into gay rights—in particular her ability to frame gay rights as a threat to American families—became the foundation for a burgeoning conservative movement. As she frequently reminded her followers, "As a mother, I know that homosexuals cannot biologically reproduce children; therefore, they must recruit our children."[25] So effective was this narrative that policymakers took up the mantle of children's welfare and family stability on their own. California passed a law preventing clerks from issuing marriage licenses to gay couples. And in Florida, Bryant's home state, the legislature passed two bills curtailing the rights of homosexuals to marry each other or adopt children. Anti-homosexual sentiments were a source of pride among the public officials leading the crusades. Boasted one Florida senator:

> I would hope they would take this as a message that we are tired of you and wish you would go back in the closet. The problem in Florida is that homosexuals are surfacing to such an extent that they are infringing on average normal people who have a few rights too.[26]

Equal Rights Amendment (ERA) opponents capitalized on increasingly public anti-homosexual sentiments by arguing that the proposed amendment would require the legalization of same-sex unions.[27] One Michigan gubernatorial

candidate attempted to besmirch the character of ERA sponsors as "proponents of lesbian marriage, homosexual marriage."[28] Even as Congress revisited
the ERA and attempted to repackage the proposed amendment in 1983, it had
to contend with the specter of gay marriage. Phyllis Schlafly and other ERA
opponents continued to remind conservative members of Congress and the
public of the amendment's slippery slope into same-sex unions.

While Bryant and Schlafly waged their war against gays and lesbians,
several advances were being made on behalf of the gay community, interestingly from mainstream straight organizations and government officials.
For instance, although the Episcopal Church expressly forbade priests
from blessing homosexual unions, during the early 1980s several factions
within the Episcopal Church began to question this policy. Some even
publicly fought the church, at great risk to their own status within the
church hierarchy. In 1984 the Unitarian Universalist Fellowship became
the first major denomination to publicly support gay unions.[29] City governments began to offer domestic partnerships to gay couples. Following
the assassination of San Francisco's first openly gay elected public official, Harvey Milk, the city's Board of Supervisors unanimously voted to
offer city employees the same benefits to both unmarried and married
couples, gay or straight.[30] As one gay rights advocate recalls of progress in
California:

> Nobody was even pushing that issue in the gay community in
> California. It was well-meaning straight people who took the debate
> away from us.[31]

There was movement in the medical field as well. Researchers began to view
gay relationships as legitimate terrain for the study of intimate, rather than
aberrant, sexual behavior. In 1978 two researchers embarked on a study of the
elements that lead to successful partnerships. The study included unmarried
and married homosexual and straight couples.[32]

Same-Sex Marriage and "the Gay Agenda"

Despite these advances, national gay rights groups did not initially pursue
marriage equality as part of their policy agenda. They either remained silent
on the subject of marriage—or expressed ambivalence about the appropriate course of action. While individual gay couples, such as a lesbian couple
in Kansas in 1980,[33] continued to apply for wedding licenses, the gay community and its advocacy organizations remained divided over whether and

how to pursue marriage equality. One gay rights advocate who had been at Lambda Legal during this period recalled:

> If you had told me in the 1980s that marriage would be an important issue, let alone achieving it, I would have thought you were crazy. To me, litigants and individuals pushed the marriage issue. When you come out here to smaller cities it is a really important issue and the gay groups kind of fought them but then realized "if you can't beat them join them."[34]

Some believed that marriage equality communicated an important "symbolic as well as legal message"[35] to gay and lesbian couples. As Tom Stoddard, then director of Lambda Legal articulated, "Gay relationships will continue to be accorded a subsidiary status until the day that gay couples have exactly the same rights as their heterosexual counterparts."[36] Others, however, questioned whether striving for marriage equality was at best "assimilationist" and would render the gay community invisible or at worst would subject gay relationships to a sexist and oppressive institution.[37] For instance, Lambda's legal director, Paula Ettelbrick, an outspoken skeptic of same-sex marriage, argued that it "will constrain us, make us more invisible, force our assimilation into the mainstream, and undermine the goal of gay liberation."[38]

It wasn't until the mid-1980s that national civil rights organizations entered the fight to expand marriage to same-sex couples. In 1986 the American Civil Liberties Union became the first mainstream civil rights group to publicly announce its intention to pursue marriage equality for gay couples. Up until its announcement in October, the ACLU avoided any explicit support for same-sex marriage and, instead, focused their advocacy efforts on employment discrimination.[39]

Even after the Hawaii Supreme Court stood on the brink of legalizing same-sex marriage, gay rights activists and leaders remained publicly divided over whether or how to proceed. Some felt that other issues needed to take priority.[40] The Deputy Director of the Gay and Lesbian Victory Fund described efforts to pursue a more diverse policy agenda:

> With the number of issues that gays and lesbians and their friends and families have to face—health care, punishing hate crimes, ending workplace discrimination—I think that marriage is a little lower on the priority scale for a lot of people.[41]

Others advocated for a more localized and incremental approach. Rep. Barney Frank, who had become openly gay in 1987, chastised the marriage "movement" and asserted that activists "made a mistake pushing for national gay marriage—it's bad law and worse politics." As Pinello concludes,

> It's no wonder these early lawsuits miscarried. Lone couples, unsupported by organized lesbian and gay interests, made ad hoc assertions of novel social and constitutional positions, often without the benefit of legal arguments orchestrated by seasoned advocates.[42]

The opposition capitalized on organizational cleavages within the LGBT community and developed their own public portrait of the same-sex marriage movement. Conservative strategists characterized marriage equality efforts as part of a broader deliberate strategy designed by gay elites to trample traditional values. In reality, the same-sex marriage movement was born out of isolated attempts by gay and lesbian couples to secure licenses—quite a few of whom were contending with complications from HIV or AIDS—in order to secure health, survivor, and other government benefits.[43] In fact, although the *Baehr v. Lewin* plaintiffs initially contacted a local ACLU affiliate for legal assistance, they decided to seek representation from a private attorney after the ACLU appeared reticent to take the case without first establishing broad support within the LGBT community.[44]

By the mid-to-late 1980s, in anticipation of a potentially pro-gay Supreme Court ruling in *Bowers v. Hardwick* (1986), the Moral Majority, and conservatives in general, had developed a series of rhetorical attacks on same-sex marriage.[45] After Anita Bryant's "Save Our Children" campaign disbanded, conservative Christians had been waiting for an issue that would catalyze Christian voters. Same-sex marriage fit the bill perfectly. Although, in *Bowers* the Court ultimately upheld the Georgia statute that criminalized sodomy, many feared that a different decision would have opened a "Pandora's Box of efforts to extend privacy rights to polygamy, homosexual marriage" and other policies that threatened religious fundamentalism.[46]

Conservatives had so successfully "harnessed panic and fear about AIDS"[47]—directly linking its onset and rapid spread to the "gay lifestyle"— that the mere possibility of gays and lesbians receiving the blessings of the state to marry and have children catalyzed political and financial windfalls. In 1989 the Family Research Council, under the leadership of Gary Bauer, stood ready to defeat any attempt to legalize marriage for same-sex couples. Bauer viewed marriage equality "as a major battleground of the 1990s" and suggested that any advancement on this issue would "undermine deeply held and broadly accepted ideas of normalcy."[48] While the Hawaii Supreme Court drafted their landmark 1993 decision, and mainstream gay rights organizations debated the merits of pursuing marriage equality, the anti-gay marriage movement had formed and was ready for battle.

The hands of early marriage equality advocates were, then, forced by well-meaning and deserving same-sex couples who wanted legal recognition and by strategic right-wing conservatives seeking to gain political momentum. What resulted was, in some advocates' eyes, a movement ill-prepared to meet the obstacles that it would face.[49] Explained one gay rights activist:

> What happened is that there were a couple of people who decided that marriage would be the next issue but didn't anticipate how it would play out politically. There was no complete understanding of state constitutional processes. There wasn't a lot of work done on the ground level to educate people about the real family issues. This was a fight that wasn't envisioned. But there was a great strategy on the part of the opposition.[50]

Hawaii: Into the Limelight

It was not a foregone conclusion that Hawaii would become ground zero for the modern fight for marriage equality. As stated earlier, similar demands for marriage licenses date back to the 1970s, and we know that at least six couples in Colorado successfully received licenses.[51] There were efforts in other parts of the country as well. In the early 1990s several couples requested marriage licenses in Chicago and one asked a Washington, DC, clerk to grant them a license. When denied, the DC couple took the issue to court. They hired an attorney, William Eskridge, and argued that the denial violated the District's human rights code, which outlawed discrimination based on sexual orientation. A District of Columbia superior court judge ruled that the issue needed to be clarified by the legislature, not a court, but found that, historically, there were specific gender differences implied in the definition of marriage.[52] The couple appealed the case, causing a fissure among local government officials. DC corporate counsel argued that the denial was valid, while the DC Human Rights Commission advised the city that the couple's rights had been violated. It was the first time in their history that the Commission and corporate counsel disagreed.[53] As the case made its way through the DC courts, Congress deliberated over a domestic partnership bill for the District, which was supported by DC public officials, including the mayor who had championed a pro-gay rights agenda.

Gay couples in Texas were making headlines as well. In 1992 an Austin newspaper ran a paid announcement celebrating the recent nuptials of a lesbian couple.[54] News of the announcement prompted local religious leaders to castigate the couple's inclusion as "an insult to the momentous, happy occasion of the other married couples whose accounts of their weddings are portrayed on this page. The purity of these pages has been marred by the stain of immorality."[55] The paper's publisher argued that it was a simple choice "to not discriminate on the basis of sexual orientation." In fact, it was national buzz on the issue in 1992 that prompted Dan Quayle to weigh in during the presidential election and state that "so-called gay marriage and . . . a heterosexual marriage are not the same thing and should not be treated as the same."[56]

Hawaii's support was largely "a matter of luck."[57] As Evan Wolfson, the attorney who managed to convince a still skeptical Lambda Legal to at least marginally support the case, recalls

> There happened to be changes in the composition of the court, really just within a few months of the case making it there, that brought us a baby-boomer bench that was ready to hear it. . . . [S]ometimes you get lucky.[58]

The Hawaii Supreme Court's ruling in May 1993 was a game-changer in the fight for marriage equality. Although the court fell short of granting marriage rights to same-sex couples and remanded the issue to the lower court for review under a higher level of scrutiny, the court's decision was tantamount to an endorsement of same-sex marriage in the eyes of the public. Conservatives panicked over what an affirmative gay marriage court ruling by a court of last resort would mean for other states. Would full faith and credit require other states to validate the gay marriages performed in Hawaii? Could traditional marriage really be dissolved by the opinion of a few state court judges?

Gay rights advocates attempted to take control of the message as they sat on the precipice of marriage equality, and faced a well-funded and tightly organized conservative coalition.[59] Gone were the days of gay couples quietly marching to city hall to request a wedding license with nary a whisper in the headlines. Gay rights organizations were forced to take a stand. Wolfson, who had been one of few representatives from gay rights organizations on the front line of the Hawaii case, confronted elites in the gay community.

> Whatever you thought before, the world has just changed. This is a major ruling. A court has said that, unless the government can show a good reason why same-sex couples shouldn't be married, the state constitution requires it. Now is our time to make that case forcefully.[60]

Many in the LGBT community, however, remained unconvinced. Some local advocates, although supportive of marriage equality, felt that pushing for same-sex marriage would overshadow other policy pursuits or displace individuals who had little interest in marriage.[61] Recalled a field organizer for Human Rights Campaign:

> It was a privileged position. Most of my folks were blue-collar workers. The field organizers in some of these states had to carry guns. They weren't talking about marriage.[62]

One advocate described the new message of elite leaders as: "Look, we have a goal. And our goal is marriage equality for everyone. In the meantime there may be some backlash. But that's a sacrifice we have to make. There was a sense that conservative or flyover states didn't matter." She recalled, "By 2005–2006 the marriage advocates just didn't see anything else."[63]

Resource allocation was a big concern among gay rights advocates. As one activist remarked in 2011, "the marriage equality movement has become the primary focus of the LGBT movement, so it sucks a lot of energy and money resources."[64] Explained another:

> There was concern about marriage within [my] organization both because of backlash and funding drain. Marriage can move resources away from other work such as passing employment discrimination legislation, which always gets overshadowed by marriage amendments.[65]

And there was a fear that opposition to marriage would bleed into other policy arenas.

> Here we are trying to keep people from being fired, from being beaten up or killed and they are talking about marriage. I thought "Man you are gonna mess everything up." . . . When the first push for gay marriage took place in Massachusetts we were trying to push for domestic partnership benefits for state employees. We were scared to death of what that would do for our push.[66]

Other gay rights activists still believed, as Paula Ettelbrick did, that marriage reified patriarchy, and wanted to move beyond heterocentric understandings of relationships and family.[67] "The LGBT marriage rights movement is relatively conservative," explained one scholar.

Sometimes people will take issue with that and say that the gay rights movement should be more progressive. But that's not what it is now. There are progressive orgs within the community but you can't talk about a cohesive political agenda within the community. You can talk about what is more visible.[68]

Conservative voters ultimately resolved this issue. The possibility of same-sex marriage quickly became fodder for political conservatives hoping to build a reputation among values voters, for pundits interested in stirring the pot of political gossip, and, in response, for activists attempting to convene a national debate about the inequities and inequalities of being gay in a straight world.

"Two Steps Forward, One Step Back"

The celebration over the landmark decision in Hawaii proved short-lived in the wake of "enormous political backlash."[69] The maps in Figure 3.1 chart the rapid spread of same-sex marriage bans across the United States between 1996 and 2006. Immediately after the Hawaii Supreme Court issued its decision, state legislators crafted legislation defining marriage as between a man and a woman, and argued that the state's interest in "fostering procreation" was compelling enough to pass judicial scrutiny.[70] Succumbing to pressure from state officials and conservative activists, Congress passed the Defense of Marriage Act (DOMA). The legislation, signed into law by President Clinton in 1996, limited marriage, for federal purposes, to heterosexual couples, and permitted states to bar same-sex marriage and disregard same-sex marriages from other states. In 1998 Hawaiian voters responded to their court's decision by constitutionally removing gay marriage from the courts' jurisdiction.[71] Recalled Wolfson, "Hawaii mounted this tremendous political resistance and counterattack and challenge that, on the ground there, we were completely unprepared to meet."[72] This advocate agreed:

There was this threat that we didn't encounter with other issues. It's like a virus. If you let Hawaii then all gays everywhere can marry. If you allow it anywhere you allow it everywhere. That's the narrative that caught on and helped nationalize it even though the strategy was specifically to minimize national attention. They didn't understand that possibility.[73]

FIGURE 3.1 . Progression of Anti- and Pro-Same-Sex Marriage Policies Across the United States, 1996–2006

Source: National Gay and Lesbian Task Force and Freedom to Marry.

2000

1. New Hampshire
2. Vermont
3. Massachusetts
4. Rhode Island
5. Connecticut
6. New Jersey
7. Delaware
8. Maryland
9. Washington, DC

■ States with Constitutional Bans
▨ States with Statutory Bans
▧ States with Marriage or Full Marriage Benefits

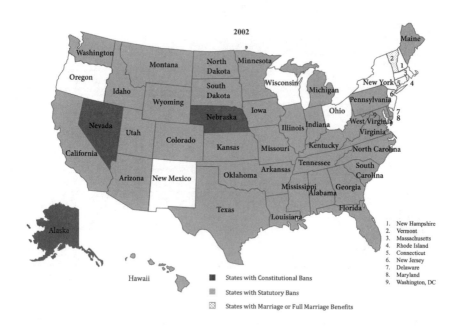

2002

1. New Hampshire
2. Vermont
3. Massachusetts
4. Rhode Island
5. Connecticut
6. New Jersey
7. Delaware
8. Maryland
9. Washington, DC

■ States with Constitutional Bans
▨ States with Statutory Bans
▧ States with Marriage or Full Marriage Benefits

FIGURE 3.1 (Continued)

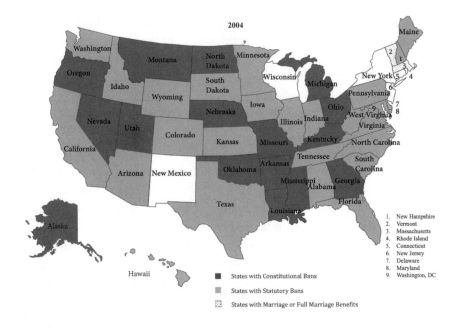

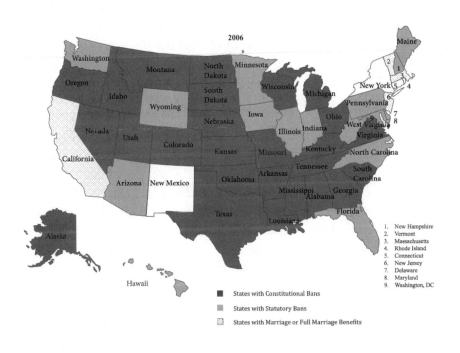

FIGURE 3.1 (Continued)

Despite the backlash, individual gay couples continued their quest for marriage equality, and the courts began to respond. In 1998 a superior court judge in Alaska defined marriage as a fundamental right, requiring the state to provide a compelling reason for denying this right to same-sex couples.[74] Once again, backlash prevailed. Before the state's supreme court could weigh in, voters amended the state's constitution to ban marriage for gay and lesbian couples.[75]

In 1999 Vermont became the third state to consider the issue. Perhaps seeing the writing on the wall, the Vermont Supreme Court adopted a more cautious approach—one that worked with, rather than against, the legislature.[76] In its decision the court permitted the legislature to enact either same-sex marriage or "domestic partnerships" that would grant same-sex couples the same benefits as those enjoyed by their heterosexual counterparts. However, encouraged by DOMA, by 2000, opponents had convinced the vast majority of states to pass state-level DOMAs or constitutional amendments barring same-sex marriage, and in some cases civil unions (Figure 3.1).

Four years after the Vermont decision and a few months after the US Supreme Court outlawed all remaining anti-sodomy statutes in *Lawrence v. Texas*, the Massachusetts Supreme Judicial Court granted same-sex couples the right to marry in *Goodridge v. Department of Public Health*. However, where the Vermont Supreme Court remained open to marriage alternatives, the *Goodridge* court left no room for civil unions. When asked by Massachusetts legislators to provide guidance as to whether civil unions would be acceptable, the court unequivocally rejected that option. Reiterating arguments from their November ruling, the Justices chastised civil unions as an "exclu[sion] from the full range of human experience." In October 2006 the New Jersey Supreme Court followed Vermont's lead and ruled that same-sex couples are constitutionally guaranteed the "full rights and benefits enjoyed by heterosexual married couples."[77]

The Massachusetts court's unambiguous validation of same-sex marriage meant that gay and lesbian claims to constitutional protections could no longer be viewed as "fringe" or "academic" musings.[78] They now had the backing of legal authority. However, "the entrenched connection between religion and state on family policy" posed a mounting threat to gay rights progress on this front.[79] Just as they had after Hawaii, opponents responded swiftly through ballot box reprisals. Between 2004 and 2006 the second phase of anti-gay marriage ballots hit the states in the form of constitutional bans (Figure 3.1). In total, by the end of 2006, same-sex marriage had been banned by either statute or constitutional amendment in more than forty states. Confirming conventional wisdom, these waves of backlash came on the heels of landmark state court rulings supporting marriage equality. Fifteen states passed state-level DOMAs within three years after *Baehr* and twenty-three enacted constitutional amendments during the three-year period following *Goodridge* (Figure 3.2).

Marriage activity was not confined to state-level politics. Each of the major political parties spent significant time and resources distinguishing their marriage equality positions on the national stage—despite their united disapproval of same-sex marriage. Democrats attempted to minimize the importance of marriage bans and actively opposed the Federal Marriage Amendment, which would have constitutionally limited marriage to heterosexual couples. They endorsed "equal responsibilities, benefits, and protections" for gay or lesbian-headed families.[80] The Republican Party, conversely, devoted a section of their platform to "protecting marriage" from judges who might "force states to recognize other living arrangements as equivalent to marriage," and limiting its benefits to heterosexual couples in order to preserve the "well-being of children."[81] In service of these goals, they supported a constitutional amendment defining marriage as between a man and a woman. Party leaders followed suit. Both John Kerry (the 2004 Democratic presidential candidate) and President Bush opposed marriage equality efforts. Yet, while Kerry pressed for a reduced national focus on marriage bans, Bush .

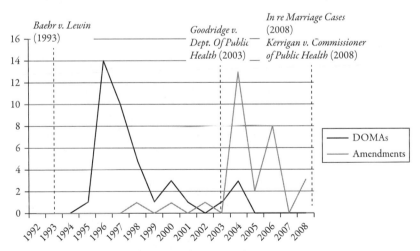

FIGURE 3.2. Same-Sex Marriage Bans by Type and Year, 1992–2008
Source: National Gay and Lesbian Task Force and Freedom to Marry.

repeatedly cast Kerry as a "northeastern liberal who is out of touch with the values of the rest of the country" because of his tacit support for civil unions.[82] He used the campaign trail to promote his support for a federal amendment and several state-wide measures barring same-sex unions.

Public Panic

Almost immediately after the Hawaii Supreme Court issued its ruling, same-sex marriage became a matter of acute public interest. When opposition to marriage equality garnered the attention of presidential candidates and party elites, interest turned into frenzy. It has been difficult at any point during the past two decades to turn on the television, read a newspaper, or follow politics in general without hearing about national debates concerning gay marriage. This was particularly true during election cycles.

One measure of the public's interest in marriage equality, aside from the more obvious proliferation of voter-driven bans presented in Figure 3.1, is media coverage. Figure 3.3 charts the number of articles on same-sex marriage published by *The New York Times* from 1996 to 2006, the height of same-sex marriage backlash.[83] Coverage of same-sex marriage reaches into the hundreds—peaking at 434 in 2004—during periods of high court activity and increased election-aided backlash. Local coverage is equally revealing, especially at pinnacle moments of marriage equality activity—in 1996 when Congress enacted DOMA and 2003 onward, after same-sex marriage was officially legalized in Massachusetts (Table 3.1).

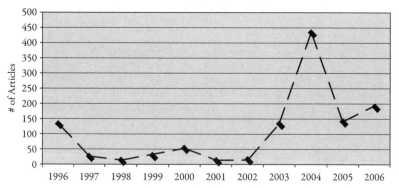

FIGURE 3.3. *New York Times* Articles on Same-Sex Marriage, 1996–2006

Source: LexisNexis search for *New York Times* articles including the following terms in headlines or lead paragraphs: same-sex marriage; homosexual marriage; gay marriage; lesbian marriage between 1996 and 2006.

Table 3.1. Local Coverage on Same-Sex Marriage

Year	Marriage Articles	Marriage Editorials
1996	594	66
1997	186	32
1998	181	37
1999	192	45
2000	202	90
2001	76	21
2002	66	0
2003	919	387
2004	2631	524
2005	861	213
2006	1304	411

Source: LexisNexis search for articles in regional newspapers including the following terms in headlines or lead paragraphs: same-sex marriage; homosexual marriage; gay marriage; lesbian marriage between 1996 and 2006.

This is not surprising, as it was during this period that same-sex marriage was both highly visible and hotly contested. Conflict and coverage provided mutually reinforcing guarantees that the issue would remain on the public's agenda.

Public officials catalyzed and capitalized on this attention. Just as Christian Conservatives had hoped when they first set their sights on same-sex marriage, the issue had, by 2004, achieved the stature of abortion as a mantra and mantle for values voters. In his re-election campaign speeches, for instance, President Bush frequently linked the two issues. In all but two instances, whenever abortion is mentioned, so, too, is gay marriage—with equal attention and intensity.[84] In more than 60 percent of his campaign speeches, Bush reminded his audience that his administration

> stand[s] for a culture of life in which every person matters and every person counts. We stand for institutions like marriage and family, which are the foundations of our society. We stand for judges who strictly and faithfully interpret the law.[85]

Toward the end of the campaign he referred explicitly to Kerry's vote against the Defense of Marriage Act in the same breath as his vote against the Partial Birth Abortion Act.[86]

Of course, this was a reciprocal relationship. Just as conservative candidates hoped to mobilize their base through public pleas to protect "traditional marriage" from rampant judicial activists, marriage opponents used this publicity to achieve their goals—to use the ballot box to define marriage as a "heterosexual-only" institution.

The ease with which opponents were able to launch a public and polarizing attack on same-sex marriage can be credited, in part, to the way they pitched their frames and appeals. Although religion and morality figure prominently in many discussions of same-sex marriage, formal appeals to preserve "traditional marriage" centered on one primary issue: children's welfare. Marriage equality opponents were able to create immediate and widespread panic about the possibility of same-sex marriage by arguing that same-sex marriage hurts children.

Focus on Family, the leading organization in the fight against same-sex marriage, asserted (and remains committed to the idea)[87] that same-sex marriage will confuse children about sexual orientation and will deny them the benefits of parents who are committed to each other over the long term. James Dobson, the group's founder, has proclaimed that gay marriage will lead to same-sex adoption, to an increase in the placement of foster care youth in gay households, and increased custody rights for gay parents.[88] In its arguments in *Goodridge*, the State of Massachusetts asserted that banning same-sex marriage helped to preserve child rearing in "two-parent biological families." Supporters of the Defense of Marriage Act and the Federal Marriage Amendment maintained that the mission of traditional marriage, and therefore the primary justification for protecting the institution, is child rearing—specifically by fathers and mothers. For instance, hearings on the Federal Marriage Amendment in 2004 highlighted the negative impact that same-sex marriage would have on child well-being and family stability.[89] Argued Senator Rick Santorum (R-PA):

> Marriage is about children. Marriage is about the glue that holds the basic foundational societal unit together, and that is the family. When we change the composition of that glue, we weaken the bonds of marriage and then we weaken the American family.[90]

Jay Sekulow of the American Center for Law and Justice framed the question as follows:

Social science, and human experience over hundreds of years, tells us marriage is best for the family, and especially for children. Children are hurt when either the father or the mother is absent ... The question must therefore be settled: is the marriage of one man and one woman, and the hope of children it provides, the cornerstone of our welfare, of our liberties, and of our responsibilities as free people; and if so, must it be protected?[91]

Rep. Steve Chabot concurred:

The thing that brings us here today, obviously, is the fact that many of us believe—in fact the overwhelming majority, I believe, in this country believes that marriage has always been a cornerstone of our society. It is an institution that is important, obviously, for raising children; and it has always been recognized as a man and a woman.[92]

Opposition advocates responsible for the overwhelmingly successful movement to constitutionally ban same-sex marriage at the state level similarly argued that traditional marriage should be preserved because "children do better with a mom and a dad."[93] A 2006 report issued by the Senate Republican Policy Committee documented these fears and warned that in the absence of constitutional protections for traditional marriage, complicated child custody battles would ensue, particularly among married lesbian and gay couples from "gay marriage states" who later moved to states with marriage bans.[94]

Concern for children's welfare and family stability is highlighted in same-sex marriage media coverage as well.[95] A content analysis of local articles on marriage equality during the height of backlash (1996–2006) reveals that, among articles citing opposition arguments, a greater percentage of articles mentioned either children's or family welfare than frames more commonly associated with the anti-marriage equality movement such as moral values (Figure 3.4).

Opponents were also mindful about appearing discriminatory or homophobic and went out of their way to develop frames that would deflect allegations of bigotry, especially after the Court's opinion in *Lawrence v. Texas* drew less opposition than expected.[96] As President Bush articulated in response to *Goodridge*, "Tolerance and belief in marriage aren't mutually exclusive points of view. I do believe in the sanctity of marriage. It's an important differentiation. But I don't see that as conflicting with being a tolerant person or an understanding person."[97] The editor of a Catholic

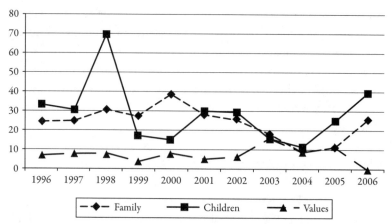

FIGURE 3.4. Percentage of Anti-Marriage Equality Frames by Type 1996-2006
Source: LexisNexis search for articles in regional newspapers including the following terms in head-lines or lead paragraphs: same-sex marriage; homosexual marriage; gay marriage; lesbian marriage.

magazine encouraged Republican candidates and the White House to be sensitive to the tone used in their efforts to defend traditional marriage. During an interview, he stated:

> There's a danger of overplaying it in the tone with which it's dealt. In defending the traditional notion of marriage, we should all avoid a condemning tone or a self-righteous one.[98]

In light of these rhetorical constraints some opponents elected to side-step the issue of homosexuality altogether, and instead cast the struggle as between activist judges and helpless state majorities. These narratives warned the American public of the perils of allowing unelected or unresponsive judges to dictate morals, and extolled the virtues of legislative or popular decision making as the most appropriate way to determine the outcome of marriage equality. As one opponent argued:

> Well the courts are the ones that have caused the problems in the first place. We never had same sex marriage until courts in Massachusetts forced it on us. Now we have judicial activism. That's why we have the problem we have.[99]

Anti-marriage equality advocates argued that whatever the merits of same-sex marriage, the courts should not be permitted to overwhelm legislative authority on the subject. Indeed, this was one of the primary arguments swaying members of Congress to enact DOMA.

> We are here today because a few judges in Hawaii, against the express wishes of the Hawaiian people, are contemplating a radical social change. Ordinary people did not pick this fight. They are not the aggressors. They are merely defending the basic morality that has sustained the culture for a long, long time. Yet good men and women of varying beliefs have been subjected to a barrage of name calling and abuse simply for saying that marriage ought to be the union of a man and a woman, and that the laws should protect this vital social norm.[100]

Same-sex marriage, vituperated James Dobson, is the product of an "oligarchy" of judges "determined to make all of us dance to their music."[101] To promote her attempt to amend the Constitution to outlaw same-sex marriage, Representative Marilyn Musgrave said she wanted "to let the people decide, not unelected judges who are virtually unaccountable to voters."[102] Bush similarly argued that he was forced to support a constitutional amendment because of the actions of "activist judges" in Massachusetts.. Lawyers in New Jersey and Maryland, in their attempts to thwart the legalization of same-sex marriage in their respective states, argued in briefs that the question is not about the merits of same-sex marriage, but rather the appropriateness of judicial involvement.[103] The issue, argued Maryland attorneys, is one best left to the "legislative forum."[104] On average, between 2002 and 2006, more than 50 percent of articles with an anti-same-sex marriage frame contained anti-court rhetoric (Figure 3.5).

Similarly, opponents focused their efforts on protecting state autonomy from pro-gay judicial tyrants. When they introduced the Marriage Protection Act, to remove from federal court jurisdiction questions concerning state-level bans on same-sex marriage, congressional supporters explained that the "bill is really a reaffirmation of states' rights."[105] In the aftermath of *Goodridge*, then Governor Mitt Romney ran to the aid of other states and attempted to make the option available only to Massachusetts residents. Through an obscure and rarely referenced 1913 state law, originally established to preserve anti-miscegenation policies in other states, Romney instructed clerks to refuse marriage licenses to out-of-state residents who were legally barred from marrying in their own states and alerted governors in all forty-nine states of his intention. Marriage equality opponents, in turn, "applaud[ed]

FIGURE 3.5. Percentage of Articles with Negative Frame Using States' Rights or Judicial Activism Rhetoric

Source: LexisNexis search for articles in regional newspapers including the following terms in headlines or lead paragraphs: same-sex marriage; homosexual marriage; gay marriage; lesbian marriage.

the governor for respecting the forty-nine other states where it is the public policy to define marriage as a union between a man and a woman."[106]

This "states' rights" argument is prominent in media coverage, particularly during periods of high movement activity. In Figure 3.5 we see this argument appear in more than half of the articles with anti-marriage frames in the aftermath of gay marriage litigation in Hawaii and DOMA proceedings, in almost 70 percent after the Vermont Supreme Court's decision in *Baker v. Vermont*, and just under 40 percent in 2003, when *Lawrence v. Texas* and *Goodridge* were issued. Ironically, this same argument would come to be embraced by marriage equality advocates in their efforts to bring down the federal same-sex marriage ban articulated in DOMA, discussed below. Perhaps this is why it becomes less prevalent among marriage equality opponents—at least in the press.

In many respects advocates for same-sex marriage had to play catch-up to what seemed to be a highly controlled message supporting same-sex marriage bans. As stated earlier, advocates at the national level were slow to join the ranks of same-sex marriage supporters. Once they did, however, they argued fiercely that the issue of marriage equality was primarily about "gay rights," a frame that appeared in more than 50 percent of the articles that included pro-same-sex marriage arguments between 1996 and 2006.

One attorney in Louisiana described the state's proposed constitutional amendment banning gay marriage as removing "rights that are inalienable and inviolate."[107] "We want equal rights, not special rights," argued a gay rights activist in Ohio after the state passed its amendment.[108] When questioned about gay marriage momentum in Washington, Matt Foreman of the National Gay and Lesbian Task Force stated "and if it's a Vermont-style civil-unions decision, the challenge will be getting the legislature to do the right thing and give people full equal rights, not just a shadow version of that."[109]

"Changing Tides"

Somewhat unexpectedly, as widespread backlash against same-sex marriage waned, leaving an overwhelming majority of states without same-sex marital options—gay rights groups began to gain traction. States without constitutional bans on marriage (particularly those with greater restrictions on voter-driven initiatives) soon became viable battlegrounds for marriage advocacy. In 2008 supreme courts in California and Connecticut validated same-sex marriage, although opponents in California quickly gathered enough votes to pass a constitutional amendment barring state recognition of LGBT nuptials. In 2009 the Iowa Supreme Court overturned the state's legislative ban on same-sex marriage. That same year the Vermont legislature decided to upgrade their civil unions to full marriage equality. Maine and New Hampshire also passed same-sex marriage legislation, and DC followed suit in 2010.

By the end of 2012, nine states and the District of Columbia had granted marriage equality to same-sex couples. One year later that number had nearly doubled, to sixteen states and the district. If civil unions states are included, nineteen states offered significant marriage benefits, if not actual marriage, to same-sex couples as 2013 came to a close (Figure 3.6).

This increased uptick in the number of states willing to support marriage equality prompted some formerly resistant public officials to "come out" and voice their support for same-sex marriage. Despite his support for DOMA, President Clinton announced in 2009 that he "was wrong" about same-sex marriage, and he later called for DOMA to be overturned.[110] Although he still supported state autonomy on the issue, he stated, in an interview with Anderson Cooper, that "me, Bill Clinton personally, I changed my position. I am no longer opposed to that. I think if people want to make commitments that last a lifetime, they ought to be able to do it."[111] John Kerry, too, once supportive of a constitutional amendment banning same-sex marriage in Massachusetts,[112] announced

Marriage

1. New Hampshire
2. Vermont
3. Massachusetts
4. Rhode Island
5. Connecticut
6. New Jersey
7. Delaware
8. Maryland
9. Washington, DC

■ States with marriage bans

▨ States with full marriage benefits

▨ Marriage equality states

FIGURE 3.6. Marriage Equality, 2013

Source: National Gay and Lesbian Task Force and Freedom to Marry.

his allegiance to same-sex marriage in 2011 and later penned an op-ed for the *Boston Globe* articulating his struggle. As he stated in a *Globe* interview:

> I don't think it hurts the things I thought it would; lesson learned. You evolve with these things. You see through experience what happens. The sort of concerns I had—that somehow it would have some impact on the quality of church teaching, or that I wasn't honoring that—I think is just not borne out by experience. Period.[113]

And shortly after Vice President Biden issued an impromptu announcement supporting same-sex marriage, President Obama became the first sitting US president to publicly declare his support for marriage equality—doing so on network television as his re-election campaign went into full swing.

These announcements from high-ranking officials (particularly President Obama) spurred a windfall of additional significant endorsements from organizations and individuals who could influence communities that were still on the fence. For instance, in addition to receiving a cue from President Obama, African American voters—who had been less supportive of the same-sex marriage movement, and its reliance on "rights" rhetoric, than other members of the Democratic Party—could take their lead from the NAACP and Colin Powell.[114] Shortly after President Obama declared his support for marriage equality, the NAACP acknowledged that same-sex marriage was a constitutionally protected "civil right."[115]

For politicians across the aisle, crises of conscience posed significant professional risks. One of the four Republican state representatives who supported New York's same-sex marriage legislation decided not to run for re-election in 2012. Believing that his position on marriage equality would place him in disfavor among some of his constituents, he decided to sacrifice his career aspirations for party unity.[116] Similarly, a high-ranking member of Mitt Romney's 2008 presidential campaign staff succumbed to calls for his resignation because of his sexual orientation, despite having support from Romney and other high-ranking campaign staffers. A spokesperson for the Romney campaign expressed disappointment over Republican reactions to his hiring (although Romney quickly reconfirmed his opposition to same-sex marriage).

> Wherever there are voices of intolerance within the party, or the Democratic Party, for that matter, it doesn't matter where it's coming from, it's disappointing. And the governor has taken the opportunity in the past to denounce those voices of intolerance. We do not take into consideration non-factors like race or ethnicity or sexual orientation. We look for the best possible people to do the job.[117]

Republican strategists saw the writing on the wall and urged the party leadership to adopt a more moderate stance on marriage equality. Citing public opinion polls that show increasing support for same-sex marriage among Republicans, a former Bush pollster drafted a memo calling for Republican support for pro-gay rights policy points.[118] Republican consultants and more moderate party leaders amplified this request after President Obama's re-election victory, and some listened. Early 2013 saw a revived interest in Republican confessions of same-sex marriage support most likely brought on by Obama's reference to Stonewall among the several landmark civil rights struggles mentioned during his second inaugural address.

What prompted this shift? For one thing, gay rights advocates retreated from using the "rights" frame that characterized much of their initial messaging. Although they had no hope of minimizing publicity, in the aftermath of their significant electoral losses marriage equality advocates began to test messaging that limited or avoided altogether any mention of gay rights. Their goal was to give those in the middle some opportunity to reflect upon the merits of marriage equality. Research indicated that by using a "rights" frame, advocates were alienating potentially persuadable voters. Third Way, a think tank working in partnership with Freedom to Marry, an umbrella organization created in 2003 by Evan Wolfson to help organize the marriage equality movement, asked heterosexual individuals what marriage meant to them and how they perceived the motivations of gays and lesbians who were seeking marriage rights. They found that heterosexuals focused on "love and commitment" when they talked about marriage, but felt that gays and lesbians, "selfish[ly]," only wanted rights and benefits.[119] This finding prompted Wolfson's group, in collaboration with a number of state-level gay rights organizations and scholars, to form "Why Marriage Matters" in 2011. Their aim was to refocus marriage messaging from "rights" to "love, commitment and family." Campaigns in Washington, Maine, and Maryland successfully tested this new language. Rather than featuring ads that focused on gay rights and the benefits of marriage, these campaigns often ran ads in which the parents of gays and lesbians implored voters to allow their children to get married or highlighted gay and lesbian families.[120] The three states became the first in the nation's history to usher in marriage equality through a popular vote.

For public relations experts, the proof of the frame's success is in the numbers. "The rapid turnaround in public support for marriage" provides clear evidence that "message really matters."[121] In just under twenty-five years, support had progressed from a 12-percent approval rating to just over 50 percent (Figure 3.7). As public opinion expert Nate Silver explains:

> If you look at the numbers on abortion they've been pretty much the same for decades. Maybe on gun rights, there's been some movement toward the pro-Second Amendment side, but not as rapidly as you see on gay rights issues or on gay marriage in particular. It's quite unusual for social issues to move even by two or three points a year, which, as we've seen, adds up to something pretty significant over a decade or so.[122]

Of course, even in late 2013, the rise in national support did not necessarily guarantee ballot box victories in the eyes of marriage equality advocates.

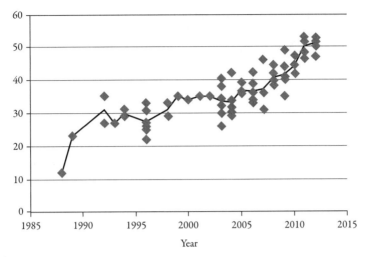

FIGURE 3.7. Average Percentage Public Support for Same-Sex Marriage, 1988–2012
*Data points represent individual polls from Gallup, Newsweek, NORC/GSS, CNN/ORC, PSRA/Pew, Yankelovich/CNN/Time, CBS/NYT, NBC/WSJ, Fox, Time/ABT/SRBI, Harris Interactive, Quinnipiac, and ABC/Washington Post. The line represents the annual average support based on polls.

For one thing, the degree to which national polls indicated an opening for advocates to dismantle same-sex marriage bans was up for debate. Since the primary impediments to same-sex marriage were state- rather than federally imposed, it was state level, rather than national, opinion that carried more weight for marriage equality supporters who were interested in overturning bans through democratic means. National support and state attitudes toward same-sex marriage varied significantly. For instance, in the same month that national public support for marriage equality surpassed 50 percent, North Carolina voters approved a broad constitutional ban on all same-sex unions with more than 60 percent of the votes.

Even state-level polls had the potential to overestimate support. "It's not that people are lying," explained one pollster. "It's an intensely emotional issue. People can report to you how they feel at the moment they're answering the polls, but they can change their mind."[123] For instance, field polls commissioned just one week prior to voters approving California's Proposition 8— which constitutionally barred same-sex couples from marrying—indicated the initiative would lose by 5 percentage points.[124] It ultimately passed with 52.5 percent of the vote. "People are conflicted," explained one advocate. "Their intellectual position can show up in a poll and their emotional position shows up in the voting booth."[125] Advocates required more than a marginal lead in the polls to consider asking the voters to remove marriage bans. As the president of Basic Rights Oregon explained of the group's decision not to pursue an initiative to dismantle Oregon's constitutional ban in 2012,

> We need to know that we've moved enough of the public in terms of their growing acceptance and awareness of what it means to extend the freedom to marry. It was clear looking at the landscape in the fall that we needed more time to have the conversation. The numbers just weren't there in terms of support for a 2012 ballot measure campaign.[126]

Back to Court

Uncertainty about public support along with growing impatience among same-sex couples prompted advocates to continue to pursue court support and turn their attention to federal judicial waters.

There were two prongs to federal marriage litigation. The first leveraged state-level marriage equality victories in order to dismantle Section 3 of DOMA. Marriage equality states—and their married gay and lesbian residents—argued that the federal ban on same-sex marriage violated both the equal protection rights of same-sex couples by treating them differently from married heterosexual couples and the spending clause by forcing states with same-sex marriage to contravene their own constitutions in order to continue to receive federal funding for services regulated by marital status.

DOMA litigation enjoyed broad support among gay rights activists. Explained one scholar early on in the appeals process, "Those are very good cases from a constitutional perspective. DOMA is so blatantly discriminatory from a state perspective . . . The federal government has always deferred to state definitions of marriage."[127] It was pragmatic. By deferring to state authority, this approach provided some middle ground for those who opposed same-sex marriage. As the First Circuit Court of Appeals conveyed in *Massachusetts v. HHS*:

> Many Americans believe that marriage is the union of a man and a woman, and most Americans live in states where that is the law today. One virtue of federalism is that it permits this diversity of governance based on local choice, but this applies as well to the states that have chosen to legalize same-sex marriage.

President Obama agreed. Although executive officials continued to implement DOMA, Obama directed Department of Justice officials to examine whether Section 3 could survive anything higher than rational basis review—the lowest standard of Supreme Court analysis for cases involving constitutional questions. Under a higher standard of review it is far more difficult for a government entity to prevail in their legal defense of legislation that may be constitutionally questionable. The Department of Justice determined that it would be impossible for Section 3 to survive anything but rational basis and, on February 23, 2011, Obama informed Congress that his administration would no longer defend DOMA in court.[128]

Ultimately it was Edith Windsor's Canadian marriage to her wife Thea Spyer that prompted Supreme Court review of DOMA. The two were New York residents and had married in Canada in 2007. At that time Canada provided one of few options for same-sex couples seeking legal marital validation. New York recognized their marriage in 2009, after Governor Paterson issued an executive order validating out-of-state same-sex marriages. Spyer died that same year, leaving Windsor her estate and—because of DOMA—a federal tax bill of $363,000. Windsor filed a complaint in the Second Circuit—which, unlike some other circuits, was not barred by existing precedent from using "heightened scrutiny" to review same-sex marriage bans. Windsor prevailed under this heightened standard and the Second Circuit joined the 1st and the 9th in ruling Section 3 unconstitutional. The government (now represented by two conflicting parties—the Obama administration, calling for DOMA's demise, and the Bipartisan Legal Advisory Group,[129] which had convened to defend DOMA) appealed the ruling to the Supreme Court. On June 26, 2013, in a 5–4 decision delivered by Justice Kennedy, the Court struck down Section 3, describing it as "injur[ing] the very class New York seeks to protect" and contravening "basic due process and equal protection principles."[130] The law, Kennedy stated, "impose[s] a disadvantage, a separate status, and so a stigma upon all who enter into same-sex marriages made lawful by the unquestioned authority of the state."[131]

The second category of federal marriage adjudication directly challenged the constitutionality of state constitutional bans and received, at least initially, only lukewarm support from gay rights advocates. David Boies and Ted Olson (the adversaries of *Bush v. Gore* (2000) fame) raised more than a few eyebrows, in 2009, when they teamed up to take on California's Proposition 8—the state's newly minted constitutional ban on same-sex marriage. In many ways, this unexpected partnership was devised specifically to rattle naysayers and fence-sitters and force them to think about the consequences of limiting marriage to heterosexuals. Explains Olson:

> The harm that that does to those loving individuals, who are our fellow citizens—they are our doctors, our lawyers, our neighbors, our friends, our coworkers—we are doing great harm by discriminating against people. And I think the more people hear what we have to say, what David and I have to say, the more people will understand that. That's one of the wonderful things about the fact that we have come together. Because people will ask . . . "Why are you doing this? What is your explanation?" And [it] gives us a chance to explain the damage that's being done by discrimination, and the great burden that would be lifted if we finally stop.[132]

However, at the time, many in the LGBT community, including leading marriage equality advocates, felt that Supreme Court review was premature. As one advocate explained,

> The national LGBT organizations were initially opposed to the Prop 8 case. They wanted to keep it at the state level. If the Prop 8 case goes to the Supreme Court I just don't see the Supreme Court telling the states that all of their mini-DOMAs are unconstitutional. I think it is a mistake to think the Supreme Court is going to lead the country. The anti-miscegenation case wasn't taken until after only 15 states had these laws.[133]

Judges seemed equally reticent. Although a district court judge issued a detailed, and scathing, indictment of the state's constitutional ban, on appeal, a three-judge panel argued that, by removing a right that had once existed—even if only for a short time, Prop 8 violated the lowest standard of equal protection review. In so doing, the appellate court sidestepped more contentious—and more broadly applicable—arguments regarding fundamental rights and suspect classifications and limited the scope of the decision to events that transpired only in California.

As the Prop 8 case climbed the ladder of appellate review, it took on a clown-car quality similar to that of the DOMA cases, as supporters began defecting from the cause and others stood up to defend it. Just as the Obama administration had decided to opt out of defending DOMA in court, so, too, did the governor and attorney general of California. After the district court overturned Prop 8, the state called it quits. The proponents of Prop 8, however, would not be deterred. They filed a motion to intervene and were, ultimately, granted permission by the California Supreme Court. By the time the case reached the Roberts Court, the question of the proponents' standing was of equal intrigue to that of the case's substantive claims. Would the Supreme Court actually permit initiative proponents to defend a policy in court even if the state has no interest in litigating? The Supreme Court disagreed with the lower courts on that count and denied the proponents standing to appeal. They were, therefore, exonerated from having to weigh in on the more controversial element—whether a state could bar same-sex couples from receiving marriage licenses. Their decision left the district court's ruling in place and the thirty-plus state bans outside of California untouched.

Post-*Windsor*, however, the judicial climate had become far more supportive of marriage advocacy efforts. State courts in New Jersey and New Mexico used the Court's language in *Windsor* to require their states to recognize the marital rights of same-sex couples. Bans were overturned in 10 additional states through federal judicial fiat—which in some instances went unopposed by state officials (Pennsylvania and Oregon).[134] On October 6, 2014 the Court refused to grant cert to any of the marriage cases that were ripe for review, letting stand these unanimously pro-marriage equality appellate court rulings. Five additional states stood on the brink of marriage equality in the wake of the decision. Bans in these states were presumed to be unconstitutional by virtue of their inclusion within the jurisdictional reach of the federal court rulings that had been validated (at least tacitly) by the Court. Only one state during this period, Illinois, legislatively affirmed the right for gay couples to receive wedding licenses. By October 2014, the total number of marriage equality states increased to 30 (plus the District of Columbia)—with at least five additional states waiting to join the ranks.

In some ways this progress is surprising. In other ways, things have unfolded exactly as conservatives had predicted at the height of the rush to ban same-sex marriage. One thing to consider, then, as we look back on the years of "marriage panic," is whether conservative, more than liberal, political officials and advocates were able to read the tea leaves of possibility. Perhaps they understood that they had only a small window of opportunity to limit marriage to straight couples—a generation, to be exact. The urgency with which they pounced on same-sex marriage—before the LGBT community had even considered pursuing it as part of their agenda—may have been based on their sense that change was imminent. They wanted to codify and constitutionalize heterocentrist conceptions of marriage because opposition to gay rights—in particular gay couples—appeared to be waning, and might soon diminish to the point of irrelevance. Rather than waiting it out, opponents wanted to impose as many obstacles as possible to protect their increasingly outdated understanding of marriage and family.

Nevertheless—whether they were based on fear or fact—their predictions about the possibility of same-sex marriage were accurate. Judges have led the charge to dismantle marriage bans. And the public is, perhaps begrudgingly, supportive. The overall trend is clear: marriage equality has attained an unyielding momentum. Whether due to increased representation of younger generations (who are generally more supportive of marriage equality) in public opinion polls, better framing, or more across-the-board exposure to gays and lesbians through friends, family, and associates, this rise in judicial and public support has prompted activists on both sides to declare marriage equality a fait accompli. The president of Human Rights Campaign recently pronounced that "the trend toward marriage equality is undeniable—and irreversible."[135] Maggie Gallagher, founder of the National Organization for Marriage—a leading opponent of marriage equality—concurred, announcing in 2014 that "we are now in the 'gay marriage in all fifty states' phase whether we like it or not."[136]

Conclusion

The struggle for marriage equality will likely be recalled as one of the most rapidly progressing, yet volatile, court-centered campaigns in recent history. Its path has been fraught with victories and setbacks. On the one hand, the notion that any state, let alone more than half of them, would extend full marriage benefits to gay couples was inconceivable even ten years ago. According to recent census data, over fifty percent of the nation's population resides in states that support marriage equality and other estimates suggest that an equal percentage of lesbians and gays now have the option to marry.[137] That number will only increase as more same-sex couples avail themselves of the benefits of marriage, and as more bans are dismantled. And any notion that courts are insignificant arbiters of social change has been rendered defunct by the sweep of same-sex marriage court decisions that have ushered in new rights and increased acceptance for same-sex couples.

That said, the path to progress was rocky to say the least. First, no matter how rose-colored one's glasses, we cannot ignore the twenty-year (and counting) period in which gay and lesbian couples were absolutely and explicitly barred from marrying in well over half the states (and the hundreds of years prior when it was utterly and universally implausible). Even in states with marriage equality, implementation has been shaky. As more states have legalized same-sex marriage, gay and lesbian couples have experienced pushback from wedding service providers—bakeries, photographers, wedding venues, stationery stores—who refuse to offer their services to gay and lesbian consumers. The next legal struggle may very well revolve around determining whether these public accommodations are required to provide services to same-sex couples. We have seen the same resistance from state officials. In the years following marriage equality in Iowa, for instance, state vital records clerks refused, on separate occasions, to list both spouses in a gay or lesbian couple on their child's birth[138] or death[139] certificates.

Nor can we dismiss the hostile campaign rhetoric that accompanied these bans as mere *surplusage*. Lesbian and gay couples have been fodder for public debates in which their private lives and their parenting skills are dissected and debased. Driven by the negative and hostile tone of these campaigns, a variety of public figures entered the fray to defend traditional marriage. Some—like Chick-fil-A—issued passive aggressive pronouncements in the hopes of capitalizing on marriage opposition. The president of the chicken empire publicly declared it "a family-owned business, a family-led business," run by men who are "married to our first wives." In response to this commitment from the fast-food chicken kingpin, Mike Huckabee branded August 1, 2012, Chick-fil-A Appreciation Day.

Others issued more violent statements. In support of the state's constitutional amendment, a North Carolina pastor referred to gays and lesbians as "perverted" and called for their prosecution.[140] Not to be outdone, shortly after that another North Carolina pastor called for opponents to

> build a great, big, large fence—150 or 100 mile long—put all the lesbians in there. Do the same thing for the queers and the homosexuals and have that fence electrified so they can't get out . . . and you know what, in a few years, they'll die out . . . do you know why? They can't reproduce![141]

A Kansas-based pastor also weighed in and asked the government to start executing members of the gay community.[142]

Even amidst the sweep of pro-gay federal court rulings, religious and conservative officials remained committed to brandishing anti-gay rhetoric to catalyze support. For instance, the American Family Association (a Southern

Poverty Law Center designated hate group) issued two verbal attacks on the gay community in mid-October 2014 to mobilize voters. On October 13, 2014, the President of the American Family Association warned his fundamentalist Christian followers of the rampant "mandatory gay brain-washing" that was overwhelming the states. Bryan Fischer issued a concurrent warning during an AFA radio program in which he referred to the rainbow flag—a symbol of LGBT rights—as "the Mark of the Beast" while bemoaning recent court decisions that required small businesses to offer their services to gay and lesbian consumers. Businesses are "not allowed to engage in commerce," he vituperated, "because they would not take 'the Mark of the Beast' on their hands or on their foreheads."[143]

Some have been inspired to act on these implicit and explicit threats. In the years since marriage equality was first legalized, scores of violent and discriminatory acts have been waged against gays and lesbians and their families. A lesbian who was highlighted in the local news after she and her partner married in Michigan was severely beaten shortly after her nuptials. The assailants recognized her from the news coverage.[144] In the year following marriage equality in New York, the state saw an overall rise in the number of hate crimes. The most frequently reported hate crimes were based on sexual orientation. Sexual orientation-based hate crimes in New York City increased by 70 percent in 2013.[145] Included in the 2013 data was one gay man who was shot and killed in Greenwich Village. The gunman made homophobic slurs at the victim and his friend, and then shot him point-blank in the face.[146]

Nationwide, in 2011, according to FBI data, hate crimes based on sexual orientation were the second most common after racially motivated crimes, accounting for more than 20% of the total single-bias hate crime incidents reported that year.[147] While other groups had experienced a drop in the number of reported incidents over time, those committed against gays and lesbians had plateaued since 1996—when the data were first collected.

Some have attributed this persistence in the incidence of anti-gay hate crimes to an overall increase in both the visibility of and support for marriage equality.[148] On the whole, hatred against gays and lesbians "is ratcheting up in direct proportion to the losses [of] the religious right" according to a Southern Poverty Law Center extremism expert. "I think what we are seeing is kind of a desperate anger coming out of a lot of the Christian right groups . . . When these kinds of groups get on TV and make statements about how gay men are pedophiles . . . ultimately it does result in criminal violence."[149] A Santa Clara County district attorney made a similar argument after the percentage of the county's hate crimes attributed to sexual orientation increased from 15 to 56 percent between 2007 and 2008—when the state was in the throes of the Prop 8 campaign. "My belief," he stated in an interview, "from having done this work for many years is that surges in types of hate incidents are linked to the headlines and controversies of the day."[150] Added a local gay rights advocate, "When there's a lot more information about gays and lesbians on TV or in the news, it brings out the worst in people who have an inherent bias against groups they don't belong to . . . It seems like visibility makes people come out of the woodwork."[151]

Although advocates are winning the war, progress on the marriage equality front cannot be understood without accounting for this contentious call and response between advocates and opponents. As one side advances, the other rallies their troops to limit or thwart any gains. As one advocate described,

> I think it is one of those two steps forward and one step back scenarios. We are ahead of where we were in the mid 90s. I do think there is movement forward. But I think it is really sad that there are people with bigoted views who are also really pushing families back.[152]

It had never been the intention of gay rights advocates to elevate the issue to the ranks of *Roe* and other polemical civil rights debates. Once foisted into the business of marriage equality, advocates had hoped to promote an incremental, state-by-state strategy. However, the instant that same-sex couples asked the state to marry (and gained sympathy from the courts) the issue became fodder for public consumption. In order to challenge state marriage laws, advocates had to convince, first state then federal, courts to reject long-held assumptions about marriage, and, in some cases, acknowledge the history of degradation and discrimination against gays and lesbians. As one advocate explained:

> The proponents of marriage equality have tried to go incrementally in states that they thought would be friendly. That has been the tactic of the national offices. We always believed that litigation was the way. But it was more high impact litigation—that was the only way you could change the law. Our opponents used the ballot box because that was the most effective tool. Just by the nature of the beast marriage equality has to be a very public debate.[153]

Opponents seized on this opportunity to declare same-sex marriage and its supporters as public enemy number one.

The coalition of "strange bedfellows"—Democrats, Republicans, moderates, conservatives, religious and agnostics—that characterized early opposition to same-sex marriage, then, is in part a by-product of the artful campaign devised by conservative strategists to mobilize their base while also speaking to more mainstream voters. Couched in the rhetoric of tolerance promoted by Bush and other "compassionate conservatives," mainstream heterosexual America could comfortably protect marriage without being discriminatory. Well-meaning voters could rely on children's welfare or states' rights rhetoric to rationalize what would otherwise be viewed as a homophobic decision to oppose marriage equality. Supporters of federal bans on same-sex marriage could shield themselves from criticism by arguing that "activist judges" forced their hand. Although their success was short-lived, these opposition frames licensed ordinarily liberal voters to block same-sex couples in their attempts to seek marriage equality and to publicly interrogate and castigate lesbian and gay couples' claims of "familyhood." The question, then, is why marriage and not parenting? How were gay parenting advocates, bound by similar substantive and public opinion constraints, able to avoid a similar public battle? This, we explore in Chapter 4.

4

The Silent Struggle for Same-Sex Parental Rights

IN 1996, WHILE same-sex marriage opponents successfully lobbied members of Congress and voters and legislators in fourteen states to statutorily bar lesbian and gay couples from marrying, parenting advocates were continuing their ten-year run of convincing local and family court judges to recognize lesbian and gay co-parenting rights. In that year, for instance, four lesbians (one couple and two single women) went to court to seek custody of their children and joined gay and lesbian parents in at least ten states where judges had validated LGBT co-parenting arrangements. K. M. and D. M. asked an Illinois Appellate Judge to reverse a ruling issued by a Cook County circuit court denying the couple's request to grant D. M. co-parental status over their three-year-old daughter Olivia.[1] Through a process now commonly referred to as "second parent adoption," the non-biological or non-adoptive parent in a lesbian or gay relationship can seek legal recognition of their relationship with their children without requiring the biological or adoptive parent to relinquish their own legal status. The procedure has become one of many ways that gay couples, in the absence of marriage rights, provide a legal safety net for their children. In Pennsylvania, A. L. asked the superior court to grant her custody rights over the child she had raised since birth, but who was born to her former partner. Despite having left the child with A. L. for months on end, the biological mother refused to acknowledge her relationship with A. L., and A. L.'s relationship with the child, and denied her access to the child.[2] Mother of two Rebecca Schroeder petitioned an Illinois court to restore custody of her children after a county judge had them transferred from Schroeder's care to their father's, out of concern for the "burden of social condemnation" caused by their mother's sexual orientation.[3]

The stakes for these parents, and the issues raised in their arguments in court, parallel those involved in the very public and hostile battle over same-sex marriage. As with same-sex couples seeking marriage rights, gay and lesbian parents seek legal recognition for psychological, legal, and financial security—and out of a sense of justice. Opponents of both LGBT marriage and parental rights argue that nothing less than the welfare of children and society are at stake when courts recognize gay relationships. Yet when K. M. and D. M. won their request for a second-parent adoption, when A. L. was granted standing as an "equitable parent" over her former partner's child, and when Rebecca Schroeder regained custody over her two children, their court cases were greeted with little of the backlash or publicity given to Nina Baehr, her partner, and the two other couples discussed in Chapter 3, who requested marriage certificates in Hawaii around the same time. As gay marriage opponents whipped the public into a lather of panic and paranoia over the consequences for children and society of legalizing same-sex marriage, gays and lesbians were parenting at an increasing rate and securing widespread judicial support. By 2006, when the country was cloaked in anti-gay marriage bans, gays and lesbians enjoyed co-parenting privileges in at least half of the states—and yet encountered only a fraction of the obstacles erected in the marriage realm.

This chapter explores how parental rights advocates capitalized on opportunities for low-visibility advocacy inherent in family law and purposely kept their intentions off the public radar in order to minimize backlash. Through the use of low-visibility strategies, advocates avoided a potentially vitriolic opposition campaign and, on the whole, safeguarded gay and lesbian parenting court victories.

The Second Front

In many ways 2006 was a bellwether year for same-sex parenting advocates and their clients. As the previous chapter explains, by the end of 2006, marriage equality bans had been implemented either by statute or constitutional amendment in more than forty states, twenty-six[4] of which were passed between 2004 and 2006. In the aftermath of the 2004 election—and the thirteen newly minted constitutional bans on gay marriage—gay rights organizations braced themselves for similar attacks on same-sex parenting. Many forecasted that, buttressed by successes on the marriage front, gay family opponents would turn their attention to same-sex parenting. A *USA Today* article warned of the impending initiatives and described the issue as the "second front in the culture wars that began during the 2004 elections over same-sex marriage."[5] These fears were not unfounded. In 2004 eight proposed pieces of legislation curbing gay adoption or parental rights were introduced in six states. Oklahoma's statute, however, was the only one enacted.[6] In 2005 at least seven states had initiated efforts to ban or curtail LGBT parenting rights, including one proposal in Texas to require child protective services to ask potential foster parents about their sexual orientation.[7] Despite failures or false starts, many of those states indicated an interest in pursuing similar legislation in 2006. All told, approximately sixteen states in 2006 were poised to initiate bans on same-sex parenting legislatively or through the ballot process.[8] These initiatives, coupled with efforts to ban marriage in the few states without a DOMA or constitutional amendment and further limit gay rights by rescinding anti-discrimination ordinances, portended a potential tsunami of anti-gay activity. As one Task Force spokesperson pointed out, "We could have roughly half of the country's population voting on us in one year."[9]

In Arkansas, legislators battled over a proposal to limit adoptions to married couples. Ohio entertained proposed legislation similar to the adoption ban in Florida passed in 1977. It would bar adoption and foster care

> if the individual is a homosexual, bisexual, or transgender individual; the individual is a stepparent of the child to be adopted and is a homosexual, bisexual, or transgender individual; the individual resides with an individual who the court determines is a homosexual, bisexual, or transgender individual.[10]

State Rep. Ron Hood, the bill's sponsor, argued that the proposed bill was supported by research that demonstrates "the optimal setting to raise children is in a traditional setting with a mom and a dad."[11] Gay rights opponents across the state believed that "now that we've defined what marriage is, we need to take that further and say children deserve to be in that relationship."[12]

In some states there appeared to be initial public support for these initiatives. For instance, a Georgia initiative to bar gay and lesbian couples from adopting children, although perceived as less important than issues like the economy or property rights, was ranked as very or somewhat important by 58 percent of participants in a Zogby poll commissioned by the *Atlanta Journal-Constitution* in early 2006.[13] Consequently, in anticipation of this onslaught of anti-gay parenting initiatives, the ABA passed a resolution in early 2006 to oppose legislation barring individuals on the basis of sexual orientation from serving as foster or adoptive parents.[14] This resolution supplemented one issued in 2003 supporting second-parent and joint adoptions for all unmarried couples.

Despite dire predictions that 2006 would serve another round of setbacks to gay or lesbian families, none of the sixteen states saw significant progress in their efforts that year. This minimal backlash came as a surprise to policy advocates on both sides of the issue. This "second wave" was dampened before it had the chance to gain the kind of momentum evident in other gay rights struggles. Legislation died in committee. Proposed initiatives never made it to the ballot. All the while family, appellate, and state supreme courts continued to grant adoptions to and recognize the parental rights of gay and lesbian parents. To be sure, aggressive campaigns were mounted, and some came close to enactment. But few ultimately succeeded. For instance, legislators in Utah passed a bill preventing non-custodial parents from seeking custody or visitation rights in 2006 in response to an ongoing lesbian custody battle in the state. However, the governor vetoed the bill out of concern for unintended and "undesirable consequences" for step-parents or grandparents.[15]

This lack of backlash is particularly noteworthy when we compare parenting opposition to that of same-sex marriage during the same period. While the handful of gay marriage court victories was met with statutory and constitutional bans in more than forty states between 1996 and 2006, efforts to advance adoption and protect parental rights for gay or lesbian parents have not produced the same level or type of backlash (see Figures 4.1 and 4.2). Despite the at least fifty favorable court decisions in existence during this period that overturned adoption bans, permitted adoption in the absence of state legislation, required that birth certificates list both parents in a same-sex couple, or granted parental rights to gay and lesbian parents embroiled in child custody battles or seeking co-parent or joint adoptions, only a handful of anti-parenting backlash efforts were successfully implemented during this period.[16] In May of 2004, for instance, Oklahoma passed legislation preventing out-of-state gay adoptions from being recognized in the state—although it was later overturned in court as violating full faith and credit. In September of that year, Michigan's attorney general issued an opinion preventing couples married in Massachusetts from jointly adopting in Michigan.[17] In March of 2006, Catholic charities in a number of cities terminated their adoption programs to avoid having to comply with city or state ordinances requiring "orientation-neutral" adoption procedures.[18]

Even in the few instances where states or private actors did implement parenting restrictions, some judges used their discretion in custody and adoption cases to work around parenting restrictions for same-sex couples.

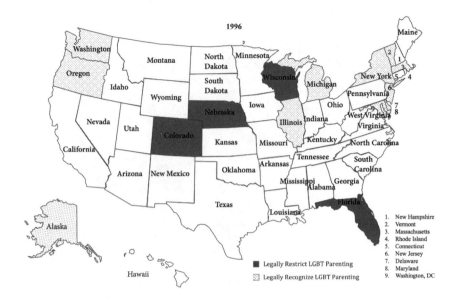

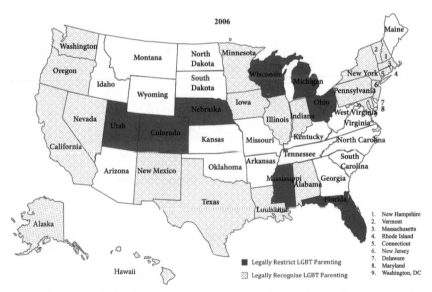

FIGURE 4.1. Progression of Anti- and Pro-Same-Sex Parenting Policies Across the United States, 1996–2006

Source: National Center for Lesbian Rights and National Gay and Lesbian Task Force.

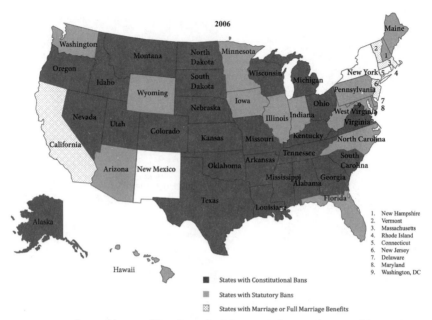

FIGURE 4.2. State of Anti- and Pro-Same-Sex Marriage Policies in the United States, 2006
Source: National Center for Lesbian Rights and National Gay and Lesbian Task Force.

For instance, an Ohio appellate court honored a joint-custody agreement that had been validated by a trial court but later disputed by one of the mothers after the couple separated. Although the state supreme court ruled in 2002 against second-parent adoptions, explicitly stating that this procedure "is not available in Ohio," the high court, on appeal, validated the appellate court's joint custody decision.[19] Similarly, in 2002 a chief county judge in Michigan issued a memo barring judges in that county from granting second-parent adoptions. This had effectively eliminated second-parent adoptions in the state, because this county was the only one in the state permitting legal recognition of both parents. Yet, in 2006 the Michigan Court of Appeals upheld a joint adoption granted by a judge in that county (albeit one that took place in 1999).[20]

To be sure, attempts to limit same-sex parenting rights did not disappear after 2006. In 2007, for instance, although only four measures opposing same-sex parenting were introduced, one, in Utah, passed.[21] This legislation privileges heterosexual married couples over single adults in foster child placement. In 2008 Arkansas voters approved a ballot measure preventing non-married couples from adopting in the state—although the initiative was

overturned by the state's supreme court.[22] In 2010 a lesbian successfully petitioned the North Carolina Supreme Court to invalidate the second-parent
adoption granted to her now-estranged partner. The decision outlawed court-
granted second-parent adoption in the state. Two courts in 2012 issued similar rulings. In *In re Adoption of KRS*, an Alabama appellate court ruled that
the state's ban on same-sex marriage barred same-sex couples from using the
state's step-parent adoption regulations to become legal co-parents. A Kansas
Court, in the context of an unmarried heterosexual couple's custody battle,
argued that strict construction of the state's adoption laws prevented anyone
but the natural parent's spouse from legally co-parenting a child. In reference
to judges in other states that had validated second-parent adoptions through
"broad judicial interpretation of existing statutes," the court stated, "we are
not inclined to judicially create such authority."[24] Even states with same-sex
marriage experienced judicial push-back in the realm of parenting. In June
2014 a lesbian mother was denied custody of the son she had raised by a New
York family court judge because, although she and her son's biological mother
married soon after New York's marriage law went into effect, she was not married to her son's biological mom at the time of his birth.[25] At the federal level,
the Fifth Circuit Court of Appeals ruled in 2011 (and the Supreme Court
declined to review) that Louisiana did not violate full faith and credit when
they denied a gay couple's request to have both fathers listed on the birth
certificate of a child who was adopted in New York but born in Louisiana.[26]

These setbacks are real, and for the parents in these states, tragic.
However, on the whole, same-sex parenting advocacy has received far fewer
battle scars than same-sex marriage. As the maps in Figure 4.3 indicate, by
the end of 2013 there were still significantly fewer states that proscribed,
and more states that permitted, gay and lesbian co-parenting compared
with marriage (although the gap was closing as the marriage movement
gained momentum). As the National Center on Lesbian Rights (NCLR)
described in a report on same-sex adoption, "Over the past two decades,
second-parent adoptions have been granted in a steadily growing number
of state and county jurisdictions"[27] and much of the growth occurred prior
to 2004 (before any state had legalized same-sex marriage).[28] Furthermore,
this graph likely underestimates the number of states in which family
courts have validated second-parent adoptions precisely because these
cases occur largely outside of public view. As NCLR states "Many more
states are moving toward permitting adoption by same-sex couples on a
county-by-county basis . . . There undoubtedly are counties in other states

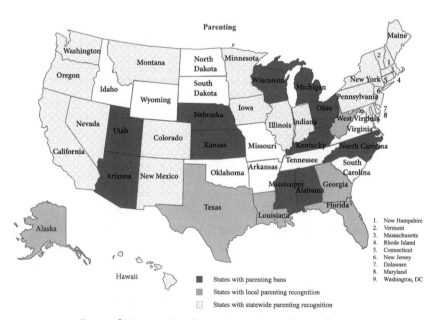

FIGURE 4.3. Status of Marriage Equality or Parenting Rights as of 2013

Source: National Center for Lesbian Rights and National Gay and Lesbian Task Force.

that have granted second parent adoptions."[29] This success in minimizing backlash and awareness while gaining court support stems, in part, from the "below-the-radar" strategies detailed below.

Early Planning

To a large degree, concerns about backlash against gay and lesbian parents informed strategic decisions for parenting advocates from the beginning. First, they were well aware that the gains they had made in the years preceding marriage panic could be swiftly dismissed if marriage opponents set their sights directly on same-sex parenting. Opponents had the political infrastructure, resources, and frames to quickly obliterate parenting victories and forestall future efforts. Advocates watched as discussions about the capacity for gays and lesbians to parent increasingly became part of the public debate on a range of gay rights issues. Second, parenting advocates were acutely aware of the risks imposed on gay and lesbian parents if anti-gay opponents successfully included parenting in their family values platform. As one NCLR representative explained, "To be denied a marriage license doesn't mean you can't be a couple. To be denied parenting rights means you can't ever see your child again … the damage done is enormous."[30] Early on, activists and advocates realized that the best strategy to help secure these parent-child relationships was a low-visibility case-by-case approach. Dahlia Lithwick describes it best in her account of one anti-gay family activist's warning about parenting advocacy: "while we are loudly and properly debating the legal change in the word marriage, the legal definition of the word parent is 'quietly' changing under our noses."[31]

The Past Informs the Present

In part this low-visibility, case-by-case approach was dictated by the nature of the controversies that typified the early years of parenting litigation. They dealt primarily with gay or lesbian individuals who had conceived children through a heterosexual relationship but who had "come out" and were struggling to obtain or maintain custody of their children. One representative from NCLR recalls the group's initial foray into parenting rights:

> When NCLR was founded in the late 70s there were lesbian moms who were losing custody of their kids in huge numbers. Much of the early parenting efforts were reactive. Bad things were happening to

queer-identified parents. Lawyers and activists were stepping in to stop
those bad things from happening. The vast majority of cases from the
late '70s through the early '90s were almost always cases where we were
representing a gay or lesbian parent who was being challenged for custody or visitation based on their sexual orientation and the children
were a product of the heterosexual union.[32]

Cases concerning the parenting potential of gays and lesbians stem back to
as early as the 1950s and were largely unsupportive of gay and lesbian parents. In one 1952 case, for instance, a mother who had recently divorced her
husband successfully dissolved the couple's joint custody agreement because
of her ex-husband's "homosexual tendencies" and potentially "harmful influence."[33] However, there were a few exceptions. A Pennsylvania judge in 1953
declined a mother's request, mostly due to insufficient evidence, to alter her
ex-husband's visitation rights based on claims that he had "exhibited homosexual tendencies and committed unnatural sexual acts" during the course of
their marriage.[34]

It wasn't until the mid-1960s that the tides against gay and lesbian parents seemed to (at least marginally) shift. In *Nadler v. Superior Court*, a lesbian mother appealed a ruling from a Sacramento Superior Court judge who
ruled that her "homosexuality . . . as a matter of law constitutes her not a
fit or proper person to have the care, custody and control of her daughter."
An appellate court in California's 3rd District overruled the decision, arguing that the lower court did not exercise its discretion when it neglected to
review evidence to determine how the child's welfare would be influenced by
a change in custody. Relying on a state supreme court decision establishing
that a trial court is permitted "wide latitude in the exercise of its discretion . . .
to determine, after considering all the evidence, how the best interests of the
child will be subserved," the court reminded petitioners that the "question
is to be determined solely from the standpoint of the child, and the feelings
and desires of the contesting parties are not to be considered, except in so
far as they affect the best interests of the child."[35] *Nadler* provided doctrinal
support for future courts to diminish the relevance of a parent's homosexuality as a stand-alone factor for determining custody decisions. Courts could,
instead, consider only what was in the "best interests of the child."

By the time NCLR opened its doors in the late 1970s, courts in at least
ten states had deliberated over petitions to deny or alter custody based on one
parent's sexual orientation. Much like the preceding years, 1970s parenting
litigation can be characterized as a long string of restrictive decisions with

moments of progressive rulings. In most cases judges curtailed visitation rights, limited the frequency of overnight visits with the gay or lesbian parent, prohibited a child's exposure to the gay or lesbian parent's partner, or terminated custody altogether. Nevertheless, in a few instances judges determined that sexuality should not be a primary factor for considering custody—even in cases where children were being raised in same-sex households. Recall that the lion's share of cases involving gay and lesbian parents during this time period dealt with parents who were fighting to defend themselves against allegations of impropriety in custody battles with their estranged former spouses. Rarely were judges required to confront the reality of same-sex couples parenting children together in a single household. In 1978, however, the Washington Supreme Court was asked to review a custody decision concerning a lesbian couple who had been jointly raising children conceived through each of their previous heterosexual marriages. The fathers were each asking the court to revisit custody, since previous determinations of custody had been predicated on the requirement that each mother refrain from exposing their children to their same-sex partners. Rather than revoking custody, however, the court ruled that

> even if the trial court had found the mothers in contempt, that alone would not justify a change in custody. Punishment of the parent for contempt may not be visited upon the child in custody cases. The custody of a child is not to be used as a reward or punishment for the conduct of the parents . . . The best interests of the child are the paramount and controlling considerations.[36]

This early focus on helping gay and lesbian parents defend themselves against custody disputes from heterosexual former spouses necessarily required the parenting movement to adopt three approaches that helped them in later years. First, the very nature of these disputes—individual spousal disputes involving children, which were handled in family court on a case-by-case basis—helped to keep even the victories off the public radar. As one attorney explained,

> thirty years ago . . . the biggest percentage of people who needed assistance were people who lost custody of their kids because of sexual orientation. In a lot of those cases there wasn't publicity. . . . A lot of the cases involved settlement and low publicity because of the kids' involvement. Parents don't want the kids to be publicized. If publicized, it is

used against the parents. Built-in institutional issues made these parenting cases not as visible.[37]

Second, these early cases placed homosexuality on trial. Typically at issue
in these trials is the simple contention that either a gay or lesbian parent cannot
properly perform their parental duties *because* of their homosexuality, or that
exposure to homosexuality would harm the child. Gay or lesbian parents in
these cases, then, were forced to defend their parenting in the context of their
sexuality and the accompanying stereotypes of the time period—assumptions that presumed, for instance, that a parent's homosexuality would be
passed on to the child. As Richman explains, "in the legal arena judges and
opposing litigants have asserted . . . that transmission of sexuality may happen
in an active or passive way" through modeling or "recruitment."[38] In some
cases, less blatantly biased arguments were used to explain the nexus between
sexuality and parenting. In *M.P. v. S.P.*, for instance, judges were asked to
determine whether a child's welfare would be hindered by her community's
condemnation of homosexuality if a lesbian were permitted to retain custody
of her children. To defend their clients against each of these arguments, in
many cases, advocates encouraged judges to look beyond their client's sexual
orientation to see their skills and contributions as a parent. For instance, in
determining that the trial court erred in denying the mother custody, the
court in *M.P. v. S.P.* chided the lower courts for modifying the arrangement
"for the sole reason that she is a homosexual and without regard to the welfare of the children." They explain further that

> the trial judge apparently weighed against defendant the fact that she
> was caught up "in an attempt to find her own identity and to deal
> with the problems" arising from her sexual status. However, he did not
> explain what problems he had in mind or in what way her problems
> or her quest for identity were different from those of most ordinary
> people; more importantly, he made no attempt to articulate a relation-
> ship between any of this and the welfare of the children. The judge also
> noted that defendant's ongoing liaison with her lesbian companion
> had "materially upset the older child and will have a slight influence in
> all probability, from the credible evidence, on the younger child." . . .
> there is nothing in the record to show any nexus between defendant's
> sexual companionship and the older girl's reaction. Nowhere do we
> find documented in the record any specific instances of sexual miscon-
> duct by defendant or evidence that she tried in any way to inculcate

the girls with her sexual attitudes. To the contrary, the evidence is affirmatively to the effect that she never displayed any sexual behavior in the presence of her children, and that she refrains from any demonstration of affection toward other women when the girls are present.[39]

As they did in cases like *M.P. v. S.P.* or *Nadler*, advocates focused on establishing the irrelevance a parent's sexual orientation when determining questions of custody. According to one advocate from Human Rights Campaign,

> that was really the first step—so that courts would say being gay is not a factor in determining who gets custody. Once we were able to surmount that hurdle, we said "now the lady who was once in a heterosexual marriage is now in a homosexual relationship—can we protect that parent-child relationship?"[40]

Third, and relatedly, the risks associated with these cases—that a parent-child relationship could be legally severed—in some ways contained and constrained legal advocates to use arguments that had previously been made in other parenting arenas. Rather than attempting to craft new arguments or doctrines from the distinct fact patterns of cases concerning gay or lesbian parents, many advocates attempted to base their arguments on family law doctrines established in cases involving heterosexual parents. In downplaying, for instance, the relevance of sexuality, advocates relied on the more universal application of the "best interest of the child" standard, which had first been articulated in a Massachusetts statute crafted in the mid-1800s and had been used to successfully thwart attempts to alter custody arrangements in cases involving parents in other socially vulnerable families. Cases concerning parents in interracial relationships, for instance, provided precedent in some instances for courts to reject categorical arguments of social opprobrium when resolving custody disputes, and instead employ a case-by-case approach to determine the best interests of the child. In response to the community condemnation argument advanced in *M.P. v. S.P.*, for instance, the court relied on a past Pennsylvania Supreme Court case involving a custody dispute between an ex-husband and an ex-wife who had entered into an interracial relationship. The trial court had issued custody to the father because of society's "almost universal prejudice and intolerance of interracial marriage."[41] Quoting the Pennsylvania Supreme Court's reversal of that decision, the *M. P.* court argued that "if children are raised in a happy and stable home they will be able to cope with prejudice and hopefully learn that people are unique individuals who should be judged as such," and found that "there is no reason to think that the girls will be unable to manage whatever anxieties may flow from the community's disapproval of their mother." In many ways, the structure of family law—its implicit case-by-case philosophy, its focus on privileging children's welfare above all other interests, and the considerable discretion granted to family and other lower court justices in considering how to determine the "best interests of the child"—make it an ideal platform for expanding the rights of an unpopular minority group without awakening an intense public countermovement.

Same-Sex Couples as Parents

By the mid-1980s the focus began to shift from cases primarily addressing custody battles between gay and lesbian parents and their opposite-sex former spouses to parenting questions or conflicts arising within the context of same-sex relationships. Despite the change in focus, however, advocates stuck to the more conservative, incremental, low-visibility approach employed in early parenting cases involving homosexual parents.

In truth it is difficult to determine when the first parenting court victories for same-sex couples occurred. Many second-parent, single, and joint adoptions were legalized in intimate family court settings with little attention beyond family and friends. In fact, in many instances the family court judges presiding over these adoptions neglected to inform their colleagues of their decisions. As one adoption advocate recalls about judges in Vermont,

> Many of the family court judges in the state kept the decisions to themselves without realizing that their colleagues were granting them as well. It was only during an annual retreat that a few of them admitted to recognizing the adoptions.[42]

However, increased parenting advocacy on behalf of same-sex couples has unearthed a number of early, unpublished decisions. According to Gay and Lesbian Advocates and Defenders[43] (GLAD), gay and lesbian couples were granted the ability to enter into second-parent adoptions as early as 1985, when a Multnomah County, Oregon, circuit court validated a lesbian couple's petition to have joint legal status over their child.[44] Arguing that the legislature granted the court wide latitude in cases of adoption, same-sex parenting advocates convinced the court that it was in the "best interest of the child" to grant the request.[45] Washington state courts granted similar adoptions in the mid- to late-1980s.[46] In one Washington case concerning a lesbian couple's second-parent adoption petition, the court referenced and relied on similar requests granted in Oregon, Alaska, and California, in order to support their decision to permit the adoption.[47] By the 1990s and through the early 2000s advocates were able to compel courts in Delaware,[48] the District of Columbia,[49] Illinois,[50] Indiana,[51] Maryland,[52] New Jersey,[53] New York,[54] Pennsylvania,[55] and Vermont[56] to use their discretion to apply step-parent provisions to same-sex couples. This allowed judges to waive stipulations requiring the legal or biological parent to relinquish their parental rights in order to make the child "available" for adoption. In general these claims rested on three determinations. First, similar to a step-parent, the non-biological parent operated as a de facto parent to the child in question. Second, the spirit, history, or intent of the law privileged the "best interests of the child" above all other considerations. Third, denying the adoption request would produce "absurd results."[57]

Even where courts had previously invalidated second-parent adoptions, they were willing to acknowledge same-sex couples and their children as family units. In 2002 a Nebraska Supreme Court upheld a co-parent agreement legalized in Pennsylvania, despite having invalidated a second-parent adoption request originating in their state in the same year.[58] Analyzing Pennsylvania adoption statutes, the Nebraska court rejected claims that the Pennsylvania court lacked subject-matter jurisdiction when it granted the second-parent adoption. Accordingly, full faith and credit compelled the Nebraska court to uphold the ruling.

Additionally, a number of states have granted visitation or custody rights to former partners who are non-biological parents and required payment of child support to the birth parent. In 1997 courts in Texas and North Carolina awarded visitation rights to the non-biological parent in a dissolved same-sex relationship. In 1999 through 2006 courts in California,[59] Colorado,[60] Delaware,[61] Indiana,[62] Massachusetts,[63] New Jersey,[64] Pennsylvania,[65] Rhode Island,[66] and Washington[67] ruled that the non-biological parent in a same-sex relationship serves as a "de facto parent" and should be awarded visitation or custody rights, or should be required to pay child support, in the event of a breakup. Courts in Indiana[68] and Colorado[69] ruled that an individual's sexual orientation could not per se be used to deny a parent custody or visitation rights.

Same-sex couples have also received help from the courts in their attempts to acquire birth certificates reflecting their joint parental status. In 1998 a Los Angeles County court granted the first ever *in utero* second-parent adoption, requiring that the county list both parents in a gay relationship on the birth certificate immediately.[70] In 2005 a New Jersey superior court[71] required both parents in a lesbian relationship to be listed on the birth certificate and a Virginia court[72] required the state to issue birth certificates to gay parents who adopted children out of state.[73]

Adoption and parenting advocates suffered significant court losses as well during this time period. For instance, a Missouri court ruled against a lesbian's petition to seek joint custody of her three children with her ex-husband. The Connecticut Supreme Court denied a second-parent adoption, arguing that the state statute only applied to married couples or children who were available for adoption.[74] However, in the same year legislation was introduced and later passed in the state to permit second-parent adoptions. Courts in Nebraska and Ohio each strictly construed their state's adoption statute and rejected a lesbian couple's request for a second-parent adoption because the birth mother did not rescind her legal rights over the child.[75] In 2002 a Michigan Supreme Court judge asked the Chief Judge of Washtenaw County to stop allowing second-parent adoptions. When the judge who had been issuing the adoption decrees refused to comply with the chief judge's request, the chief judge took over adoption duties, effectively ending the availability of second-parent adoptions in the state.[76] Two years later the attorney general explicitly outlawed all adoptions by unmarried couples.[77] And in perhaps the most highly publicized same-sex adoption case of the period, *Lofton v. Secretary of the Department of Children and Family Services* (2004), the Supreme Court refused to hear an appeal involving several Florida families who were attempting to overturn legislation that categorically prohibited any household containing gay or lesbian members from adopting. In this case the Eleventh Circuit upheld the Florida ban.[78]

On the whole, however, the trajectory of same-sex parenting rights within the United States is marked by significant progress, with occasional (but devastating) losses. Where same-sex marriage progress (including civil unions) is really a twenty-first-century phenomenon and was met with significant public backlash, same-sex parenting progress has a longer history, was more immediately widespread, and has been relatively less contested.

Explaining Low Levels of Backlash
Public Opinion

Of course, the first place to look for an explanation as to why gay parenting rights decisions have inspired lower levels of backlash relative to marriage is public opinion. It is possible that the public had a higher tolerance for gay parenting relative to other gay rights struggles that provoked more broad-based and visceral forms of opposition. Similar to public support of civil unions (to which a majority of the public lent its support), it is conceivable that, by 2006, a large enough margin of the public accepted or at least tolerated gay or lesbian-headed households. The results, however, suggest a more complicated story. Analysis of support over time for same-sex adoption suggests that it follows a similar, but accelerated, pattern relative to support for marriage equality (see Figure 4.4). Both issues enjoy less than majority support through 2006. Support for adoption rights plateaus at just over 50 percent in 2007. Support for marriage equality reaches the 50 percent mark four years later.

A survey conducted by Pew Charitable Trusts provides an interesting snapshot of individual attitudes toward marriage equality and adoption in 2006. Results indicate that 57 percent of participants who were asked their opinion on both marriage equality and gay adoption oppose adoption by gays and lesbians, while a slightly (although insignificantly) higher percentage, 62 percent, oppose marriage equality for same-sex couples (see Table 4.1).[79]

The poll also provides a large enough sample to compare opinion toward marriage equality and same-sex adoption in states that banned gay marriage through the ballot process as of 2006. As stated earlier many predicted that

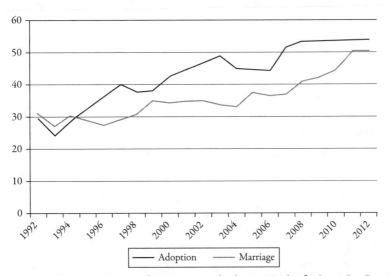

FIGURE 4.4. Percentage Support for Marriage and Adoption Rights for Same-Sex Couples
Source: Mean annual support derived from polls conducted by Newsweek, CNN/ORC, Pew, Quinnipiac, Gallup, NBC/WSJ, CBS/NYT, ABC/Post.

Table 4.1. Opposition to Marriage Equality and Adoption Rights

	Same-Sex Marriage*	Same-Sex Adoption**
Mean Opinion	61.62	57.29
Mean Opinion in Ballot States	65.29	60.59
Strongly Support	9.33	9.11
Support	23.21	29.72
Oppose	29.72	31.45
Strongly Oppose	37.74	29.72

*The question was worded as follows: "Do you strongly favor, favor, oppose, or strongly oppose allowing gays and lesbians to marry legally?"

**The question was worded as follows: "Do you strongly favor, favor, oppose, or strongly oppose allowing gays and lesbians to adopt children?"

Source: Pew July 2006 among participants who were asked questions about marriage equality and same-sex adoption. N = 846; ballot states N = 461.

same-sex parenting would meet its demise in 2006. In the end, none of the efforts were enacted into legislation.[80] Lower *successful* backlash on the parenting front during this period could be explained by diverging opinion on the two issues within anti-marriage equality ballot states (among which the sixteen states that attempted to initiate adoption bans or restrictions are included). However, the data suggest that, within these states, opinion on marriage equality and adoption rights for same-sex couples is statistically equivalent. Of the 460 participants residing in ballot states in 2006, just over 60 percent oppose both practices.[81]

The benefit of this survey, in addition to its timing, is that participants are asked to identify their degree of opposition or support on both issues. Evaluating differences in strength of support or opposition is particularly important in matters of political contestation. It is far more likely that individuals who have strong attitudes toward a given policy will show up at the polls to register their opinion than individuals who hold less stringent beliefs. We see that, as with overall opinion, individuals residing in states that banned same-sex marriage through the ballot box were just as *strongly opposed* to adoption rights as they were to marriage equality in 2006.

We also see similarities in the structure of public opinion on adoption rights to that of marriage equality (see Table 4.2, Model 1) Multivariate analysis reveals that gender, party identification, ideology, whether one believes the Bible to be the "word of God," and one's opinion on the immutability of homosexuality, each play a significant role in opinion formation

Table 4.2: Structure of Opinion on Same-Sex Marriage and Adoption

	Model 1 Adoption	Model 1 Marriage	Model 2 Adoption	Model 2 Marriage
Age	0.004	0.010***	0.001	0.008**
	(0.003)	(0.003)	(0.003)	(0.003)
White	-0.060	-0.230	-0.099	-0.160
	(0.117)	(0.119)	(0.122)	(0.124)
Gender	-0.265**	-0.273**	-0.125	-0.180*
	(0.086)	(0.088)	(0.088)	(0.090)
Married	0.157	0.157	0.075	0.056
	(0.087)	(0.089)	(0.089)	(0.091)
College Grad	-0.285***	-0.109	-0.285**	0.023
	(0.087)	(0.091)	(0.091)	(0.094)
Religious Attend	0.084	0.310**	-0.065	0.318**
	(0.116)	(0.120)	(0.122)	(0.124)
Party Id	0.260*	0.460***	0.090	0.359**
	(0.111)	(0.115)	(0.116)	(0.117)
Ideology	-1.300***	-1.189***	-0.866***	-0.555*
	(0.213)	(0.218)	(0.222)	(0.226)
Word of God	0.885***	1.092***	0.413***	0.813***
	(0.147)	(0.151)	(0.153)	(0.154)
Gays can change	0.474***	0.487***		
	(0.095)	(0.098)		
Same Sex Marriage/ Adoption			3.050***	2.995***
			(0.185)	(0.087)
Ballot state	0.174*	0.234**	0.070	0.135
	(0.083)	(0.086)	(0.086)	(0.087)
N	732	707	751	751

for both same-sex adoption and marriage equality. Living in a state that limited marriage to between one man and one woman through the ballot process is also positively correlated with opposing adoption rights. All of this, again, begs the question as to why 2006 was not more of a windfall for opponents of same-sex parenting rights.

Finally, when opinion on same-sex marriage is substituted for the variable on "immutability," we find that opposition to marriage equality is positively correlated with opposition toward adoption rights. Substituting opinion toward same-sex adoption in the marriage model produces similar findings (see Table 4.2, Model 2). This is not surprising, as 73 percent of the participants who oppose adoption also oppose marriage and 77 percent of gay marriage opponents oppose adoption.[82]

Visibility

A more compelling explanation for the failure of same-sex family opponents to gain traction on the issue of same-sex parenting is its low visibility. Supplementing the *New York Times* analysis introduced in Chapter 3, we see that same-sex marriage receives much more public scrutiny than cases concerning same-sex adoption or parental rights between 1996 and 2006 (see Figure 4.5).

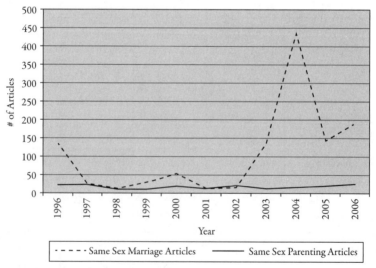

FIGURE 4.5. *New York Times* Coverage of Same-Sex Marriage and Same-Sex Parenting, 1996–2006

Similarly, at the local level we see that same-sex marriage consistently receives far more attention than same-sex parenting in articles, editorials, commentaries, and letters to the editor (see Table 4.3). Coverage on same-sex parenting remains consistently low, despite numerous court victories for same-sex parenting advocates.

Through the use of specific low-visibility tactics, and aided by institutional and policy characteristics that promote below-the-radar advocacy in family law, same-sex parenting advocates were able to shield their victories from public scrutiny. For many advocates it is simply common sense to utilize below-the-radar strategies to advance rights for children raised in same-sex households. As one journalist pointed out during the movement's early years, "lawyers have found that when it comes to the controversial subject of adoption by gay and lesbian parents, keeping out of radar range of both the media and the legislature has been the best way to challenge traditional notions of what constitutes a family."[83]

Table 4.3. Same-Sex Marriage and Parenting
Local Coverage, 1996–2006

Year	Marriage Articles	Parenting Articles	Marriage Editorials*	Parenting Editorials
1996	594	20	66	2
1997	186	30	32	7
1998	181	12	37	4
1999	192	55	45	6
2000	202	36	90	1
2001	76	38	21	8
2002	66	51	0	15
2003	919	34	387	3
2004	2631	92	524	12
2005	861	99	213	14
2006	13041	44	411	7

*This figure includes editorials, commentaries, and letters to the editor.

Source: LexisNexis search for articles in regional newspapers including the following terms in headlines or lead paragraphs: same-sex marriage; homosexual marriage; gay marriage; lesbian marriage; same-sex parent!; lesbian parent!; gay parent!; homosexual parent! between 1996 and 2006.[75]

Under the Radar and Off the Grid

In many ways, unlike same-sex marriage, the issue of same-sex parenting lends itself to (or even calls for) low-visibility advocacy. As one advocate described of same-sex marriage:

> If a couple filed a marriage lawsuit everybody knows. No one has ever quietly filed one. You are asking to undo or eliminate a law that says you can't participate in this part of civil society. You can't do one of those quietly.[84]

Conversely, just as in most heterosexual parenting cases, in same-sex parenting cases it is each party's intention—regardless of their personal goals—to minimize harm to the children who at the center of these controversies. Furthermore, in most instances (at least at the trial level) the court records are kept sealed and confidential. Explained one advocate:

> When you are talking about children in general, you are talking about cases in small courtrooms with sealed records, so no press. The judge can make a decision without visibility. Once the judge makes the decision no one will know about it. It is done with confidentiality, a sealed record, closed courtroom, no publicity. One of the things about marriage is that it has to be public. A family court judge is not faced with that.[85]

However, these characteristics cannot entirely account for its low visibility and lack of backlash. For one thing, journalists manage to cover a variety of cases concerning child custody and adoption rulings. Nor are all same-sex parenting decisions unpublished. Instead, evidence suggests that many advocates leveraged the issue's low-visibility characteristics and developed specific below-the-radar strategies to avoid any publicity that would thwart their progress—and bring harm to their clients and community. As one advocate explained when comparing marriage and parenting:

> [with marriage] you are asking for something that has never been extended, so you don't gain any advantage to keeping it quiet. With adoption you do. You don't want to look like you are politicizing the parent-child relationship. A court hostile to gay parents would not look kindly on the perception that you are grandstanding.[86]

The decision to employ below-the-radar strategies when pursuing same-sex parenting litigation was not the product of a few lone advocates operating in isolation. Instead, advocates nationwide shared their strategies with each other through word-of-mouth correspondence with scholars, advocates, and judges[87] and, eventually, through more organized events and channels facilitated, in part, by NCLR's Family Law Advisory Council.[88] Their hope was to incrementally develop positive precedent without politicizing their efforts. Advocates recognized that increased visibility had the potential to invite more players into the fray, which would minimize the degree of control that advocates could exert over same-sex parenting policies. One advocate admitted to keeping a low profile out of concern about negative spillover in the legislature or in other courts.[89]

> Nowadays—I try to do everything I can under the radar. If I get publicity, then the [individuals] in our legislature are more likely to screw it up to take away the victory . . . My fear is that if there is more publicity and more lawyers try this stuff and they aren't sophisticated about these issues, they will set bad precedent.[90]

Both gay rights advocates and opponents consider the issue's low visibility as critical to its success. A staff person at Basic Rights Oregon (BRO) attributes the organization's success with parenting, in part, to the fact that "BRO was able to keep the issue under the radar."[91] Likewise, a staff member at Focus on Family—a leading anti-same-sex family advocacy group—confirmed that the issue was "not high on the radar for pro-family conservatives."[92] Anti-marriage advocates in Ohio concurred, stating that the issue "is not on our radar screen right now."[93]Instead, opponents seemed resigned to the progress made on the parenting front. Explained one: "The issue has been settled in our state for 30 years."[94] Added another: "It is already permissible in our state. It is a done deal. We are fighting the current battles now."[95] Anti-same-sex family advocates argued that "gays and lesbians now have tremendous opportunities to adopt kids into their homes."[96]Others downplayed the importance of parenting to their cause: "The same sex community is really tiny. Only a fraction of them are actually quote unquote parenting."[97] Echoed another:

> The fact of the matter is that in reality homosexual households are such a small fraction of the population. It's tiny. And then homosexual households with children represent an even smaller percentage.[98]

These arguments were made despite an overwhelming reliance on children's welfare arguments to oppose marriage equality.

Legal Tools

Advocates took advantage of a number of legal resources to keep same-sex parenting off the public radar. For instance, as in the early years when gay and lesbian parenting cases typically involved custody battles from heterosexual marriages, advocacy for same-sex couples also borrows heavily from heterosexual family law precedent. One individual described parenting advocates—especially in the early '90s—as "cautious." "We didn't have statutes on which to base what we were trying to do," he explained. "We were trying to handcraft something off of what was there. We didn't want to go to the legislature because we thought it was problematic in terms of what we would get there."[99] Echoed another, "we were able to work with the law that we have. We didn't want to develop a new law because we were afraid of the backlash."[100]

This reliance on commonplace methods for advancing same-sex parenting has rendered court decisions fairly unremarkable—despite high public disapproval for their outcome. Advocates describe these cases as "a dime a dozen. They are filed every day in court. You are seeking the same rights that everybody else gets. You want the same custody laws that determine the best interests of the child applied to you."[101] Similarly, as another lawyer explained relative to same-sex marriage,

> a lot of those cases . . . aren't as sexy or jazzy. Now the issue of children is more accepted within the gay community. It wasn't as interesting to people even though they were precedent-setting issues.[102]

For one thing, parenting cases tend to rely on statutory and administrative, rather than constitutional, arguments to advance their issues. As described above, many advocates were loath to create "new rights" and opted instead to use the legal framework in place in their counties and states to encourage judges to grant custody and adoptions to gay and lesbian parents.

The issue of whether or not to constitutionalize same-sex adoption has been debated considerably by gay rights advocates. People in favor of establishing constitutional protections for same-sex parents point to the often arbitrary and inconsistent rationales used to deny or support same-sex adoption petitions. Although there have been rulings in favor of same-sex adoption, the argument goes, parental rights vary significantly by state and, often, within a single state. This legal uncertainty renders gay parents "second-class citizens" with respect to their ability to have a legally recognized relationship with their child.[103] The parent-child relationship, argue advocates, is too important and too fundamental to allow any room for its denial. Additionally, inconsistency in litigation only breeds more litigation. In the absence of a constitutional decree declaring either the right to adopt or that gay parents can litigate under equal protection, gay parents will continue to shoulder the heavy costs of litigation.[104] Others have referred to the lack of codified language explicitly granting same-sex adoption or parental rights. This, coupled with the fact that statutory decisions (compared with constitutional rulings) are easier to overturn legislatively, requires that same-sex adoption decisions obtain a stronger legal foundation.[105] Finally, reviewing same-sex parenting cases in purely statutory terms invites more room for judicial discretion and judicial ideology to play a role in decisions.[106]

When considering constitutional arguments in parenting cases, judges have been typically presented with one of four options. The first requires judges to apply the "fundamental right to parenthood" established in *Stanley v. Illinois* (1972) to gay and lesbian biological or non-biological parents. In the second, advocates articulate a right to "familial privacy" that prevents judges from using sexual orientation as a basis to consider adoption or custody outcomes. Less common are free association arguments, stemming from the First Amendment, that protect the "parent-child relationship" from state intervention. Finally, advocates have employed a children-centered constitutional narrative that asks judges to recognize a child's right to receive care from their parent or guardian. On the whole judges have generally been skeptical about applying these constitutional frameworks in ways that would advance same-sex parenting. In constitutionally derived decisions pertaining to gay or lesbian parents who conceived children during the course of a heterosexual relationship, courts have refused to use a fundamental rights argument to grant custody to the gay or lesbian parent. In the context of custody or adoption disputes within same-sex relationships, biological status has typically prevailed, leaving non-biological parents without standing to invoke these constitutional protections.[107]

In statutory, administrative, or common law cases, which constitute the lion's share of same-sex parenting decisions, judges either tinker at the margins with technical family law doctrine or invoke the "spirit" of a statute or rule in order to validate the claims of gay or lesbian parents and their children. Standards such as "the best interest of the child" allow judges to expand

same-sex parenting rights through the long-standing lens of children's welfare without focusing on the question of sexual orientation and raising the
ire of opponents.

According to interviews with same-sex parenting advocates, it was a con-
scious and deliberate decision to advance lesbian and gay parenting protections within the context of statutory language, common law, and family law
in order to keep the issue off the public radar. As one advocate explained
about second-parent adoptions in the early years, "none of them are constitutional—all depend on state statutory law and how the judges interpret and
tweak the statutes."[108] As of 2006—when the opposition had launched their
full-scale attack against same-sex parenting—the vast majority of successful
attempts to secure same-sex parental rights (either through traditional adoption, second-parent adoption, or custody/visitation) had been accomplished
without constitutional support. On the few occasions where gay rights organizations used constitutional language to bolster their argument, the decision
either rejected their position[109] or was ultimately framed (where petitioners
used both statutory and constitutional language) solely in terms of statutory
claims.[110] In *Lofton*, for instance, advocates challenged the constitutionality
of Florida's ban on gay adoption. However, the case was considered a failure
among gay adoption advocates because of its departure from statutory rea-
soning.[111] One prominent parenting attorney and scholar stated:

Meanwhile you get the horrible Florida case, which is constitutional.
The story is because it was a frolic of its own by the ACLU it didn't
bring in children and it pursued a constitutional approach on behalf
of gay parents.[112]

Gay rights advocates would have preferred, the lawyer commented, "a statutory approach" or, if constitutionally pursued, a "claim on behalf of the
kids."[113] Advocates in California had feared that a case poised to reach the
state's Supreme Court would rely on similarly value-driven constitutional
language. However, in the end they made their pitch to the court using "statutory interpretation of adoption laws and the history of their interpretation."
By design, the approach was "very technical."[114]

Advocates have also attempted to exert control over which judges and
courts will preside over these cases. Initially, when adoption advocates first
started advancing rights for gay and lesbian parents—and when gay rights
groups took up the issue—the goal was to keep the issue at the lower court
level to reduce public attention. In Vermont, for instance, where adoptions

are handled by probate court, judges had been granting same-sex couples adoptions on an individual basis without creating any fanfare. As stated above, judges "confessed" to granting these adoptions solely in the comfort of judicial retreats in the 1990s. In fact, the issue only landed on the state supreme court's agenda because one probate court judge strategically refused to grant an adoption petition filed by a lesbian couple in order to encourage its review (and its validation) by the state's highest court. The judge felt the timing was right.[115]

Advocates took advantage of the fact that trial court judges typically finalized adoptions. Recalls one attorney, the approach was

> to keep it quiet and get as many granted at the trial level before getting an appellate decision. In California, this was twenty years after gays had been adopting. Approximately 20,000 kids would be impacted.[116]

When California gay rights advocates were confronted with an opportunity to take even a statutory claim to the state's highest court, they hesitated. "Why rock the boat?" argued one California attorney. "People were getting adoptions through random judges in the state."[117] One advocate who took on a case involving uncharted legal territory for second-parent adoptions in a state that is more hostile to gay rights admitted, "I do that with some trepidation because it won't rest at a lower court. Doing it below the radar is better for the parent. Parents risk losing their kids."[118] Recalled another:

> There is a fear that if it isn't case-by-case there will be consequences. A county-by-county basis sometimes means not even appealing bad lower court decisions.[119]

Many of the advocates interviewed cited the local nature of parenting litigation as critical to maintaining a low-visibility approach.[120] One scholar, comparing parenting with marriage, stated

> in contrast to the issue of marital exclusion to same sex couples—the across the board, self-conscious, planned, strategic efforts to open marriage on a grand scale ... [the parenting cases] come out of the lives of men and women and children and they are posed for the most part in state courts around the country—courts of original jurisdiction—family courts, superior courts, juvenile courts. These are the local

judges who in almost all issues affecting the parent child relationship have an enormous amount of discretion . . . There is an enormous range of discretion that a local judge can exercise in interpreting and applying the meaning of best interest in a particular case.[121]

This local focus also privileges the role of local lawyers (over national organizations) who are familiar with the legal frameworks and arguments that are most palatable to family or county court judges and the community at large.

> The downside to having a national organization do this work is that they have a tin ear to the politics. The success of [our state] is that it is [state] advocates doing the work and knowing when not to appeal. It is a very different approach from impact litigation.[122]

For some members, the development of NCLR's Family Law Advisory Council was significant because it acknowledged the important role that local attorneys play in same-sex family litigation. As one advocate stated:

> NCLR has been easy to work with because they have a totally different philosophy about working with individual local attorneys. That is why they formed this group. They realized the benefits of locals.[123]

For these advocates, local is synonymous with incremental. Explained one:

> National groups lost the thread of incrementalism [with marriage]. It got nationalized by the opposition, which they should have realized. But something just got crazy. Family issues are the norm of incrementalism—the rule. The scary thing is what if there's a case that nationalizes adoption.[124]

Local and lower-level advocacy allows attorneys to have tighter control over how frames and narratives are articulated to judges and other policy elites who can influence same-sex family policy.

Additionally, because of their relationships with judges and their intimate experience with the local family court system, local advocates are able to develop mechanisms for educating judges who are likely to hear their cases. The parenting advocates featured below worked with judges by offering seminars, developing bench books, meeting with judges to reassure them that their rulings will not be politicized. Testing the waters of judicial support, however, could only occur in the context of these local relationships. As this advocate described of efforts to keep parenting off the radar in her hostile state:

> I make huge efforts to keep it on the down low—I go and talk to the judge who does adoptions, explain the theory, and see if the judge would be comfortable. The one time the judge wouldn't do that, he ruled against me and we had to appeal it. I do that in counties where I am not familiar . . . . That makes a really big difference. You have to take steps to keep it under the radar. I make sure to tell these judges that this is not a test case. "We are not going to put you on the spot. I appreciate that you are an elected judge and I am not going to do something that will hurt you."[125]

These advocates recognized that—especially in the period preceding rapid marriage equality progress—judicial discretion was both a prized and risky component of parenting litigation.

Children's Welfare, Not Gay Rights

In addition to choosing low-visibility legal resources and relying on local expertise to promote low-profile advocacy, same-sex parenting advocates have also employed specific frames to avoid public attention. There is a natural opportunity, and according to some advocates, a clear advantage, for same-sex parenting advocates, to steer the focus away from gay rights and toward children's welfare. As one marriage scholar described:

> Same-sex adoption has never been dealt with as a rights issue for gays. Gay marriage is inevitably a rights issue, which makes compromise harder. However, it wouldn't be on the radar if it hadn't been a rights issue.[126]

According to another scholar, same-sex parenting cases focus on

> protect[ing] the child in the context they are already in. It is all about the child. It is not about protecting the parents. That's where it is different [from marriage]. The relationship between the parents is irrelevant. It is ignored.[127]

By keeping the focus on children, particularly in the early days, advocates could make individual case-by-case claims rather than arguments on behalf of the entire LGBT community. Decisions in the custody arena, for instance, "depend on the child's circumstances, needs, perceptions, and passage of time."[128] As one spokesperson from the National Center for Adoption Law & Policy explained, the issue was framed as an "individual concern, not a gay rights issue."[129]

The children's welfare frame served multiple purposes. First, focusing on children's needs rather than parental rights depoliticized many of the issues at stake in the cases concerning same-sex parents and, consequently, kept the argument within judges' comfort zones.[130] Richman argues, in her analysis of appellate cases involving gay or lesbian parents between 1952 and 1999, that any appearance of privileging parental rights over children's needs backfired in court. When confronted with assertions of parental rights, she contends, judges often positioned themselves as guardians of children's welfare *against* parental rights claims, which were perceived as a statement of "ownership" or a "power play." Instead, she finds that parents were rewarded for "subvert[ing] their own interests and rights to those of the children."[131]

Second, by focusing on the *children* of same-sex couples rather than the parents themselves, advocates attempted to cast these decisions as unremark-able or an extension of firmly established and widely accepted precedence and principles of family law. As one advocate explains, these cases involved, "very invested parents protecting their children, looking at what exists and try-ing to work within these boundaries."[132] Before marriage equality was even a thought, recalls one attorney, the basic principles of these early adoption cases were simple:

> The issue was if one woman invites another woman to share parenting and the non-biological parent agrees, and during this period the child perceives the person as a parent, there has to be some way for the court to protect the child's relationship with the non-biological mother. The relationship between the parents doesn't matter.[133]

This remained true when advocates began seeking second-parent adoptions.

> There was a more determined effort to use the court to determine these relationships while the couple was together. People really weren't thinking about marriage. Again, we focused on children's rights.[134]

On the few occasions when gay parenting cases made the press, advocates consistently reminded the public of what was truly at stake. As one attorney described:

> The court is now going to decide whether children born to same-sex parents must be given the same legal protections as children born to straight parents.[135]

And judges used this frame in their decisions. One judge noted in his opinion that

> this case is not about gay and lesbian rights. This case is not about gay marriage. This case is not about gay adoption. What this case is about is whether or not a child is better off in this rather uncertain world with as many people as possible taking an interest in the child, both financially and emotionally.[136]

Steering the conversation away from same-sex parental rights and toward children's needs was a strategic move utilized by legal advocates on both sides. As one Republican political strategist explained,

> There has always been, among people who work in adoption, a concern for what is best for the child. Among these people, having kids grow up in a loving home is better, regardless of demographics.[137]

Where marriage advocates and opponents disagreed about the debate's relevant reference points (at least during peak periods of marriage contestation), opponents and advocates of same-sex parenting have each focused almost exclusively on children's welfare.[138] Focusing on children, rather than same-sex couples, constrains messaging and framing options for opponents—thereby reducing the potential for successful public backlash campaigns like those used to battle marriage equality. "It hinders the ability to create an anti-message against protecting children," stated one East Coast advocate. "The people on the right know those points aren't super palatable."[139] As the Family Research Council concedes, the issue was low on the "radar for pro-family conservatives" because of the "confusing rhetoric of same-sex adoption, the media bombarding the public with images of happy gay couples taking in disadvantaged kids" and the argument that "this kind of family is better than no family."[140] Added another opponent, "trying to take the kids away . . . it's a ridiculous battle to fight."[141] On the few occasions where conservative political elites were questioned about their views on same-sex adoption, they provided the canned response that typified public debate on marriage. President Bush, when asked about adoption, shifted the focus to marriage, and reiterated that "the ideal is where a child is raised in a married family with a man and a woman."[142] In 2008, during his bid for the presidency, Senator John McCain sidestepped specifics when asked about gay adoption and focused instead on "family values . . . the values that two parents, the traditional family, represent."[143]

For advocates, focusing on children's welfare instead of gay rights also offers partnership-building and legitimizing payoffs.[144] A National Center for Adoption Policy & Law spokesperson stated:

> [between same-sex marriage and adoption] the difference is that chil-
> dren are involved. There is a recognition that children should have
> homes and children in the public system need homes. People are will-
> ing to put aside their own views on type of home. Organizations like
> mine are opposed to categorical bans.[145]

Attracting non-gay rights groups to participate in these same-sex parent-ing cases, in turn, further legitimizes claims that sexual orientation and gay rights are irrelevant to the best interests of the child. One children's rights advocate showcased in Richman's analysis argued:

> I think one of the reasons . . . why we were able to create such a strong
> opinion [on appeal], was that it was coming from a legal clinic that was
> associated with children's issues, rather than from an organization or
> a party that was clearly representing one parent's issues over another.
> . . . The court clearly look[ed] to the fact that this was a legal clinic
> involved in it, and . . . this doesn't appear to be part of a legal strategy
> aimed at getting, increasing rights for gay and lesbian parents.[146]

In order to maintain the focus on children's—rather than gay—rights, some high-profile gay rights organizations have opted to minimize any association their organization has with specific same-sex parenting cases.

> There are many cases where we don't even put our name on the brief.
> We don't want them to misapprehend that this is a political issue—
> with the name of a major gay rights group on the cover. It is solely the
> best interest of the child.[147]

On the whole, focusing on children's welfare rather than gay rights allowed advocates to highlight in sharp relief the consequences of denying kids access to two legal parents. They argued that a negative adoption or parenting decision would only strip children of their right to have a *legal*, rather than an *actual*, relationship with their parents. Remarked one attorney, "kids are living with the families regardless of the decision. So you will be leaving the kids vulnerable. It is not about recognizing the parental relationship."[148]

In some ways opponents are as reticent as parenting advocates about focusing on sexual orientation—despite their clear disdain for same-sex parenting. Although, during interviews, opponents reiterated their firm support for research that they believe demonstrates that children should be raised by a married mother and father (and their commitment to continuing this research), they described their campaigns against lesbian and gay parents as an opposition to all "third-party parents." In other words, where opponents are involved in blocking same-sex parenting litigation or advancing restrictions on parenting, they are often supporting the position of the biological parent—regardless of their sexual orientation. Because the nature of same-sex parenting litigation has shifted toward addressing custody issues within same-sex couples, in order to remain active on this issue, opponents have mounted litigation-based campaigns advocating on behalf of gay and lesbian *biological* parents who are attempting to deny their former partners access to their children, creating yet another set of "strange bedfellows." As the Family Research Council described of a custody dispute between two lesbian parents, "here you have the rights of the biological parent being violated by someone who is not the biological parent at all."[149]

The Liberty Counsel's advocacy efforts in support of "traditional" families exemplify this somewhat schizophrenic strategy. On the one hand, in custody battles involving "ex-gays" or heterosexual former spouses they characterize homosexuality as a "harmful and destructive lifestyle."[150] In response to a 2009 Georgia custody ruling in favor of a gay father against the heterosexual mother, a Liberty Counsel attorney stated:

> Obviously it is not in the best interest of a child to be taken by his father and introduced to a group of people who are engaging in abhorrent sexual behaviors, who are modeling abhorrent sexual behaviors and celebration of that [which is] demonstrably dangerous from a medical, spiritual, and emotional standpoint—modeling those behaviors for the child.[151]

Yet this organization has also teamed up with gay and lesbian biological parents to protect them from intrusions by "third-party parents." For instance, in *In re Mullen* (2011) —a custody dispute involving two lesbian former partners and their child conceived through in vitro fertilization—the organization successfully argued that any biological parent has a "constitutional right to parent their children without interference from a third party."[152] The Liberty Counsel has filed similar briefs in a number of other appellate court custody and second-parent adoption disputes involving same-sex couples. Other opposition groups have adopted the same philosophy. For example, this west coast opposition group argued that it is "our position that the biological parent or adoptive parent has the final say over the types of relationship they want their children to have . . . We go for the objective measure. This is the person's child. They should be able to decide."[153]

To be sure, these organizations are far more eager to defend the rights of birth mothers or fathers who have renounced the "gay lifestyle." In these circumstances opposition groups can continue to unabashedly oppose homosexuality, support an individual's efforts to reclaim their heterosexuality, and still defend a child born into a gay or lesbian-headed household. For instance, the Counsel defended the rights of Lisa Miller, in the now infamous custody case between Lisa Miller and Janet Jenkins, to seek sole custody of their daughter after she became a Born Again Christian and rejected her homosexuality. Because Miller rejected her lesbian past (in service of her new religious beliefs), the Liberty Counsel could frame the battle as between a Christian mom and a lesbian "legal stranger" who believes that "Christianity is harmful to children." [154] When the birth mother eventually absconded with her daughter to Nicaragua, the opponents applauded the "courage" of fellow anti-gay-parenting activists in supporting her efforts.[155] However, opposition to homosexuality has not prevented groups like the Liberty Counsel from seeing the precedential value in defending the rights of birth parents who continue to identify as gay or lesbian.[156]

Marriage

In theory, at least some of the legal uncertainty inherent in same-sex parenting could be lessened if same-sex couples were able to have their relationships legally recognized through marriage. Some opponents, in fact, suggested that promoting and safeguarding marriage bans would help de-legitimize both same-sex couples *and* their plans to parent. As one opponent from a national anti–gay rights organization indicated: within the context of marriage, "we are not opposed to non-biological parents being given rights, but definitely, for gay people, our marriage strategy limits this."[157] Added another, "Marriage is the foundation for family. We lose it, we lose everything."[158]

Many parenting advocates, however, questioned the degree to which marriage equality resolved their clients' parenting status—a concern that portended the 2014 New York family court decision referenced above. For instance, Joan Heifetz Hollinger, a legal advocate for children raised in same-sex households, counsels gay and lesbian couples to seek second-parent adoptions regardless of whether or not they have a legally recognized marriage. As she explained,

> The most guaranteed default approach to parenting is to have a child in the midst of marriage. No one challenges your parentage because it accompanies the marital territory. Same sex couples who are married have that presumption. They have the advantage, supposedly, of marriage. The problem is Part 2 of Federal DOMA that lets the states off the hook in regard to recognizing same-sex marriages . . . and the further problem is the states that have their own DOMAs. The question is whether the married same sex couple has a child without an independent court order based on adoption or parentage and they cross a state and seek to be recognized as parents or split up in a hostile state—will they be recognized as the parents to that child? Will state courts in hostile states treat parentage as an incident or arising from or based upon their marriage? And if so, would those courts refuse to recognize it? This is not a phantom. This is beginning to happen, which is why many of us who work on behalf of children in these situations find ourselves in the ironic and sad position of congratulating couples on their domestic partnerships or their marriages and for having the security and protections for their family, but on the other side saying you are in trouble. If you want to protect your child or the child you will have, you really need to get independent protection based either on adoption or a parentage order.

As stated above, early in the marriage campaign parenting advocates feared that backlash on the marriage front would spillover into other areas. Advocates in particular worried that marriage opposition would paralyze their parenting gains. As one latecomer to marriage advocacy admitted:

> I would not be at all surprised if there was a concern that gains on marriage would lead to losses on parenting or artificial insemination. A lot of people including myself were concerned about how it would impact all sorts of things.[159]

Recalls one parenting advocate of an early meeting among gay rights activists regarding the decision to prioritize marriage equality:

> They were so single-minded about marriage that they didn't realize that the hostility towards marriage was going to extend to parenting and family issues ... especially in fly-over states, which will result in bans.[160]

Added another:

> There was tremendous fear in the organized gay rights movement and among gays and lesbians in the country about what the push for gay marriage would do in general—that we weren't ready. That it would lead to backlash. That it would get gays and lesbians harmed or even killed.[161]

Consequently, although the two issues are clearly interrelated, advocates have "worked very hard to decouple these issues from a legal perspective" by focusing on the children instead of the parents.[162] This explains why advocates have been so successful despite marriage bans and anti-marriage rhetoric. Nevertheless, when the nation erupted into a frenzy of anti-same-sex marriage fury, same-sex parenting advocates expected the worst and, on occasion, attempted to dampen calls for same-sex marriage litigation in their states. As one advocate admitted, "we have actively been discouraging marriage litigation here. We believe it would cause a backlash in other areas where we have had success ... If we have a marriage case there will be high publicity."[163]

No Contest, No Coverage

While there are multiple prongs of conflict that animate media coverage of same-sex marriage, parenting coverage is less controversial. Comparing the sample of marriage articles reviewed in Chapter 3 with the entirety of parenting articles published in local newspapers between 1996 and 2006, we see that where marriage coverage strikes a pitch-perfect chord for promoting interest and provoking conflict, parenting coverage appears more detached. [164]

Each article is analyzed to determine how the arguments are framed, whether opponents and advocates are evenly mentioned or matched, whether court decisions generate out-of-state interest, and whether the articles appear to have an anti-court bias.[165] The data reveal, first, that where marriage litigation, and its concomitant coverage, pit "gay rights against children's needs," parenting advocates and opponents are, as predicted, primarily in agreement about the issue's most salient factor: children's welfare. Similar to legal proceedings, arguments supporting and opposing same-sex parenting were framed primarily in terms of children's welfare. Of the parenting articles that include arguments opposing same-sex parenting, children's welfare appears as an opposition frame in well over half during eight of the eleven years included in the analysis. Children's welfare dominates arguments in support of same-sex parenting as well—appearing in more than 60 percent of articles that include a pro-parenting perspective. Figure 4.6 graphically displays an annual ratio of opponent and advocacy children's welfare frames in articles on marriage and adoption. This graph allows us to identify the degree to which opponents and advocates utilized conflicting or congruent frames in their arguments. Opponents and advocates appear to be relying on far different frames in the realm of marriage. Specifically, there is, at minimum, a two-to-one difference between opponent and advocate reliance on children's welfare frames in marriage articles. In the parenting articles, however, they appear to be evenly matched; the ratios hover around 1:1 in most years.

Second, where marriage advocates focus more heavily on gay rights, parenting advocates do not. Terms like discrimination, equality, and gay rights appeared in only 11 percent of the articles featuring arguments supporting same-sex parenting (Figure 4.7).[166] In fact, in most years, parenting advocates appear to be decidedly rejecting the gay rights approach. Articles

FIGURE 4.6. Ratio of Opposing and Supporting Arguments Invoking "Children's Welfare" in Marriage and Parenting Articles, 1996–2006

Source: LexisNexis search for articles including the following terms in headlines or lead paragraphs: same-sex marriage; homosexual marriage; gay marriage; lesbian marriage; same-sex parent!; lesbian parent!; gay parent!; homosexual parent! between 1996 and 2006.

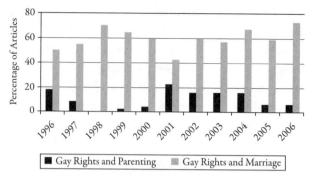

FIGURE 4.7. "Gay Rights" in Marriage and Parenting Articles, 1996–2006

Source: LexisNexis search for articles including the following terms in headlines or lead paragraphs: same-sex marriage; homosexual marriage; gay marriage; lesbian marriage; same-sex parent!; lesbian parent!; gay parent!; homosexual parent! between 1996 and 2006.

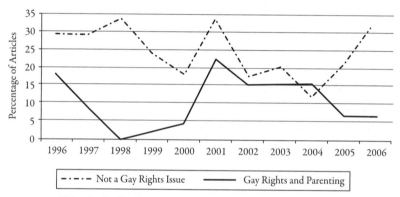

FIGURE 4.8. "Gay Rights" v. "Not 'Gay Rights'" in Parenting Articles, 1996–2006

Source: LexisNexis search for articles in regional newspapers including the following terms in headlines or lead paragraphs: same-sex marriage; homosexual marriage; gay marriage; lesbian marriage; same-sex parent!; lesbian parent!; gay parent!; homosexual parent! between 1996 and 2006.

focusing on the fact that same-sex parenting *did not* center on gay rights outpaced those utilizing a "gay rights" frame (Figure 4.8). Parenting arguments, like their marriage counterparts, did talk about the specific benefits that accompany legal validation of parent-child relationships, but at a lower rate. Interestingly, the "benefits" argument played a decreasingly prominent role in both marriage and parenting arguments during the last four years of the study period, confirming research that suggests a public distaste for this approach.

Another platform of contestation in the marriage articles that receives scant attention in parenting arguments centers on perceptions of judicial activism and elitism. As discussed in Chapter 3, in marriage articles and arguments, judges bore the brunt of anti-same-sex marriage rhetoric and activity. Pro-marriage judges were perceived as instigating or, at the very least, buttressing the assault on traditional marriage and majoritarian values. Same-sex parenting articles focus far less on judges as a source or target of conflict—a likely byproduct of the highly technical and statutory (rather than constitutional) arguments used by parenting advocates. Between 1996 and 2001 articles on same-sex parenting were more likely to include anti-judicial rhetoric than were articles on same-sex marriage. However, starting in 2001, gay marriage articles containing anti-court language outnumbered anti-court gay parenting articles (Figure 4.9). Coverage also differed in terms of the source of anti-judicial rhetoric. In the marriage articles opponents were often responsible for court-centered criticism, while in the parenting articles court critiques were delivered by judges through excerpts of dissenting opinions.

The type of anti-court rhetoric differed as well. In the case of same-sex marriage, early articles described the courts as "forcing" or "threatening" states to accept same-sex marriage. Opponents justified the passage of state DOMAs by arguing that states were "protecting" their citizens from the Hawaii Supreme Court. They described judges as "legislating from the bench," "arrogant," "too liberal," and a "danger to democracy." In 1998 opponents began to regularly accuse the courts of "legislating from the bench" and to admonish them for "overstepping their bounds." They argued that the issue should be left to the

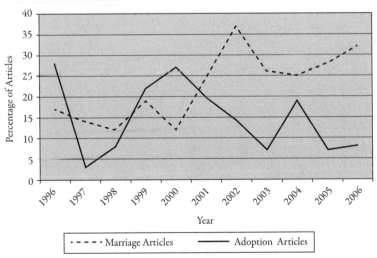

FIGURE 4.9. Anti-Court Rhetoric in Marriage and Parenting Articles, 1996–2006
Source: LexisNexis search for articles in regional newspapers including the following terms in headlines or lead paragraphs: same-sex marriage; homosexual marriage; gay marriage; lesbian marriage; same-sex parent!; lesbian parent!; gay parent!; homosexual parent! between 1996 and 2006.

state legislatures. By 1999 opponents started to refer to judges as "judicial tyrants" or "judicial activists," accused them of "creating law," and called for measures to remove same-sex marriage from the courts' jurisdiction.[167] In 2003 opponents added to this rhetoric the notion that citizens should determine the contours of this debate rather than the courts, and censured the courts for "creating divisiveness" and becoming "too politicized." Anti-judicial rhetoric in discussions of same-sex marriage continued along this vein through 2006.

In the same-sex parenting articles, anti-judicial rhetoric took on a more muted tone. Courts were primarily criticized for "creating policy" and "legislating from the bench," and were sometimes described as behaving "irresponsibly." While these critics encouraged the use of legislatures over courts to resolve the issue of same-sex parental rights, judges were rarely referred to as "activists" or "tyrants"; measures to curb their involvement in the issue were not mentioned. During the entire period of the study, the term "judicial activist" was used three times to describe judicial involvement in LGBT parenting rights, which is somewhat surprising given the quantity and scope of cases promoting these rights.

Third, and relatedly, despite the large number of cases on same-sex parental rights, relative to marriage, significantly fewer parenting articles covered cases that occurred outside of their media market. This suggests that court decisions on same-sex parenting were of little incidence or import to individuals residing beyond the decision's jurisdiction or direct reach—unlike marriage litigation. Out-of-state coverage on parenting peaks in 2000, where 22 percent of the articles discussing cases mention decisions outside of their media market (Figure 4.10). In 1996 through 2000, however, the percentage of marriage articles covering

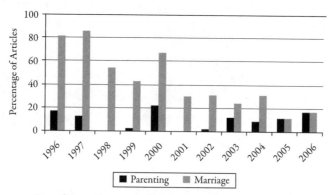

FIGURE 4.10. Out-of-State Coverage of Marriage and Parenting, 1996–2006

Source: LexisNexis search for articles in regional newspapers including the following terms in headlines or lead paragraphs: same-sex marriage; homosexual marriage; gay marriage; lesbian marriage; same-sex parent!; lesbian parent!; gay parent!; homosexual parent! between 1996 and 2006.

out-of-state cases ranges between 43 and 86 percent. By 2005, newspapers had diminished coverage of out-of-state cases in the realm of same-sex marriage to 12 percent, on par with parenting articles.[168] High out-of-state coverage may have exaggerated the success and, therefore, the "threat" of marriage equality. Despite the presence of far fewer marriage cases, coverage of out-of-state opinions raised public awareness and increased the significance of the handful of gay marriage victories. Likewise, low out-of-state coverage in the realm of same-sex parenting minimized knowledge of the breadth and pace of judicial victories. Not only were readers provided limited information about cases in their own cities and states, but they also remained ignorant of significant progress on the issue in other locations across the country.

One final factor contributing to the low-conflict quality of parenting articles is the ratio of opponents to advocates featured in these articles. As stated in Chapter 2, journalists, in an attempt to appear impartial, will go out of their way to balance supportive arguments with narratives that contradict these perspectives. In this sense, the media can exacerbate conflict by creating the image of a standoff, even if none exists. The marriage articles, not surprisingly, tended to equally showcase supporters and opponents. Journalists hardly had to seek out conflicting perspectives on this issue. Parenting articles, however, quoted far fewer opponents than supporters, on average. Supporters of same-sex parenting were two-to-three times more likely than opponents to appear in parenting articles. This skewed focus on supporters of same-sex parenting as experts and sources in articles suggests to readers that the issue is not highly contested. Without contestation the topic seems less important or newsworthy.

In sum, same-sex marriage and parenting coverage differs in several important ways that may illuminate why parenting advocates faced lower levels of backlash. Media coverage of same-sex marriage is abundant, is inclined to represent supporting and opposing perspectives equally, pits gay rights against the interests of children and family, highlights the issue as one involving states' rights, is anti-judicial, and is likely to cover out-of-media-market cases. On the other hand, parenting articles are relatively scarce, frequently showcase supporters over opponents, and frame both sides as a children's rights issue. While still critical of judicial involvement, gay parenting articles are less likely to disparage courts and judges as judicial activists and generally present these criticisms as the products of judicial dissents. Cases on same-sex parenting, although in greater supply when compared with same-sex marriage, are less likely to receive coverage beyond their state (and are therefore less likely to be used as fodder for a state-by-state campaign to restrict gay parenting rights.)

Conclusion

The evidence discussed in this chapter (and in Chapter 3) demonstrates that same-sex parenting advocates devised strategies to reduce public awareness of parenting litigation and protect court victories from the torrent of backlash so common in the struggle for same-sex marital rights between 1996 and 2006. Parenting advocates made a concerted effort to keep adoption and custody decisions out of the public eye. This was facilitated, in part, by supporting their positions with statutory or family law doctrine, which permitted judges to review petitions on a case-by-case basis, and by removing "gay rights" from the equation, choosing instead to frame their arguments in terms of children's welfare. This redirected conversations about the issue away from negative gay stereotypes and toward the neutral or positive discussions regarding children's rights. Without the controversial focus on gay rights, newspapers lost interest. With decreased public focus, the potential for backlash was reduced, further minimizing issue-visibility.

Some advocates, however, are concerned that their ability to keep their victories off the public radar is diminishing—especially as more federal courts allude to state parenting cases in arguments and decisions regarding marriage equality. "It is becoming more visible," lamented one advocate. "There are more people who know about it and more lawyers who are asking me about these issues. I think that there is more visibility and frankly that worries me."[169] Evidence suggests that there is reason to be concerned. Perhaps out of fear that they are losing the battle for public support on the marriage front, gay rights opponents have recently taken off their gloves regarding same-sex parenting. In a radio show, Matt Barber of the Liberty Counsel characterized gay adoption as "egocentric."

> Homosexuals who can't through the natural biological process have children, trying to acquire children, they're basically purchasing children. It's like having little pets or something, I guess. It's egocentric. It's selfish and it hurts children.[170]

Opponents have also realized the benefits of low-visibility advocacy. The Liberty Counsel and other right-wing organizations are retreating from (or supplementing) their trademark public campaigns and are utilizing the same below-the-radar strategies that have been so effective for parenting advocates.[171] Explained one advocate, "We have seen a sustained, over time and recent, uptick in bad court rulings and legislative activities. . . . Even though it is less above the fold, the damage done is enormous."[172] Recent state court rulings in North Carolina, Alabama, New York, and Kansas certainly validate these fears. Although marriage equality is reaching the point of inevitability, its visibility—and its increased linkages to parenting—may inspire smaller, localized pockets of anti-parenting backlash. Opponents seem to realize that the only way to fight incremental gains in parenting is through incremental opposition—one case at a time.

On the whole, though, this approach may be ill-timed. With over thirty states in support of same-sex parenting, mounting evidence debunking the presumptive heterosexual parenting ideal, and public opinion polls and court cases highlighting a sustained shift toward majority support for, and state validation of, same-sex marriage, it seems unlikely that same-sex parenting will suffer lasting losses.[173]

Yet to be answered through this case study is the degree to which below-the-radar strategies can shape the influence, rather than simply the incidence, of backlash. For issues where backlash is inevitable, can low-visibility advocacy help soften the blow of opposition efforts? The following chapters on group housing advocacy address this issue.

5

Group Homes in Gridlock

LITIGATION AND BACKLASH OVER GROUP HOME LOCATION

ON CHRISTMAS EVE 1996, amidst countless holiday celebrations, a group of neighbors congregated in the quiet community of Carrboro, North Carolina. This, however, was no ordinary yuletide gathering. These homeowners were meeting to develop a plan to oust a group home for three developmentally disabled adults and their in-home caregiver from their neighborhood.[1] They worried about how the house—and its residents—would affect their children. "We have nine children in the neighborhood," explained one mother to the Board of Alderman reviewing the project. "They might ask 'Was I naughty? Will I become like he is?'"[2]

The weeks before Thanksgiving that same year witnessed similar levels of hysteria in Wauwatosa, Wisconsin, when a group home for two elderly residents with Alzheimer's announced its intention to invite six additional residents. The house, argued homeowners, would interfere with the community's commitment to "safety" and "strong family values." As one homeowner agonized, "I would not be happy with my two daughters in the front yard like they are now if this place was to have a lot of mildly mentally handicapped or severely mentally handicapped people."[3]

When Florida developed an initiative, in the mid-1990s, to shift care for those with developmental disabilities from institutions to smaller community-based facilities, the homes (and their adult and underage residents) were harshly criticized. One Upper Pinellas neighbor defended his position on fiscal grounds. "I have nothing against these children. And I am not saying they should be put in an institution. I just feel that money could be spent in a much more efficient manner for these children."[4] A homeowner from a nearby community that hosted a group home for disabled adults argued that the home clashed with her neighborhood. Although she conceded that the neighbors were "no bother" and that their "yards always looked nice," it came down to a question of fit. "I feel sorry for these people but I don't think they should be in a neighborhood like this."[5]

These examples are not relics from a more intolerant past. In 2012, more than twenty years after Congress passed legislation effectively making group housing for the disabled a legally protected right, residents in a quiet upscale Palatine neighborhood organized to oppose a possible group home for individuals recovering from gunshot or brain injuries. Residents were concerned that the house would alter "the whole dynamic of the neighborhood" and would "reduce property values." They asked the zoning board to enact a policy restricting the number of group homes. One resident suggested that "ordinances should work to protect residents' safety, enhance property values and prevent adverse living conditions."[6]

Nor are these incidences solely the workings of the uneducated or ill-informed. A University of Pennsylvania psychology professor led a community-wide effort to obstruct a proposal to open a group home in Bucks County for mentally ill adults. The group home ultimately abandoned its efforts when the mob-like cabal of angry neighbors threatened to destroy the house if the group home forward with its plan.

Group home opponents have made good on their threats. In 1987 individuals set fire to a single-family home slated for use as a foster-care home for six infants. Officials arrested and charged several community homeowners who had publicly opposed the project, some of whom had openly threatened that they would "burn it down before we let the city have that house."[7] In December of the same year, a group home for the mentally ill, scheduled to open in Hempstead, New York, met the same fate. The home, which had been the subject of significant neighborhood protest, incurred more than $100,000 in damages.[8] Although no one was charged with that fire, two years later the town was the site of another arson investigation against a proposed group home for the mentally ill.[9]

Stories of backlash and opposition against group homes for the disabled are as varied as they are widespread. Despite the passage of the Fair Housing Amendments Act in 1988 (FHAA) and other legislative or judicial decrees supporting the group housing rights of individuals with disabilities, property owners from all walks of life continue to attempt to block group homes from locating in single-family neighborhoods. Backlash against group homes—even those serving "sympathetic" clients—is now the norm rather than the exception. Similar to the marriage equality advocates featured in previous chapters, group home operators devote much of their siting efforts to devising strategies to minimize fall-out from opposition campaigns.

However, group home advocates (and opponents) face a far different policy landscape than do those battling over gay family rights. As explained in Chapters 3 and 4, same-sex rights opponents often pursue voter-driven mandates to block rights advancements.[10] Marriage equality opponents successfully convinced voting-age majorities in most states to enact constitutional and statutory provisions barring same-sex couples from legalizing their marriages. To stay off the radar—and out of voters' reach—gay parenting rights advocates sought lower court support based on family law doctrine to secure wins that attracted little public attention and few public reprisals.

Group home opponents, conversely, do not typically pursue broad policy enactments to block group homes.[11] Instead, they often engage in episodic neighborhood-based attempts to block a specific group home. They need only delay the siting process long enough to prevent a single group home from obtaining property in their neighborhood. To that end, they consult legal venues (zoning boards, county commissions, licensing boards, courts) and engage in guerrilla tactics to impede a sales or rental agreement between the property owner and the group home, or otherwise render the property unworkable or unavailable. Any tactic that could burden the group home and delay their efforts—regardless of whether these strategies could be sanctioned in the long run—is fair game for the most strident NIMBY warriors. Consider this excerpt from Michael Winerip's investigation of NIMBY protests in Long Island, recounting the experience of one attorney (Seth Stein) who advocated on behalf of group homes.

> Trying to be good citizens, Seth and the director of [the] agency had gone to [the] mayor and confided that they planned to soon buy 312 Melbourne Road. Forewarned, these wealthy, enterprising Great Neck neighbors banded together, formed a corporation and bought 312 Melbourne first, so it could not become a group home. The state attorney general had to drag them through the courts to get the house back. The opening of that group home was delayed years.[12]

In many ways, group home opponents have access to a wider range of backlash tactics than do those who actively oppose LGBT family rights. This leaves supporters with fewer options (and different goals) than LGBT advocates have for minimizing opposition fallout. Although legislation and court victories can provide group home operators with leverage in their fight to protect their housing rights, the lengthy process of safeguarding housing rights through litigation alone often leaves group home residents vulnerable to housing instability. To manage backlash, group home supporters have two choices: either attempt to reason with community members early on in the siting process in the hopes of pacifying NIMBY concerns, or go off the grid and secure their housing before the public is alerted. Parenting and group home advocates also have differing expectations about what low-visibility advocacy can accomplish within their policy fields. Where same-sex parenting advocates use subterranean tactics to *prevent* backlash, low-visibility group home advocates stay off the radar in order to *stem its effects*. Notes one scholar,

> The opportunity to affect the location decision is limited if neighbors learn of the location after the home has been established. [Neighbors] can still attempt to drive the home from the neighborhood, but the opportunity to influence the initial location decision, for example, to convince the owner not to sell or rent to the group home provider, is lost.[13]

This chapter reviews the history and current status of legal protections for disabled individuals who wish to live in congregate or group home settings and the backlash they commonly encounter. Chapter 6 explores how group home advocates manipulate visibility in order to offset NIMBY effects.

The Group Home Controversy

Although shared housing spans the history of urban planning, the concept of using group or congregate housing as a therapeutic tool for individuals with disabilities was born of a 1970s national trend toward deinstitutionalization. The passage of President Kennedy's Community Mental Health Act of 1963 led to an unprecedented shift in the way that state and local agencies cared for mentally ill or disabled patients. Although Kennedy's proposal called for a 50-percent reduction in the number of clients in custodial care within twenty years, by 1975 the population of individuals in psychiatric facilities had decreased by 62 percent. Both scientific and philosophical shifts, as well as fiscal concerns, prompted an end to the "dark age of institutional confinement" and the beginning of community living arrangements.[14] At the same time, budget cuts to drug rehabilitation and halfway houses also forced those in recovery to develop alternate sober-living arrangements. Again community living emerged as the most viable alternative, allowing those transitioning from drug treatment programs to continue to have peer support while minimizing their expenses. The question immediately arose as to where to locate these smaller home-based facilities. Property owners pushed for group homes to locate in mixed-use or business districts. Group home operators, however, planned on opening their facilities in single-family neighborhoods and ignited a battle that has persisted over forty years.

Communities zoned for residential, rather than business, development offer disabled residents the safest, most stable, and most familial environment within which to continue their therapy and live as independently as possible.[15] The concept is simple, argued one group home operator to his opponents. "We want a safe environment for our people."[16] A home's physical space can be extremely therapeutic, explained another operator who works with disabled children. "It's important for kids to live in settings that do not look like institutions. We think they should be living in residential settings."[17] And community involvement is critical. "We've become much more community based and community oriented," offered a senior living facility operator.

> The goal is to provide people an opportunity to live in the least restrictive setting possible. If they can be maintained and provided support in a community environment where they can interact, that's the best place for them.[18]

The Single Family Ideal

In many ways the battle between single-family and other forms of housing dates back centuries. The introduction and quick proliferation of multi-family housing in the early 1800s through many of the country's cities spawned a national movement to zone out high-density housing in favor of single-family development. By the late 1800s cities had established building codes and zoning ordinances limiting the construction of multi-family housing to specific areas of town and privileging single-family housing units. The Supreme Court, in *Euclid v. Ambler*, upheld these regulations in 1926, holding that zoning land for specific uses and types of housing was an appropriate use of local police powers and a justified response to the "evils of overcrowding." In the minds of reformers multi-family housing did not simply increase risks for fire or exposure to illness. It also posed a risk to the formation of a sophisticated citizenry. Multi-family housing interfered with "rearing the best type of children" and "could never be a wholesome place for families."[19]

By the 1940s the country's firm philosophical commitment to single-family dwellings gained federal financial support and expanded through increased suburbanization. Experiments in exclusionary housing began to appear in many of the country's suburbs in order to bring the American Dream to less affluent families. Vanport City, Oregon, was designed to provide single-family housing to wartime female industrial workers and their families. Levittown, New York, became a model for accommodating male workers and their stay-at-home wives. In designing this single-family community, William Levitt marketed his development to "the beribboned male war hero who wanted his wife to stay at home" and raise children.[20] Vanport and Levittown represented two very different outlooks on single-family housing. Where the former offered single-family rental housing for individuals who could not obtain mortgages, coupled with social and employment services for employees and their families, the latter privileged ownership, privacy, and autonomy. Levitt opted to use land for private yards rather than shared green space or social services—offering returning veterans respite from "the communal style of military barracks" and an opportunity to expand their homes to accommodate a growing family.[21] In the end the Levittown model stole the hearts and minds of the American public.

Due in part to an almost exclusive investment of government housing resources in single-family units during the latter half of the twentieth century, by 1999 two-thirds of the post-1940s housing stock had been designed for single families.[22] However, recent studies indicate that the desire for single-family housing may be waning. The allure of single-family living is increasingly challenged by urban revitalization and commuting costs—each of which has inspired a multi-family housing renaissance. Policymakers understand the trend, but the major obstacle seems to be the now shrinking population of single-family homeowners. As one study's author explains, "What's in the way, really, are the established neighborhoods who don't want change or are fearful of change—even if it's change that's good for them—until they understand it fully."[23]

Against this backdrop it makes sense that single-family homeowners would fight tooth and nail to maintain their plot of paradise, and why group home operators would equally vehemently defend the housing rights of their clients. The belief, so rampant in the late 1800s, that anything other than the single-family model will diminish the quality of our citizenry still runs strong today among those seeking single-family living. Homeowners harbor a massive distrust of the types of individuals who reside in non-traditional housing and have escaped to single-family neighborhoods in order to shield themselves from this population. And just as they did in the nineteenth century, homeowners wield zoning laws like a sword in order to forestall the onslaught of group homes on their neighborhoods. At the same time, government investment—both legal and fiscal—seems to be shifting toward multi-family and non-traditional forms of housing, posing a threat to what now may be an outdated version of the American Dream. An increasing number of cities are prioritizing high-density housing developments over single-family new construction. Relatively significant funds have been devoted to mixed-income and mixed-use housing projects. Single-family neighborhoods are increasingly vulnerable to these multi-family goals. Court decisions have privileged the rights of disabled individuals to live in group or community settings in single-family neighborhoods over the rights of property owners and government officials to zone out anything but traditional families. In many ways, then, for single-family homeowners, group home residents are the flesh-and-blood incarnation of the risks of this national trend against 1950s Americana, and they are fighting to ward off this threat.

Perhaps ironically, the real "problem" for homeowners is that group home residents share their belief in the superiority of single-family neighborhoods. They target single-family neighborhoods—and eschew mixed-use or mixed-housing districts—specifically because they believe in the elixir of middle-class communities. Sober-living facilities want to locate in single-family neighborhoods because they believe it will offer their residents the best chance for recovery. Those residing in assisted-living facilities choose smaller houses over apartments because it feels more like a home than an institution. Many group home residents would be equally skeptical of a push toward larger housing structures or higher density housing. In other words, their intention is to partake in the single-family American Dream, not to destroy it. Like their single-family neighbors, many group home operators and residents will fight to the end to secure their legal rights to live this dream. However, although group home operators are united in their commitment to securing single-family housing, they are divided in their approach to minimizing or managing the backlash that often accompanies their housing efforts.

Group Home Opposition

Deinstitutionalization prompted federal and state demand for congregate housing. But local government—fueled by homeowner opposition—has become a formidable obstacle. Almost immediately, at the onset of the community living movement, property owners in the vicinity of group homes leaned on zoning ordinances and boards to restrict group homes from accessing single-family neighborhoods. These ordinances require group home providers, regardless of whether they will rent or own their properties, to apply for a zoning variance to live in a single-family neighborhood. Cities may impose a cap on the number of unrelated individuals living in a single-family residence (typically ranging from four to eight). These maximum occupancy restrictions place hardships on group homes that require some minimum number of individuals to live in the group home as part of the treatment and in order to reduce costs. Zoning regulations may also classify a group home as a business or boarding house, which often results in operators being forced to locate in neighborhoods zoned as business or mixed-use—denying residents the treatment benefits of living in a single-family neighborhood. Finally, a more recent phenomenon requires group homes to abide by minimum spacing requirements.[24] These limit the proximity between group homes, and can severely curtail their siting options.

In the early years, group home opposition often entailed using the courts to validate the long-held belief that zoning authority held absolute power— and that neighborhood opposition held legitimate sway. However, when homeowners lost the bulk of these battles—particularly in states with legislation protecting group homes from exclusionary zoning—they resorted to intimidation, harassment, violence, or arson aimed at sellers, landlords, and group home residents. As the President's Commission on Mental Health reported in 1978,

> Mentally ill and mentally retarded persons discharged from hospitals face difficulties in being accepted by people in their home communities. Too often, they return to find ignorance, prejudice, . . . discrimination and social ostracism. . . . The movement to treat in their own communities people who once would have been cared for in state mental hospitals has been a difficult idea for many individuals and communities to understand and accept. Surveys continue to show that a large portion of the public is both frightened and repelled by the notion of mental illness, even though it is less socially acceptable to say so.[25]

Group homes, in many ways, became the "most visible targets of discrimination."[26]

This backlash took its toll on would-be group home residents. In addition to denying those with mental illness or other disabilities "the single most basic need," group home opposition also reproduced the isolation and segregation of institutional living. In order to find a community willing to accept their residents, group home operators had to settle for neighborhoods that offered a far less than ideal therapeutic setting—often in "psychiatric ghettos."[27] By the mid-1970s, planning experts had concluded that exclusionary zoning and community opposition posed a significant threat to community integration. "As more mentally disabled citizens exercise their legal rights," one report noted, "a backlash is developing."[28] The Mental Health Law Project—which had been formed in 1972 to combat discrimination against the mentally ill— estimated that as many as 50 percent of group home sitings were thwarted by backlash efforts.[29]

Beginning in the 1970s, prompted in part by congressional support for the rights of the mentally ill and in response to increased publicity documenting the atrocities of institutional care, disability rights advocates filed a flurry of lawsuits on behalf of institutionalized clients. These cases focused on establishing constitutional rights for those who were institutionalized and diminishing barriers to community living. In pursuing the first strategy, advocates relied on the principle of "normalization," which, according to experts, was "the only successful method for habilitating" individuals with mental illness or developmental disabilities.[30] Normalization required individuals with mental illness to "be cared for, trained, and educated in a normal community environment."[31] Despite legislative and scientific backing, these cases yielded mixed results. Advocates had few statutory or constitutional authorities to reference in their attempts to establish the rights of individuals with disabilities. They were unable to convince judges that Kennedy's push for "least restrictive settings" imposed on states an affirmative obligation to provide community living arrangements for institutionalized individuals. In the first case of its kind, for instance, the Supreme Court argued that Congress did not intend "to require the states to assume the high cost of providing 'appropriate treatment' in the 'least restrictive environment'."[32] Disabled individuals, the Court argued, can claim "no substantive rights" to community-based housing or services.[33] Legal victories regarding the rights of mentally ill individuals to be treated in the "least restrictive settings" varied, often turning on the availability of more explicit state legislation and the willingness of legal adversaries to settle their cases.

Litigation concerning exclusionary zoning specifically—and its obstruction of group home development—was equally ambiguous. Although a wide range of cases detailed the persistent threat of exclusionary zoning practices to community integration efforts, a paucity of legislative support again yielded a hodgepodge of judicial doctrines. The Supreme Court remained committed to the zoning autonomy of local governments. Fifty years after their *Euclid* decision, they reaffirmed zoning authority in *Village of Belle Terre v. Boraas* (1974), this time specifically in the context of housing for unrelated individuals.[34] The Court upheld an ordinance restricting the number of unrelated individuals that could reside in one housing unit. Although courts were willing to diminish zoning authority when neighbors sought to exclude "protected classes" (categories that were not permitted for use to justify housing exclusions), without protected class status, disabled individuals faced an uphill battle in challenging zoning decisions.[35] Any neighborhood opposition could be viewed as a permissible exercise of one's rights in the zoning process.

There were some bright spots of constitutional adjudication. The Supreme Court had ruled in favor of group homes on at least two occasions. In *Moore v. East Cleveland* (1977), the Court invalidated a local ordinance that restricted the definition of "family" to specific types of related individuals.[36] Eight years later the Rehnquist court ruled against a City of Cleburne decision to reject a group home's siting plans based on a city zoning ordinance.[37] However, for the most part, disabled individuals seeking group home settings had no guaranteed constitutional protections. Without explicit statutory support providing courts with ammunition to protect group home residents, the best advocates could hope for was a sympathetic judge willing to dismantle a city ordinance under rational basis—the lowest standard of review.

It became immediately apparent to advocates litigating in federal court that, in order to prevail against zoning boards, they would need to challenge, at least in the group home context, the presumption that neighborhood outrage served as legitimate grounds for denying a zoning variance.[38] For instance, the Fair Housing Act of 1968 provided civil rights advocates working on behalf of racial minorities with ammunition to not only identify but to override any opposition that was motivated by racial animus.[39] Although some courts expressed skepticism as to whether neighborhood opposition could serve as a legitimate basis for determining group home zoning requests, these cases were hit or miss in the absence of clear statutory standards. [40]

At the state level, group home protection depended on the availability of state legislation exempting group homes from zoning ordinances—or defining group homes as "families" for the purposes of delineating access to single-family units. Without these provisions, the legitimacy of group home

arguments rested on the inclination of individual judges to apply state constitutional provisions to group home arguments. In short, prior to 1988, while
opponents seemed to have endless motivation and opportunity to block
group homes from locating in single-family neighborhoods, there were few
clear judicial options to protect those who required their benefits.

Legislative Support

In response to what had become intractable opposition toward community
housing, mental health and disability rights advocates sought legislative
support. Fairly early on in the deinstitutionalization movement, advocates
realized that they could not achieve community integration without explicit
federal legislative support. In 1979 both the House and the Senate considered bills to amend the Fair Housing Act (passed a decade earlier) to include
"handicap" as a prohibited basis for housing discrimination. Of the many
issues discussed, group homes were among the most important and the
most controversial. Advocates implored members of Congress to protect the
principles of deinstitutionalization and handcuff neighborhood opposition
through federal legislation. As one presenter argued,

> in the course of our litigation we have learned of serious impediments
> to the establishment of group homes for handicapped persons who are
> being deinstitutionalized. These impediments are raised through the
> use of land use or occupancy laws.[41]

The amendment, argued this advocate, would provide individuals with
disabilities the same legislative tools for addressing exclusionary zoning
and housing discrimination that were available to advocates litigating race
discrimination cases.

> Zoning to fence out group homes because of the handicap of the prospec-
> tive occupants would be prohibited just as zoning to fence out a housing
> project "because of" the race of its prospective tenants is banned.[42]

Of central concern to those on the House and Senate subcommittees who
commissioned the hearings was the degree to which legislation would protect
alcohol and drug addicts and truncate local zoning authority.[43] Proponents
adamantly refuted any interpretation of the proposed legislation that suggested that *current* drug addicts or alcoholics would be protected by federal

law. Members of Congress were equally concerned about preserving zoning authority. The original legislation included language that would have constrained zoning authorities by outlawing regulations that limited the rights of state-licensed facilities housing eight or fewer residents. However, members of the House Judiciary Committee felt that this constituted federal overreach and called for its removal.[44]

In the end, although it passed in the House, the legislation failed to muster enough votes to end a Senate filibuster. It was reintroduced (and re-debated) several times over the following ten years before it finally passed in 1988 (in much of its original form). Ostensibly, individuals with disabilities would now have sufficient statutory leverage to challenge the discriminatory behaviors of NIMBY forces. In the words of one advocate, "the FHAA created a much better legal tool with a clearer articulation of standards in order to make changes more easily than arguing a constitutional principle."[45]

While the 1988 Act does not directly attend to the needs of group home residents, it contains several provisions that have been favorably interpreted and applied by the courts in group home cases. Specifically, the Act makes it unlawful "to discriminate in the sale or rental, or to otherwise make unavailable or deny, a dwelling to any buyer or renter because of a handicap." It also prohibits any attempts "to discriminate against any person in the terms, conditions or privileges of sale or rental of a dwelling, or in the provision of services or facilities in connection with such dwelling, because of a handicap."[46] The Act further stipulates that individuals with disabilities must be provided with "reasonable accommodations in rules, policies, practices or services when such accommodations may be necessary to afford such person equal opportunity to use and enjoy a dwelling."[47] For group home operators and residents, then, the Act prevents landlords and sellers from refusing to rent or sell property to a group home if their refusal represents an unreasonable or discriminatory encroachment of their housing needs.

Advocates hoped that the reasonable accommodations provisions would similarly limit local governments and communities from using zoning laws to bar group homes from single-family neighborhoods. However, faced with mounting opposition from property owners and locally elected officials, the bill's drafters included a number of important caveats to protect local autonomy. First, the Act would not impinge upon local autonomy to preserve any "reasonable maximum occupancy restrictions" nor impose any "fundamental alteration" to zoning laws. Second, accommodations were not required for anyone "whose tenancy would constitute a direct threat to the health or safety of other individuals" or where modifications would "impose an undue burden or expense on the local government." Third, the Act excluded from its definition of "handicap" any "current, illegal use of or addiction to a controlled substance."

During the same year as the passage of the FHAA, advocates working on behalf of individuals recovering from substance abuse scored an additional victory. Due in large part to the efforts of Oxford House—an organization created for the sole purpose of establishing group homes in single-family neighborhoods to help those in recovery maintain their sobriety—Congress passed the Anti-Drug Abuse Act of 1988. Paul Molloy, the organization's founder, had once worked as Republican counsel for both the House Energy and Commerce Committee and the Senate Commerce Committee prior to entering treatment for alcohol addiction. His connections, along with the organization's impressively low recidivism rate, encouraged members of Congress to craft legislation requiring states to provide small loans to cover start-up costs for group homes dedicated to sober living.[48]

Two years later President Bush signed into law the Americans with Disabilities Act (ADA), which bars employers and public entities from discriminating against individuals on the basis of an actual (or perceived) disability. Together, these two bills filled a number of significant legal loopholes left open in the FHAA. The Anti-Drug Abuse Act provided additional support for advocates challenging municipal proscriptions targeting sober living homes. Not only did Members of Congress tout the benefits of the Oxford House approach but, in mandating fiscal support, they were also actively invested in its expansion. The Anti-Drug Abuse Act made it difficult for Congress (or any court interpreting its edicts) to argue that they did not intend to support the efforts of group homes for those in recovery. The Americans with Disabilities Act formally put these doubts to rest by affirmatively defining disability to include any individual who is not currently engaging in substance abuse, but who is participating in (or has completed) a drug rehabilitation program.[49]

Back to Court

Despite these important legislative victories, interpreting their mandates and application to group home advocacy presented a challenge. It often took clear proclamations from federal and state judges to convince local governments and incensed neighbors to relax restrictions against group home operators serving disabled residents.

In the first two years after the Act was passed, the Department of Justice (DOJ) and private attorneys worked quickly to establish that the definition of "disability" provided a wide net of inclusion. As stated above, although most communities were equal opportunity discriminators when it came to group home backlash in the immediate wake of the FHAA, there were particular groups who bore the brunt of the opposition. In 1989 the City of Belleville refused to grant a special use permit to a group home operator who planned to open a hospice care facility for individuals with AIDS.[50] Advocates convinced a district court judge that (1) having AIDS or being HIV positive constituted a disability, (2) a group home was a dwelling under the Act, (3) denying Baxter the special use permit was an actionable offense, and (4) the city could not evade responsibility under the "health or safety" provision of the amendments. That same year the Department of Justice filed suit in the Fourth Circuit against Southern Management Corporation for refusing to rent apartments to a drug rehabilitation program, which would be used by individuals who were completing the "re-entry" phase of their recovery.[51] Relying on the medical definition of addiction—which suggests that individuals who develop a dependency on a controlled substance will always contend with an addiction—Southern Management argued that individuals in drug rehabilitation programs were "addicts" and, therefore, excluded from the Act. The court, however, referenced legislative history, HUD regulations, and the unambiguous language of the ADA, to argue that Congress's use of the word "addict" differed from the clinical definition and protected those who were in recovery.

Advocates also moved to expedite the application of race-based precedent to cases of discrimination against those with disabilities. This precedent would, first, reify the importance of their "protected class" status and, second, assure that disability-based housing cases would be reviewed under strict scrutiny. In the first case to test the FHAA, the DOJ filed suit against Chicago Heights for refusing to certify a group home simply because it served individuals who were mentally ill. Relying on race-based precedent establishing that an individual in a protected class could not be summarily denied access to housing opportunities solely because of their membership in that class, the DOJ convinced the city to settle and certify the home.[52] Advocates were able to use arguments raised in race-based and other Fair Housing Act discrimination cases to push for a higher standard of review. In many jurisdictions (although not all),[53] group home advocates can prevail if they can demonstrate that the non-intentional actions of officials or private actors have a discriminatory effect on their residents.[54]

Race cases were especially helpful in challenging the presumption that local authorities were free to enact or implement exclusionary zoning to block group homes. It was not clear, initially, whether or how the courts would relax zoning obstacles for group homes. For one thing, in most instances the language of zoning regulations is not facially discriminatory. Rarely do ordinances restrict group home location based specifically on the nature of the residents' conditions. Instead, claims of discrimination are triggered when the group home is denied an exemption to these regulations.

Advocates argue that zoning officials are expected to modify or relax these restrictions for group homes serving disabled residents in order to facilitate access to a range of resources that are otherwise unavailable in more segregated or institutionalized living arrangements. However, the legislative history regarding zoning and local autonomy is complicated, as indicated above. Although the FHAA requires entities to make reasonable accommodations to policies and practices, and the ADA enjoins local governments from discriminating against individuals with disabilities, the issue of zoning had been explicitly removed from the FHAA's original language in 1979 to preserve local autonomy. Race-based precedent, therefore, proved critical. Advocates could apply cases like *United States v. Yonkers Board of Education* (1987), which relied on 1968 fair housing legislation to outlaw the use of zoning ordinances to maintain racially segregated neighborhoods, to the group home context. This precedent established that both the purpose and effect of zoning is to promote racial segregation and that persistent patterns of racial segregation in housing are, in part, the product of concerted municipal efforts to isolate neighborhoods by income and race.[55] Once civil rights advocates began to focus on exclusionary zoning as the primary engine of state- or city-induced housing segregation, disability rights advocates could adapt that precedent to zoning targeting group homes. As one attorney explained

> The foundation for the group home cases had been the race cases. You could take the body of good case law developed pre-Reagan and apply this to the disability context because in either race or disability cases zoning is the issue . . . when you look at the race cases you see the same NIMBY language.[56]

Using this precedent, advocates have convincingly argued that zoning laws are, similarly, used to segregate those with disabilities, and have tied the hands of local officials and zoning boards. Courts have generally struck down overly restrictive zoning policies—particularly those explicitly targeting group homes serving the disabled. Localities, for instance, are limited from classifying group homes as businesses and, therefore, relegating them to business or mixed-use districts.[57]

Maximum occupancy restriction ordinances, however, have caused more judicial controversy. In the mid-1990s two different circuits had deduced entirely contradictory interpretations of the Act's ability to usurp the power of communities to establish ordinances limiting the number of residents permitted in a dwelling. In 1992 the Eleventh Circuit, argued that the Fair Housing Act *did not* apply to a city's ordinance limiting only the number of unrelated persons occupying a dwelling.[58] In this case, The Potter's House, an alcohol and drug rehabilitation center, had entered into negotiations to rent two single-family dwellings in Athens, Georgia.[59] The organization planned to house twelve residents, exceeding the eight-person occupancy cap. The owner of the property approached the planning department to inquire about rezoning the property to allow the organization to obtain the lease. While planning officials could not find any evidence that the group home would place a burden on the infrastructure of the neighborhood, they refused to rezone the house. They argued that "the rezoning would set a negative precedent for the neighborhood and would constitute spot zoning."[60] The lower court ruled that the occupancy cap was exempt under the Act and on appeal the decision was upheld.

In 1994 the Ninth Circuit took an opposing position on a similar set of facts in *Edmonds v. Washington State Building Code Council.* In 1990 Oxford House rented and moved into a house in a single-family neighborhood in Edmonds, Washington. Upon learning about the house, after an Oxford House resident handed out flyers introducing himself and his housemates, neighbors complained to the city. When the city investigated they found that Oxford House had violated the city's occupancy restrictions, which limited occupancy to "five or fewer persons who are not related by genetics, adoption or marriage."[61]

The City issued criminal citations against both the owner of the property and Oxford House. Edmonds sued Oxford House in federal district court to obtain a ruling that the city's occupancy restriction was exempt under the FHAA. Oxford House filed a counterclaim against the city, stating that Edmonds violated the Act by refusing to make reasonable accommodations. The Department of Justice filed a similar suit against Edmonds (which was consolidated with Oxford House's case). The district court, following the law established by the Eleventh Circuit, ruled in favor of Edmonds. On appeal, the Ninth Circuit reversed the decision, stating that a maximum occupancy restriction was only exempt under the Fair Housing Act if it applied to all occupants, not simply those who are unrelated.

In 1995 the Supreme Court granted cert to requests for an appeal and upheld the Ninth Circuit's decision, stating that maximum occupancy restrictions are exempt under the Fair Housing Act only if they are enacted to "prevent overcrowding of a dwelling."[62] Ordinances implemented to "preserve the family character of a neighborhood" by focusing on "composition of households"[63] rather than on absolute total number of occupants, as Edmonds did by only placing occupancy limits on unrelated persons, are not exempt. In the years that followed *Oxford House*, courts have generally overturned policies placing different occupancy standards on unrelated individuals.[64]

"Deferral, Delay, and Defeat"

Still, NIMBYism persists. Backlash to group homes (or other social service facilities) locating in single-family neighborhoods remains the rule, rather than the infrequent exception. Recent studies estimate that as many as half of all group home sitings incite some degree of neighborhood opposition.[65] As one city councilman argued when neighbors asked him to move a proposed group home to an alternate location: "Every neighborhood will voice objections. There is not one single neighborhood that will say, 'Yes, please house these families here.'"[66] Group home operators have come to expect potential neighbors to attempt to impede the siting process and now view it as one of many hurdles they need to overcome when establishing their homes. "This has been done before," explained a sober living group home operator in response to neighborhood opposition. Communities "start treading on federal law." In response, the "group home or sober-living facility will get an attorney and cite certain cases where you can't tread on federal law."[67] Against this backdrop of backlash, scores of researchers and practitioners have explored the causes, features, and consequences of group home NIMBY protests in order to diminish their influence or effect.[68] Housing groups and agencies have developed countless "toolboxes" and "how-to guides" for providers and advocates to use in order to combat NIMBY outbursts.[69]

To a large degree, group home opposition continues to play out through disjointed (but widespread) attempts to prevent individual group homes from locating in a neighborhood, much as it had prior to the 1988 amendments. Dear describes this opposition as unfolding in three stages: vitriol upon learning about the group home; strategic rhetoric; and stalemate.

Neighbors initially react with unabridged anger toward the group home residents, sometimes casting their disabilities in discriminatory terms. Once the opposition forms a strategy for halting the siting process, the rhetoric typically shifts from blatantly discriminatory or hostile accusations to pretextual explanations that only infrequently or indirectly invoke the residents' disabilities (property values, traffic, architectural integration).[70] The fight between homeowners and group home residents often proceeds in a long, protracted battle, sometimes with the aid of the courts, and the party left standing (if any) wins.

The incentives to stay the course until a resolution has been reached, however, are skewed between group home operators and community opponents. For those opposing group home location, the benefits of continuing the fight—even if they ultimately fall short of a legislative or legal victory—are significant. They simply need to stay engaged long enough to permanently block the group home from moving into their neighborhood. "Deferral, delay, defeat is what NIMBY is about," explained a planning official. "If you can increase costs, delay and hope to raise hurdles, you may cause the project to be abandoned." NIMBY backlash, "is not just a reaction to a project," he emphasized. "It is a concerted strategy."[71]

Group home opponents, as stated above, commonly rely on zoning to block group homes. Despite judicial distaste for zoning-imposed group home barriers, zoning boards and city officials still often succumb to the discriminatory motives of angry homeowners and will deny a group home's zoning accommodation requests. In order to appease NIMBY-induced opposition, many hide behind zoning ordinances to impose delays on the siting process (and ultimately discourage group home operators from proceeding with their application) even when they know they will not prevail in court.

It is difficult for zoning officials to avoid having to answer to their local constituents when a group home has declared their interest in a community. Electoral threats loom large in their decisions regarding group home siting plans. Codified procedures and societal norms often mandate that officials or group home operators permit or invite community feedback. For instance, community input is the cornerstone of many zoning requests. Some cities require public hearings as part of their zoning processes or permit the public to attend zoning hearings. A survey of group home opposition found that 82 percent of neighbors who opposed group home location made their opinions known through public hearings. Communities also explore alternate routes such as contacting their elected representatives, drafting a petition, or organizing a community association to file a lawsuit against the group home.[72]

In some instances, pressure to comply with community opposition may be so great that zoning and city officials feel compelled to revoke a zoning variance that has already been issued. Sioux Falls officials, for example, issued a conditional use permit for a sober living group home, only to withdraw it a few weeks later (after the group home had already purchased the property). Community members filed a petition protesting the permit, inducing the city to deny the permit in a re-vote.[73]

With an increasing number of courts ruling against zoning ordinances, some cities and communities have shifted to mechanisms other than zoning regulations to obstruct group homes. In Massachusetts, one community attempted to impede the location of a group home for four disabled adults in their neighborhood by blocking a construction permit to build a fire escape.[74] An Albuquerque mayor tried to pull the license of a rehabilitation center for recovering alcoholics operating a group home, despite the fact that the home complied with all state-mandated licensing requirements.[75] Residents in Greenwich, Connecticut, argued that a group home for mentally ill individuals should not locate in their neighborhood because they had concerns about the group home's septic system.[76] Momence, Illinois, shut off the water supply to two group homes for the developmentally disabled that were managed by Good Shepherd Manor, two days before the bishop was scheduled to arrive for their opening.[77] One town used a policy that restricted trash pickup for businesses and large residences against a group home serving four developmentally disabled adults. It took one year for trash pickup to resume at the home.[78]

Community members also employ more surreptitious means for thwarting group home providers in their efforts to obtain property. These range from simple tactics to more elaborate schemes. One low-cost but effective method used by NIMBY forces is to mischaracterize the nature of the group home to nearby neighbors and communities in order to mobilize opposition. Community members attempting to oust a house for elderly individuals suffering from Alzheimer's, for instance, described the house as serving "drug addicts, rapists, [or] any criminal" suffering from head trauma and warned, in a flier posted in the neighborhood, that the home may include "a person who sets fires."[79] Others have maligned or pressured sellers or landlords who were interested in negotiating with group home residents. Homeowners in a suburban New York community succumbed to neighborhood pressure and withdrew their offer to sell their home to a group home operator serving developmentally disabled adults.[80]

As indicated above, the free market provides a powerful platform for group home opponents. Neighbors in a rural Pennsylvania community offered to purchase a property at the original purchase price from a group home provider serving individuals with developmental disabilities in an attempt to block residents from moving into the neighborhood. One group home made a $10,000 profit after neighbors purchased their newly obtained property above the original sales price.[81] Members of a Lincoln, Nebraska, neighborhood collected enough funds to offset a group home's pre-purchase expenses. The group home accepted the payment and backed out of the purchase agreement. In a number of instances, homeowners have interceded in a sale before the purchase agreement has been completed and either procured other, "more acceptable," tenants for the seller to consider or purchased the property themselves.

Cities, too, have employed these tactics. In one particularly egregious instance of city subterfuge, a provider had secured federal funding through a county agency to open a facility for mentally ill individuals. Within twenty-four hours of learning about the project, the city had purchased the slated property.[82]

On many occasions NIMBYism has even spread beyond group homes serving individuals with disabilities. In an effort to restrict the use of single-family housing to specific configurations of residents, otherwise reasonable individuals find themselves protesting a range of populations not typically perceived as threatening, and employing extreme tactics to prevent the location of group homes in their neighborhoods. For instance, in the fall of 1998 three nuns residing in a middle-class neighborhood in Joliet, Illinois, approached the zoning board of their town to add a fourth sister to their single-family home. At the time, zoning laws in Joliet permitted only three unrelated individuals to live in a single-family home. Much to their surprise, the request to accommodate an additional nun in their quiet home ignited an explosion of protest from nearby neighbors. Out of fear that the group house for nuns would set precedent for future, "less acceptable," group living arrangements, more than a hundred individuals signed a petition to encourage the zoning board to deny the nuns' request. Opponents argued that the variance would undermine the "single-family character of their neighborhood" and reduce their property values. At a public hearing, several neighbors described the resulting residence as a "mini-hotel" and argued, "the nuns will come and go, novices will come and go, visitors will come and go. The result will be that our property values will decrease."[83] Although the board ultimately approved the variance, they did so with a slim (4-3) majority.

"Nobody Gets a Pass Anymore"

All group homes, not simply those serving the least sympathetic populations, are vulnerable to backlash. However, we know that individuals develop hierarchies of preferences for or attitudes toward certain populations. Accordingly, we would expect a group home serving "dependents"—those who are disadvantaged but well-regarded—to grapple with fewer constraints than a similar home serving "deviants"—individuals who are the least sympathetic.[84]

A number of surveys explore the degree to which individuals hold "hierarchies of acceptance" in their perceptions of disabilities.[85] In general, findings demonstrate clear preferences for individuals with physical rather than mental ailments. Those with more pronounced physical impairments—particularly disabilities with an accompanying "aesthetic impact" or "sensory problem"—are slightly less preferred than those with more acceptable physical challenges. Individuals suffering from intellectual disabilities or mental illness occupy a middle rung on these hierarchies, while those struggling with substance abuse or AIDS/HIV, or those who exhibit more serious psychiatric disorders, typically receive the least public acceptance. These individuals are often regarded as either "morally corrupt or potentially dangerous,"[86] responsible for their circumstances, and threatening. Accordingly, we would expect that a group home serving the elderly should be less vulnerable to backlash than a group home serving individuals in drug or alcohol recovery.

These studies, however, do not specifically address the willingness of individuals to share their communities with each of these disabled populations. It is conceivable that, while individuals may have sympathy for the physically disabled and elderly (two groups who appear at the top of the hierarchy), they may still vigorously object to living in close proximity to these groups. An increasing number of studies and surveys have attempted to address this issue. In general they find that individuals prefer small over large facilities and, as predicted, those serving individuals with physical disabilities over those housing individuals living with AIDS/HIV, addiction, or mental illness. For instance, according to a report issued by the National League of Cities in response to the growing NIMBYism around group home location:

> By and large, local elected officials have acknowledged the need for, and permitted the siting of, group homes for people with mental and

physical disabilities and foster care group homes for children. The same officials have expressed greater concerns about group homes for people recovering from addiction and those for juvenile offenders.[87]

This attitude is echoed among participants in the 2006 General Social Survey segment on mental health, comprised of a random sample of more than 1,300 adults organized into four groups. Members of three of the four groups were asked to consider a vignette that described an individual and their difficulties struggling with depression, schizophrenia, or alcohol addiction. The fourth group was presented with a description of someone who is generally struggling but who is not explicitly contending with issues stemming from mental illness or addiction. Participants were asked to answer a range of questions after hearing the vignette, one of which probes their support for a group home serving individuals similar to the one described in the prompt. The question reads as follows:

How willing would you be—definitely willing, probably willing, probably unwilling, or definitely unwilling—to have a group home for people like [the person described] opened in your neighborhood?

Only those who received the alcoholism prompt demonstrated a statistically significantly higher likelihood to oppose the group home relative to those who received the "no disability" prompt (see Table 5.1). These findings remain true when controlling for party identification, ideology, race, gender, income, religion, and whether the participant owns their own home. Not surprisingly, being conservative, having a high income, and owning a house also significantly predict opposition to group homes (see Appendix B).

**Table 5.1. Willingness to Have a
Group Home in Neighborhood**

	Willing	Unwilling
Alcoholism	0.57	0.43
Major Depression	0.66	0.34
Schizophrenia	0.63	0.37
No Problem	0.68	0.33

Source: General Social Survey 2006.

That said, case studies and analyses of media coverage and court opinions regarding group home location offer a different perspective. They suggest that abstract rankings or feeling thermometers may overestimate the degree to which group home resident characteristics—namely their disabilities—determine opposition. In a set of case studies evaluating whether proximity plays a key role in inciting backlash to group homes, Wilton argues that public opinion surveys or other methods of attitude aggregation may overstate a person's ability to "distinguish between disabilities within the context of everyday life."

> Presented with a list of discrete disabilities or facilities in a survey, respondents are instructed to distinguish. Yet when people are confronted with difference in the course of daily life they may do the exact opposite.[88]

In his analysis of group home siting conflicts in San Pedro, Wilton found that, although in the abstract certain groups were viewed more favorably than others, proximity and likelihood of location seemed to be the overriding factor in determining whether and how much opposition a group home would encounter. Rather than following the hierarchies of acceptance proffered in the literature, "considerable conflation occurred between different client groups and facilities."[89]

Content analysis of articles on group home opposition confirms these findings. In the ten-year period since the *Edmonds* decision was issued, there have been 426 separate instances of group home opposition reported in local newspapers. While public opinion data predicts that group homes for individuals with HIV/AIDS, recovering substance abusers, and emotionally disturbed youth will top the list of reported incidents, Table 5.2 demonstrates that group homes serving youth or individuals with developmental or intellectual disabilities each account for more reported incidences of opposition relative to other group homes, including those housing recovering alcoholics and drug addicts.[90] Similarly, as Table 5.3 indicates, among the seventy-seven group home cases that have been resolved through court decisions in the ten years since *Edmonds*, providers serving the elderly top the list.[91]

In total, these data suggest that, although recovering substance abusers and the mentally ill may engender greater hostility in the abstract than more sympathetic individuals with disabilities, *all* group home providers should be concerned about the effects of NIMBYism on their ability to obtain housing. With an increased supply of group homes across the board, explained one

Table 5.2. Opposition Toward Group Home Sitings, 1996–2006, by Population

Population	Number of Incidences[*]
Developmentally/Intellectually Disabled	95
Youth	93
Recovering Alcoholics/ Drug Addicts	52
Mentally Ill	42
Alzheimer's/Elderly	39
Physically Disabled	8
AIDS/HIV	4

[*]Totals are less than the overall total of opposition incidents because articles either (1) did not list the population characteristics, or (2) described the population as generally "disabled."

Source: LexisNexis local newspapers in US, 1996–2006. Search included "group home" and (court! or oppos!).

Table 5.3. Group Home Cases, 1996–2006, by Population

Population	Number of Incidences
Elderly	22
Mentally Ill	16
Recovering Alcoholics/ Drug Addicts	14
Developmentally/Intellectually Disabled	9
General Disabilities	8
Youth	6
HIV/AIDS	2

Source: Bazelon Center for Mental Health, Digest of Cases, March 2006.

advocate, the current climate is one in which "general anxiety towards some group homes has led to general and global opposition to group homes in any form. Now the harsh treatment is applied to all operators. Nobody gets a pass anymore."[92] Even when more sympathetic groups are seeking group housing in single-family neighborhoods, group home opponents generally feel that granting the variance would set bad precedent. As one opponent explained:

> If one group home is allowed, then there is little legal leverage for the residents to prevent the proliferation of boardinghouses and other group homes, which are legally, specifically and originally excluded from the neighborhood by its developers.[93]

Regardless of the type of population served, advocates operate under the assumption that they will have to confront some level of opposition or backlash as they attempt to open their house in a single-family neighborhood. Determined this operator, "If I tried to find a neighborhood that didn't have objections, I would be spinning around for the next 50 years."[94]

Advocacy Strategies

On their own, litigation and legislation are ill-equipped to minimize the incidence and damaging effects of NIMBYism in group home location. As with same-sex marriage and parenting rights, legal advocates attempting to secure housing rights for disabled group home residents are cognizant of the need not only to produce positive policies and precedent but also to utilize tactics that will minimize the imposition of backlash. This is particularly important in the housing context where, in order to prevail, NIMBY activists need only prevent a group home from moving into their neighborhood.

Litigation and legislation, however, establish a backdrop of opportunity and feasibility for advocacy tactics. For instance, in the time period prior to the passage of the FHAA and its accompanying litigation, group home operators and advocates had little recourse when confronted with backlash. Consequently, as NIMBYism became the norm in the 1980s, advocates began to push for more transparent and "good neighbor" strategies when attempting to locate their housing in single-family neighborhoods. Notifying neighborhood associations, canvassing communities, and working with zoning boards prior to renting, developing, or purchasing properties became the standard. Group home advocates felt it was in their best interests to prioritize the concerns of community members and consult them early in the process—and hoped that, in return, municipalities would grant their requests. As Dear explains, "'outreach' had become the buzzword for a successful siting."[95] However, the risks proved to be significant. Public hearings subjected clients to vitriolic and stigmatizing rhetoric and often did little to convince zoning board officials to support group homes.[96]

In the 1990s, once the FHAA was in full swing and courts had made a clear commitment to granting "broad coverage and narrow exceptions,"[97] many group home advocates began to call for "autonomous"[98] approaches to group home sitings. Rather than focusing on appeasing homeowner attitudes, advocates were committed to advancing the rights—now firmly rooted in legal and legislative doctrine—of their residents. Instead of promoting transparency and notification, then, these advocates argued that advance notification was not only unnecessary and burdensome, but also counterproductive. Advocates counseled the use of more low-visibility tactics for finding and locating homes in single-family neighborhoods—an approach that would be far riskier in the absence of court precedent.

Within the group home community, the current debate over which tactics group home operators should use is almost as polarizing as the NIMBY fights themselves. Some providers and advocates remain committed to the value of transparency in the group home siting process and believe that the best way to cope with backlash is to attempt to diminish it through early and frequent open dialogue with officials and would-be neighbors. Others share the opinion of same-sex parenting advocates and believe that advertising their intentions too early may only derail their housing prospects. These advocates and operators believe that the best way to fight backlash is to try to blunt its effects and hold off on publicizing their housing plans until after they have procured their property. If pushed, these group homes will seek zoning approval or notify neighbors only after their lease or purchase agreements have been finalized.[99] The next chapter further explores these debates over the best strategies to pursue—a high-profile strategy promoting transparency and collaboration or an approach that flies below the radar until group home residents obtain housing.

6

To Tell or Not to Tell

SECRECY OR TRANSPARENCY IN
GROUP HOME SITINGS

YOU COULD HAVE heard a pin drop as Sehl Burns spoke intimately and fondly of his mother, who had passed away from Alzheimer's complications, at a planning board meeting in support of an Alzheimer's-focused group home zoning application. Neighbors were given the opportunity to raise objections to the facility and, although some had concerns about the project's details, the tone of the meeting was supportive and respectful. As he finished his presentation, Burns was greeted with applause and admiration. "We never wanted this not to happen," insisted one neighbor who had opposed the project. "We just wanted to make sure that it was done properly."[1]

For Helen Fitzsimmons, a group home manager, these types of public hearings are an essential component of any siting process—especially if group home residents want to feel welcomed in their new neighborhood. After opening more than sixty group homes, she is convinced that

> the way to avoid conflict is to meet with the neighbors ahead of time and spend as much time with them as you can explaining that this house is not going to look, feel or smell any different than your house does.[2]

If that requires delaying an opening or accruing additional expenses, so be it.

Sarah Groth, too, thought it would be prudent to hold a series of early informational meetings with neighbors in order to garner support for her plan to develop a group home for eight recovering alcoholic women. Rather than building support for her project, however, the informational meetings dissolved into dissent. During subsequent public hearings for Ms. Groth's conditional use permit application, neighbors turned out by the dozens to oppose the plan and submitted a petition with more than two hundred community resident signatures to the planning commission charged with reviewing Groth's request. The commission declined the proposal, arguing that the home would compromise "the comfort and general welfare of the neighborhood."[3]

Lynn Shea and Claudia Coonrad became avid supporters of delaying notification when, as with Sarah Groth, their attempts to open a group home were derailed after neighbors found out about their plans. In the midst of negotiations with the seller to procure the property, neighbors harassed the owner into taking the proposed property off the market. When presented with an opportunity to purchase a different property for their group home, Shea and Coonrad, at the advice of other agencies in the state, made sure to delay community notification until after they had obtained "control of the property."[4] Once they purchased the home they launched an extensive community outreach campaign. Argued Coonrad, "the NIMBY response is almost primal and requires experience to overcome."[5]

It was this philosophy that inspired a group home operator in Embassy Hills, Florida, to postpone community outreach until after residents had moved in. Only upon noticing a large number of cars parked outside the home did community members find out that the property housed a group home for four adults with intellectual disabilities. Neighbors expressed outrage about being excluded from siting process negotiations, and pledged to fight the group home. Although the group home was not required to notify neighbors, they currently maintain an open-door policy, and frequently invite neighbors and community members to tour the house and meet the residents.

The High Stakes of High-Visibility Advocacy

One of the most pressing concerns that group home operators face when establishing a home in a single-family neighborhood is how best to handle community opposition. Group home advocates and managers operate under the assumption that backlash is a possibility in any siting decision. As highlighted in Chapter 5, many have come to view NIMBY responses as part and parcel of the group home siting process. Devising strategies to minimize the sting of opposition becomes of paramount importance for many operators, and their decision about how best to manage backlash often centers on one main consideration: when to inform either zoning officials or community members of their housing plans. In so doing, they must balance the probability of backlash against its costs. Some choose to be up front and open with neighbors and officials about their housing plans, in what is regarded as "high-profile outreach."[6] Others feel it is in their best interest to keep community members and officials in the dark, at least until after they have rented or purchased the property.

On the one hand, as early notifiers would argue, keeping neighbors and city officials in the loop early in the process may actually reduce the *incidence* of backlash. Following the principles of deliberative democracy discussed in Chapter 2, early and frequent interaction with neighbors and officials could pacify any initial knee-jerk opposition to a group home's siting plans. As one community member suggested when admonishing a group home in his neighborhood, "If HOUSE had given early notification and worked more closely with the residents, there might never have been any neighborhood opposition."[7] Added another homeowner in reference to a group home for teens,

> Boys Town in this particular application didn't do what other successful projects have done: try to bring the neighborhood in, in advance of their application (for building permits). When that's done, people don't throw up roadblocks.[8]

Community members want their feedback incorporated into the group home planning process. As one neighbor suggested, the group home's managing company "has a good reputation, but if we would have known ahead of time, we would have had some input."[9] Even when group homes are supported and vetted by the state, community members and local officials still want to participate in the decision-making process. "Residents," maintained one property owner, "should have an airing of their concerns. Instead, if they get a license (to operate a home) from the state, they don't have to talk to anyone. I think that's unfair."[10]

Homeowners feel they have a right to be consulted about any group home siting decision that affects their neighborhood, even if zoning approval is not required. Rather than simply wanting to provide feedback and participate in the planning process, these individuals feel that, as a matter of principle, their voices should be heard.

> I think we have a right to know what they're going to do and should have something to say about whether it's a good idea for our neighborhood.

They're planning an institution in a residential neighborhood and any-body's negative comment is just shut out.[11]

The notification process provides them with an opportunity to ask questions and obtain information about the group home and its residents. As one homeowner articulated:

I'm very upset that they could do this without me knowing about it. More than anything, I need answers. [The clients] will have the right to take walks. Are they unsupervised walks? I don't know.[12]

There may be other pragmatic reasons to invite public participation early in the group home siting process. For instance, group home operators whose livelihood relies on municipal or state support will need to go beyond the call of duty to promote ongoing relationships with local officials. Early and frequent communication with neighbors may be a critical step in that process. Explained one operator, "Our funding depends on our compliance with the regulations, and we are heavily monitored. We're in the community using government money. We're in a fish bowl."[13]

For many, early notification signifies a gesture of goodwill. Substantive benefits aside, alerting community members to a group home's potential arrival, and seeking out input early in the process, helps facilitate trust and confidence between group home residents and nearby homeowners. Explained one neighbor, "For these things to work you have to have absolute confidence in the provider and you have to be up front with the community so there aren't any surprises."[14] When a group home fails to notify the public, offered another, "it's like they've done this whole thing in secrecy, like they have something to hide."[15] Remarked one operator who had come to embrace transparency over secrecy, "We should be good neighbors and let people know we're coming."[16]

Homeowners in communities where group homes have neglected to be forthcoming feel that they "can't trust" the operators and perceive them as "that bully on the playground."[17] In fact, some opponents argue that their trepidation about group homes has little to do with disability but instead centers on the advocates. "This is not about the residents," insisted one mental health professional who opposed a group home moving into his neighborhood. "[It is] more about Opportunity Knocks, which should have introduced itself as a new neighbor . . . The bottom line is that these folks did an end run. . . . They want this to happen without any public comments."[18]

For these reasons, argue early notification advocates, delaying notification is counterproductive and only promotes, rather than dissipates, animosity between group homes and their neighbors. Explained one state official who conducts group home oversight, "if you're not going to have community acceptance for the facility...clients won't be welcomed in the community and that...would be starting with a strike against you."[19] Community members need exposure to their new neighbors and time to acclimate. Sympathized one advocate, "It's human nature to be afraid of something you don't know about. I think it is important to have ongoing communication."[20]

Those who would rather maintain a low profile until after they have secured their property, however, would argue that the costs of early notification—if backlash ensues—are far too high. These advocates would prefer to devise strategies to minimize the *impact* of backlash rather than its incidence. They believe that, although early notification may have the potential to decrease the frequency of opposition outbursts, the likelihood is low. Low-visibility advocates believe, instead, that transparency is far more likely to catalyze the opposition early in the game—imposing irreversible costs on group home operators and residents. For low-visibility operators the likelihood and impact of the costs and risks associated with early notification far outweigh the slim possibility of its payoff.

There are clear practical concerns associated with early notification—not the least of which is tipping off the opposition too early in the game. Simply put, "telling the neighborhood too far in advance only gives them more time to be mad and angry."[21] Rather than fostering goodwill between neighbors and group home residents, alerting potential naysayers about housing plans may hasten the project's demise. As one report on group homes argues:

> Experience has shown that the notice and public hearing requirements bring out a vocal and determined opposition who do not want "those people" living in their neighborhoods. Faced with strong neighborhood opposition to the group home, decision-makers most often bow to this opposition and deny the project, or condition it on so many conditions that it becomes infeasible.[22]

For below-the-radar advocates, public hearings are regarded as "the principal vehicles for fomenting and channeling community opposition" rather than a venue for reconciliation.[23] Although only a small number of neighbors may oppose the group home and attend the hearings, they are likely to be more vocal than those in support of the facility and "may have the effect of biasing local decision makers."[24]

Purely informational hearings may also be problematic because they "provide opportunities to organize opposition around the homes."[25] Consequently, any permit or zoning process that includes a public notification component can deter group homes from establishing themselves in single-family neighborhoods. For instance,

> An applicant may spend significant money processing the permit and complying with additional requirements that may be imposed by staff. If there is an appeal involved, more money will be spent. Frequently, the final decision is to deny the project.[26]

In some cases these restrictions are imposed to intentionally steer group homes away from certain neighborhoods. As one Maine official confessed, "By encouraging (housing providers) to go through a process they were not enthusiastic about going through, we've prompted them to look outside Portland."[27]

Even if the project is approved, argue some group home advocates, unleashing a storm of opposition against the group home and exposing group home residents to this opposition before getting them settled in their new surroundings may impede their care. Pondered one group home operator about the consequences of awakening the opposition, "I can't imagine what it would be like living in that neighborhood."[28] Although early notification can minimize fear—as its proponents would suggest—it may also propel it. "I've seen it go both ways," explained one provider. "I don't personally think it's a good thing. I think it could stigmatize the household."[29] Described another:

> Over the past six years, I have helped open about 16 of these homes throughout Wisconsin and, in all but two of them, the neighbors have packed the meeting and called me every name in the book. And in every one of these cases, we haven't had a single complaint of any substance. It is fear and the worst kind of ignorance that feeds this. These are the worst kind of NIMBYs.[30]

Additionally, some argue that notification of any kind places the privacy of group home residents at risk because "the neighbors will all know, because of the public notice procedure, the nature of the disability of the persons who will reside there."[31]

A Los Angeles County "how-to" guide summarizes these costs in a section that counsels, where possible, against engaging in conditional-use or variance procedures.

> Developers and providers of housing for people with disabilities know well that the public nature of the conditional use permit and variance process can be a catalyst for organizing opposition, and NIMBY sentiments can delay or even stop the development or siting of housing for people with disabilities. Strong opposition can persuade an elected official to vote against a housing project or lead a developer or housing provider to abandon a project because of the hostility that future residents with disabilities will have to face in the neighborhood.[32]

The guide argues further that any form of public information should be used with caution because it will "increase the visibility of the project itself, thereby increasing the potential for new opposition."[33]

Others are less motivated by pragmatic concerns, basing their resistance to early (or any) notification on principles of equity, fair treatment, and the rule of law. For one thing, some group home operators maintain that anti–group home hysteria is simply another way to express and enact racial hostility. Long-time advocates contend that anti–group home, rather than racially charged, rhetoric provides homeowners and officials with a less overtly hostile and discriminatory platform to save white neighborhoods from incursions by black or Latino residents. In the early years of the group home movement, recalled one advocate, opponents were more open about their reasons for opposing the siting of group homes (often inhabited by African American residents) in single-family (and primarily white) neighborhoods. During an East Coast siting skirmish over an Oxford House, for instance, a mayor unapologetically declared, "this is a white neighborhood. We worry about white flight and now you are threatening that."[34] Low-visibility advocates contend that, although opponents have become more sophisticated about announcing their racial hostilities, their motives remain the same.

Second, group home advocates dispute the often-proffered notion that group homes should be treated as businesses or boarding houses rather than single-family homes. "This is a home," countered a group home operator. "Individuals with disabilities have the right to live in nice homes in nice neighborhoods." Group homes are not profit-making enterprises. They operate "as a family of adults that happens to live together."[35] As one advocate described,

The reality is the people in group homes are clearly not biologically related. However, they are the functional equivalent of a family if you just watch and document what they do all day. What they do is what you and I do all day.[36]

Through this lens, argue low-visibility group home advocates, there is a double standard against group home residents. Noted one advocate, "I don't know of any family that announces to the neighbors, 'Hey I'm thinking of moving in. Do you want me here?'" When asked why he deliberately avoided public notification, this group home operator asserted, "they are going to be people's homes," and asked:

When you build a new home, do you write to everybody in the neighborhood to tell them about it? Why should we treat those individuals any different than anyone else getting a new home?[37]

In the end, then, for many group homes, the decision to avoid notifying zoning officials or homeowners is about identity, respect, and justice. Insisted one advocate,

We have always operated under the philosophy that what goes on inside [our homes] is no different than what goes on in any family. They always view themselves as a family. Whenever there were complaints the arguments would be 'we are no different from any family.' We instill in our residents family values, everybody pulling their fair share, upkeep, becoming responsible.[38]

Of course, the Fair Housing Act and other civil rights laws figure prominently in this debate. Where homeowners assert a right to be consulted or informed about a group home's plans, group home advocates insist that the Fair Housing Amendments Act prohibits required notification. For instance, in response to a city's request to keep the public informed, an operator wrote,

Notification of neighbors by any form of government for the purposes of funding, licensing or any approvals is a violation of the Fair Housing Act.[39]

Another asked pointedly, "Would you be notified of other kinds of minority groups moving in?"[40]

In a way, argue some city officials, requiring public input as part of the group home siting process gives homeowners an inflated sense of their power to stop the process. "The opposition of the neighbors could not be a basis for denying the location," explained one city planner.[41] And in some jurisdictions city officials have elected to discard any public notice requirements.

Ultimately, group home providers and advocates who oppose early notification remain skeptical about its intent. "What's the purpose of the public hearing, if not to exclude?" asked one parent of a group home resident during state legislative hearings in support of a bill requiring public notification.[42] Added a group home manager,

> Ask yourselves right now, when you choose to move to a new neighborhood, are you willing to subject yourselves to a hearing? Are you willing to see if you pass muster with the neighbors? Willing to see if you are acceptable?[43]

Similar to the gay rights advocates featured in earlier chapters, group home supporters rest their decisions about visibility on pragmatic considerations of backlash and more value-driven questions of rights. Whereas supporters of early notification view transparency as the key to minimizing backlash and promoting strong community ties, late notifiers believe that it only exacerbates the influence of backlash and infringes upon residents' rights. Diminished opposition, these advocates argue, can only come when ongoing exposure and communication begins *after* residents have moved in. This divide is captured most succinctly in the diverging opinions of the National League of Cities and the Coalition to Preserve the Fair Housing Act. On the one hand, argues the National League of Cities, "notification procedures . . . constitute the single most important vehicle for reaching neighborhoods affected by a group home." On the other, challenges the Coalition, notifying the public "without thorough public education only inflames public opposition."[44]

In reality, there is no avoiding community input. Group home residents and operators know they will, ultimately, have to reach out to their neighbors and acknowledge community concerns in order to feel at home in their new surroundings. If they do decide to postpone informing their future neighbors about their housing plans, they will have to work to "make amends" with their neighbors after they have settled into their new house. But, as this attorney stated, "it is much better to ask for forgiveness than to beg for permission."[45]

The Legal, Political, and Social Backdrop for Group Home Advocacy

Legal advocates do not make strategy decisions in a vacuum. The same-sex parenting advocates featured in Chapter 4, for instance, developed their game plan against a backdrop—and with full consideration—of a public and hostile values war that pitted gays against kids. They used below-the-radar legal venues and well-worn family law doctrine to leverage judicial support without arousing public suspicion. Group home advocacy calculations were, similarly, developed with both the nature and frequency of backlash—and the judicial and legislative response—in mind.

The Legal Consensus

Just as they did for LGBT parents, courts articulated what was possible and permitted for group home residents in their search for the perfect single-family home. Widespread court support for the mandate of the FHAA (and its implied protections for group home residents) made it feasible for operators, advocates, and residents to make claims and demands in their search for adequate family housing. Unlike the pre-amendments years discussed in Chapter 5, group homes now had clear congressional support and an invitation from the courts to locate in a wide variety of neighborhoods. However, litigation and legislation could not fully protect the rights of group home residents.

First, judges responded to the increased NIMBY ingenuity of the post-amendment years with mixed reactions. On the one hand, as they have with other zoning policies targeting group homes, courts have overruled spacing and overconcentration stipulations, which tend to limit the number of group homes that can locate in a particular area.[46] As one judge argued, "The location of 49 individuals into an area which houses hundreds of thousands can hardly constitute unnecessary concentration."[47] Courts have also continued to respond unfavorably to municipalities that rely on neighborhood opposition to deny zoning variance requests to group homes. Zoning denials based either on direct statements that stereotype group home clients—even if they express a concern for client welfare—or on less overtly discriminatory rationales, such as decreased property values or increased traffic, have been admonished in court as "pretext for unlawful discrimination."[48]

However, where judges have been, generally, unconvinced by municipal rationales for using zoning or occupancy restrictions to limit group homes, they have been less willing to find fault with obstacles erected through utility provision or permits. Recall the incident in Momence, Illinois—discussed in Chapter 5—when a city shut off the water supply to two group homes for developmentally disabled individuals hours before a bishop was due to visit the property. Both a Seventh Circuit district court judge and the court of appeals affirmed the city's defense, arguing that the residents of Good Shepherd were not denied water *by reason of their disability*. Rather, the city had shut off the water supply because Good Shepherd had not taken necessary measures to extend the pipes. The court of appeals reasoned that the property in question was uninhabitable not only for the group home residents, but for any residents who wanted to use the property—unless the appropriate structural changes were made.[49] Similarly, a group home serving residents with Alzheimer's lost their request for sewer service, thwarting their expansion plans. The court argued that the request was not a necessary accommodation for the group home residents.[50] An Arizona state court sided with community residents who sued the owners of a group home for the elderly for failing to erect a garage to store the group home's RV. Although the group home argued that the RV was necessary to transport the residents and their medical equipment (and that building a garage would impose burdensome costs), the court found that waiving the garage requirement listed in the community association's covenants did not amount to a necessary accommodation.[51]

Judges have also been reluctant to punish private or individual opposition against group homes. Those who engage in free market subterfuge have been met with a mixed judicial response. In 1994, for instance, a Sixth Circuit court argued that neighbors did not violate the Fair Housing Act when they contributed funds to purchase a property away from a group home. The court argued that this act constituted "normal economic competition."[52] During the same year a district court in Nebraska held that a lender who knowingly provided a loan to an individual to purchase a home for the purpose of prohibiting a group home had violated the Fair Housing Act.[53] Judges have been equally tenuous about balancing NIMBY opponents' First Amendment protections. Courts remain committed to upholding the First Amendment rights of neighbors to publicly oppose group home sitings through hearings, public meetings, canvassing, and a whole range of speech-centered activities. These protections end, however, when the tactics interfere directly with the procurement process.

Both the increased complexity of group home sitings and the inability of legislators or judges to stem the tide of opposition have prompted group home operators to assert that the process of securing reasonable accommodations or exemptions to zoning policies is punishment in and of itself. They argue that the process (not just the outcome) of seeking zoning variances, special use permits, and other accommodations from municipal officials interferes with their housing rights—particularly when these procedures require community notification. In addition to exposing group home residents to significant opposition-imposed delays that could cost them their property, advocates contend, requiring group home residents to divulge their disabilities in a public forum and then subjecting them to the ugly rhetoric that often accompanies siting hearings constitutes discrimination under the FHAA. Again, these advocates question why other families who wish to purchase a home in a particular neighborhood are not held to the same kind of scrutiny.

In these cases the question centers on ripeness. Is a group home permitted to forgo seeking approval from a zoning board before raising their claims in court, or must they have attempted to receive a variance (and have been denied) before asking a court to intervene? In a 1994 Seventh Circuit case involving Palatine Village, the court ruled that a city ordinance requiring group homes to seek a special use permit in order to locate in a single-family neighborhood did not violate the reasonable accommodations provision of the FHAA.[54] A US district court judge in Virginia ruled that a group home's complaint against a Virginia Beach ordinance restricting the number of individuals living in a single-family home was not ripe because the operator had not utilized the city's exemption process.[55] Courts in the Second and Eighth Circuits have ruled similarly.[56] Some courts have even gone as far as requiring group home providers to introduce Fair Housing Act arguments during the zoning process before raising them in court.[57]

That said, there are courts that have been willing to admonish zoning variance requirements and community notification regulations. In *Potomac Group Homes v. Montgomery County* (1993), a US district court in Maryland struck down neighbor notification requirements. The court argued that

> The neighbor notification rule, and defendants' proffered justifications for it, necessarily assume that people with disabilities are different from people without disabilities and must take special steps to "become a part of the community." This requirement is equally as offensive as would be a rule that a minority family must give notification and invite comment before moving into a predominantly white neighborhood.

In 1996 the Sixth Circuit, in ruling that a Michigan community notification requirement violated the FHAA, argued it "would facilitate the organized opposition to the home, and animosity towards its residents."[58]

Of course, the legal backdrop for group home sitings is not shaped by court opinions or litigation alone. In many cases the final judgment is ironed out in mediation or through consent decrees rather than court opinions. For instance, protracted litigation involving senior housing in Wall Township, New Jersey, resulted in a consent decree where the provider would not only provide senior housing but also low-income housing for the township.[59]

Nor is the sole benefit of legal advocacy securing a particular property in a single-family neighborhood. As one attorney from the Department of Justice explained, "getting a decision has a value well beyond whether a provider gets a house."[60] Court cases have spillover effects. Based on their understanding of case law, some cities have expanded their definition of disability and modified zoning regulations to comply with judicial interpretations of the FHAA— particularly after the Supreme Court's verdict in *Edmonds*.

Group home advocates have used precedent to threaten legal action and maintain momentum. As one advocate stated, "Sometimes you need even the threat of, if not actual, litigation to reach the right players and bring them to the table" in order to facilitate a workable solution.[61] For instance, one city opted to negotiate a settlement rather than continue to pursue litigation. The settlement ended up containing significantly more important provisions than would have been possible through court order—including ongoing and required training for the municipality and a mechanism for rewarding businesses and other enterprises who work with individuals with disabilities.[62] As one advocate bluntly stated, "There is a pretty strong argument that litigating will make them respect you in the morning. Standing up to your bullies decreases the chances that they will bully you in the future."[63]

Zoning officials, too, have relied on court precedent in their negotiations with angry neighbors and constituents. Because legal precedent has significantly shaped the reach of the FHAA, municipalities regularly refer to legal experts to determine how much latitude they have in the zoning decision.

> Zoning board members and city council members are inclined to succumb to constituent pressure but they are bound by law to ask their lawyer. Lawyers use cases to advise them. So, good litigation helps give city attorneys ammunition to convince cities to grant zoning requests.[64]

This, in turn, allows officials to punt responsibility for denying the requests of group home opponents to "activist judges" or lawyers—even if they support the group home's position.

Sometimes it is helpful to educate the local government on the federal law and case law. This way the city can say they are constrained by law. With strong precedent the risks of moving forward against group homes are much greater. You can explain to your constituents that these federal civil rights laws are constraining your choices.[65]

As one city supervisor explained to his constituents, after reading through cases where residents and municipalities opposed group homes, "I can't find one that ever won."[66]

Political and Organizational Factors

Where the legal and federal backdrop is largely supportive of group home residents, the local political and social context remains hostile. As one Department of Justice attorney put it, "there is no place in the country so politically liberal that a group home will not rouse opposition."[67] Communities "know what the FHA is and know what the law is," explained another attorney, who represents sober-living group homes, "but because of local politics will say 'we want to fight this.' Zoning is driven by local politics, period."[68] This is especially problematic in smaller towns where, "notwithstanding litigation on the Fair Housing Act, the story of denying conditional use permits goes on and on." He added:

> The city council goes to church with these people, they belong to the same civic organizations, who do you think they are going to listen to? We are a disenfranchised people. We don't have a say. We are not plugged into the system. Even though it is supposed to be a democratic process, local politics rules by constituent pressure. Who do you want to risk pissing off, the people who vote you into office and the people who you sit next to on Sunday, or a group of recovering alcoholics?

"Fair housing law," added this early notification advocate and scholar, "is still running up against the assumption of private property owners that they have a right to say who lives in their neighborhood. Will a decision-maker bow to local prejudices or will they go with the advocates?"[69]

Although we know that all group homes must contend with the specter of local opposition, local siting politics may be exacerbated by the specific nature of the group home—the populations they serve, the type of housing they need, and their design options. Recall, from Chapter 4, that the higher one's ailment on the hierarchy of acceptance, the more sympathetic they may appear to would-be NIMBY opponents. Where homeowners will have little compunction about aggressively attacking a group home for recovering drug addicts and alcoholics, they may be less motivated to lead an assault against a group home for the elderly or physically disabled. Although statistically all group homes face a strong likelihood of encountering some degree of backlash, anecdotally, providers have noticed clear divisions of derision. For instance, one Oregon advocate has found that although, in recent years, "NIMBYism has accommodated the moderately mentally ill and the quiet individuals, they haven't made the same accommodations for the severely mentally ill."[70] Another argued, more generally, that group homes serving individuals with mental illness or who are in recovery face a more pronounced and enduring backlash.[71] As mentioned above, race, too, plays an important "triggering mechanism" in sparking group home opposition.[72] As one Oxford House advocate remarked,

> When OH enters an all white neighborhood and there are black Oxford House residents, sometimes the residents go ape*!@$. And even where it is a mixed community, but affluent, and you have a black Oxford House resident, there is still backlash.[73]

In some instances, all-white neighborhoods were forced to desegregate only because a group home (often an Oxford House) with Black or Latino residents has set up shop on their block.[74]

For these reasons, a group home's target population may determine how forthcoming an operator will be about their housing plans. Group homes serving more controversial populations—ones that reside lower on the "hierarchies of acceptance"—may be more likely to remain below the radar because public awareness poses a significant obstacle. The lower one sits on the hierarchy, the less acceptable or more threatening they are to neighbors and the more likely the backlash—regardless of how transparent they are during the siting process.[75] If they stand little chance of preventing backlash, they will place a premium on tactics that reduce its sting. A group home for recovering substance abusers, for instance, who sit low on the hierarchy, may be more likely to privilege secrecy over transparency out of fear that neighbors will derail their housing plans before they take ownership.

Resident characteristics will also determine the type of housing or the degree of structural alterations required. The more physical accommodations required to render a house accessible to its residents, the greater the interaction with the city, and the more likely the group home will be required to keep community members in the loop. In this case opportunities to reduce visibility are limited. For instance, a housing provider for the elderly may elect to build (or purchase and renovate) a house for their clients rather than rent, in order to have the freedom to make modifications to accommodate the physical limitations of their residents. This provider will likely need building permits and a variety of amenities from the city in order make the necessary modifications.

Similarly, variation in property procurement (whether organizations rent or buy, whether they develop properties or acquire existing properties) can also determine how they will manage backlash. Organizations whose finances, mission, and structure require renting rather than purchasing homes may face fewer municipal and procedural constraints than organizations that purchase property or develop homes. In theory, a group home that rents simply has to identify a landlord willing to rent to the residents and then move their residents into the home. Renting properties typically takes very little time and requires very little paperwork, and any zoning issues that a renter may face can be resolved after residents have moved in.

Organizations that purchase property have to follow a more rigorous process in securing loans, negotiating with the current owners, and transferring deeds. If group homeowners require modifications to the existing structure (to allow for more parking, accommodations for disabled individuals, more living space), they may need to apply for a permit, which involves city input. However, unlike renters, owners have greater housing security. They are not dependent upon the whims or comfort of prospective landlords.

Group home operators who develop properties are forced to interact with city and zoning officials to a much higher degree. Not only do individual projects require the blessing of the city, but cooperation with city officials will facilitate the development of future projects. When developers operate locally, their reputation among city officials is critical. Explains one fair housing scholar,

> The developers don't want to bite the hand that feeds them. There are innumerable ways that government can deny you a permit where there won't be any legal recourse. Generally their first strategic issue is what city do they want to site in. They know the staff at city council and planning council. They don't want to get a reputation for being adversarial.[76]

Of course, an operator's sensitivity to risk also depends on their funding. Those who receive funding from local government will likely tread carefully. Participant or privately funded homes may feel more at liberty to buck community demands.

To Tell or Not to Tell

In short, group home operators employ a variety of strategies to overcome NIMBY-induced obstacles. Some pursue fully transparent and public strategies through which neighbors and public officials are apprised of the group home's housing plans before the property has been rented, purchased, or built. Others utilize more low-profile and stealth strategies. In these instances, group home operators will rent or purchase the property without first notifying neighbors or officials and will stand ready to invoke their legal rights if the need arises. These choices may depend, in part, on the level of regulatory oversight required by the city and a range of group home resident characteristics. Often these two factors go hand-in-hand.

If we organize group home providers along a continuum from transparent to low-profile siting strategies, we find that, generally, providers cluster into three camps: collaborative, cooperative, and stealth (see Figure 6.1). Collaborative organizations work closely with city officials and community residents to make sure that all stakeholders involved in the siting decision are comfortable.[77] These organizations go out of their way to notify neighbors of their intention to locate in their neighborhood. Collaborative organizations will also work closely with zoning officials prior to purchasing or renting the property to secure all permits, variances, and exemptions. Collaborative organizations employ a variety of tactics to gain the support of community residents, ranging from informal meetings with community members to gather feedback and provide information, to more official public hearings. For instance, Pine Street Inn, a housing provider in Boston, planned to purchase and develop a duplex in a single-family neighborhood to house homeless men with disabilities. In order for them to receive zoning variances and construction permits, the city required PSI to hold public hearings. In preparation for the hearing, staff

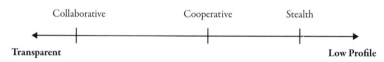

FIGURE 6.1. Visibility Continuum

conducted intensive door-to-door canvassing . . . in order to 1) meet the majority of residents and explain the project; 2) answer questions about all aspects of the project; and 3) determine the extent of initial opposition.[78]

The neighborhood eventually wrote a strong letter in support of the project.

In Portland, Oregon, collaborative group home providers used the (now defunct) Community Residential Siting Program for assistance with notification. This program stressed early interaction between group home operators and potential neighbors and recommended that operators research neighborhood demographics before developing an outreach plan. CRSP staff also provided group home operators with help identifying key community contacts and advised operators to have a series of fact sheets on hand to distribute to community members, businesses, and zoning board officials. The organization helped mediate and facilitate a range of meetings with homeowners and zoning board officials and advised group home operators to develop committees comprised of group home staff and neighbors to ensure ongoing communication and joint-ownership.

In order to appease neighborhood skepticism about a group home's siting decision, collaborative operators sometimes enter into "good neighbor agreements" with nearby homeowners. These agreements serve as contracts that bind group homes to specific conditions and provide neighbors with some degree of assurance that the facility will remain accountable and answerable to local homeowners. Often these agreements are crafted with the aid of municipal or other third-party facilitators. The contents of the agreement can then be made available to homeowners or on the group home's website.

Iglesias describes collaborative group homes as attempting to "manage" rather than "overcome" group home opposition. Their goals are to

> 1) respect the legitimate concerns of the local community and neighborhood; 2) respect the rights of current and prospective residents whom it desires to serve; and 3) advance the prospects of future affordable housing proposals in that community.[79]

They defer to local zoning authorities, prioritize the needs and concerns of property owners, and help to maintain a community's "distinct sense of local control"[80] by utilizing available channels of participatory decision making. This approach, argues Iglesias, focuses on establishing points of agreement among the provider, city officials, and community residents, and adhering

to established protocols for group home development, to educate stakeholders, and to negotiate their position.[81] In the event that communities remain
unyielding in their opposition, truly collaborative group homes will look for
alternate locations and begin the process anew. Iglesias suggests that group
home providers who develop units (rather than purchase or rent existing units)
may be more likely to use collaboration to manage opposition, particularly if
they require an ongoing relationship with city officials for future projects.

Cooperative organizations will either notify neighbors or work with zoning officials prior to procuring their home, but will not do both. They want to
be perceived as acting in good faith, but they also have concerns about being
too forthcoming with their intentions. These providers will follow zoning
procedures: attend public hearings, apply for zoning variances, and accept
conditional uses to the extent that these constraints do not significantly
impede their ability to provide treatment, but they will engage in a portion
of these activities after the property has been acquired. In the event that they
are denied the variances, cooperative organizations will take their claims to
court. After losing a bid to establish a group home because of rampant community opposition, for instance, operators in Texas sought (and received)
approval from a city official to use the single-family property for its residents,
but elected to bypass community notification until after they moved in.[82]

Stealth organizations will purchase or rent their properties before contacting neighbors and zoning officials. Like cooperative group homes, some
stealth operators are willing to apply for variances if required, but will only
do so after securing the property. Some operators simply skirt the zoning process altogether, arguing that the requirements are discriminatory. If forced to
apply for zoning, these operators head straight to court.

Interestingly, although both collaborative and cooperative providers
support some form of early notification, neither believes that public hearings or community meetings are the best vehicles for informing the public.
Presenting a group-housing proposal to a packed room of angry or scared
homeowners only facilitates the opposition by giving them a readily available
mechanism to transform anxiety into action. As this collaborative advocate
explains, "The knee-jerk notion of most developers is to have a community
meeting. This is a bad idea because you organize the opposition." They prefer
more intimate face-to-face interactions, as this advocate suggests. "Try to find
one neighbor who is a supporter and have them go door-to-door with you.
Put a human face on the organization."[83]

Cooperative and stealth providers are guided by practical as well as philosophical motivations. For instance, the Los Angeles County guide referenced

above includes, among several advantages to "low-profile group home out-reach[,] minimizing public scrutiny and criticism of the project [and] ensuring that people with mental illness are guaranteed the same rights to privacy and confidentiality that are to be expected in a free society."[84] From a practical standpoint, providers want to obtain a house and move their clients in as quickly and efficiently as possible. If they go through the zoning process before procuring a house, they stand to lose the property; zoning procedures often last several months and can take up to several years, especially if appeals are involved. For organizations that rent, this is particularly problematic. It is unlikely that a landlord would be willing to forfeit rent for the duration of the zoning process in order to support the group home residents. Philosophically, these under-the-radar providers feel that it is their right to locate in any single-family neighborhood without needing to ask for permission. As one provider articulated, "the facility is a residence . . . and the two residents and twenty-four-hour staff qualify as a family. Zoning approval isn't needed."[85]

In order to assess, on a larger scale, the degree to which advocates and operators pursue low-visibility strategies, I analyzed more than three hundred incidences of group home sitings reported in local newspapers between 1996 and 2006. Figure 6.2 provides two snapshots comparing low-visibility and transparent group home providers. The "notification ratio" compares group

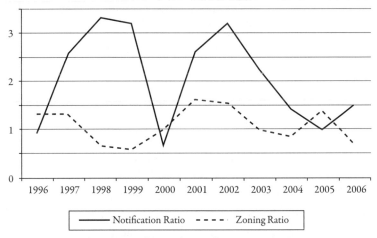

FIGURE 6.2. Ratios Comparing the Incidence of Group Home Strategies

Source: This figure represents ratios of non-notifiers to notifiers and ratios of group home operators who rent or purchase their homes first compared with operators who apply for zoning variances before renting or purchasing. Based on search of LexisNexis local newspapers in US, 1996–2006. Search included "group home" and (court! or oppos!).

homes that elected not to notify neighbors prior to renting or purchasing their home with those who chose to notify. Those who delayed notification outnumbered early notifiers, on average, 2 to 1.[86] The "zoning ratio" compares group homes who procured housing first with those who sought zoning approval before purchasing or renting their housing. Group home operators who secured housing before seeking a zoning variance or permit only slightly outnumbered operators who sought approval before procuring their house.

Twenty-five percent of the incidences included in the sample used collaborative strategies.[87] These group homes opted for full transparency and both notified and sought zoning approval prior to obtaining their houses. Another 25 percent can be classified as cooperative. These group homes were willing to either skip notification or forgo the zoning process, and proceed first with renting or purchasing the house or property. A remaining 50 percent used stealth strategies and neither notified nor sought zoning approval prior to securing their housing.

More than half of the sample is comprised of group home operators who owned (or were planning on purchasing) the property in question. An additional third intended to build or develop their properties. A small number (approximately 10 percent) of group home operators rented (or were planning to rent) their homes. Among operators who elected to purchase their homes, those who delayed notification outnumbered proponents of early notification almost 2 to 1. These group home operators were one and a half times more likely to delay zoning requests until after they purchased their property. Group home developers, however, were more likely to pursue "good neighbor" strategies—as predicted above. These operators were roughly split between early and late notifiers, and those who sought out zoning approval early in the process outnumbered those who delayed zoning 2 to 1. In general, owners were far more likely to pursue "stealth" strategies, while those who developed properties leaned slightly more toward cooperative or collaborative tactics.

In terms of population, the largest proportion—almost a third—of siting incidences included in the sample involved group homes serving individuals with developmental disabilities. A roughly equal number referred to homes serving kids with varying disabilities. The remaining stories covered, in roughly equal percentages, group homes serving the mentally ill, those recovering from substance abuse, and the elderly or those with Alzheimer's. The relationship between population and below-the-radar strategies is mixed: only group homes serving individuals recovering from drug or alcohol addiction demonstrate a clear inclination to delay notification and zoning requests until after the property has been secured. While group homes serving the elderly (or individuals with Alzheimer's) were more likely to delay notification, these operators were also inclined to request zoning approval early in the process. Similarly, while only 30 percent of group homes serving the developmentally disabled, children, or mentally ill individuals alerted community members of their plans, almost half applied for variances before securing their properties.

Oxford House: Low-Visibility Pioneers

The stealth philosophy is best exemplified by its pioneering organization, Oxford House. In October 1975, Oxford House opened its first home out of sheer necessity. A group of recovering alcoholics, only sober for a short time, had just learned that their halfway house was closing. Among them was Paul Molloy, who, just prior to receiving treatment for substance abuse, had served as Republican counsel for the Senate. The residents negotiated with the landlord, a recovering alcoholic, to take over the lease. The first Oxford House was born.

The organization's primary concern was finances. Because the men had lost their incomes to drinking and drug abuse, they could afford little rent. In order to cover the rent they opened the house to a larger number of residents and required that each resident share a bedroom. The cost of a supervisor, they decided, was too much—even if it was divided among ten to twelve people. Using the halfway house rules as a guide, the men established a concrete system for maintaining the house through group supervision.[88]

The first home, in Silver Spring, Maryland, housed thirteen people—enough to cover all of the expenses as well as create a fund to open a new Oxford House in the area. During its first thirteen years, twenty Oxford Houses opened up in the Washington, DC, area. In 1988 the Oxford House Service Board was formed to provide technical assistance to people starting their own Oxford House.[89] Today there are approximately 1,200 houses in operation nationwide.[90]

Oxford House has played an integral role in the group home community, not only for the services they offer, but also for the precedent they have established in the courts by testing the language of the FHAA. As one advocate recalled of the nascent years of group home litigation, "Advocates of the ADA were looking for a group and Oxford House was the perfect player."[91] Oxford House has been unwavering in its commitment to the following principles: (1) they require at minimum between six and eight tenants in order to operate their facilities; (2) they only rent, in order to keep costs down; (3) they locate their homes in "good neighborhoods"; and (4) they move into their homes prior to getting zoning approval. Additionally, Oxford House serves as the ideal organization to represent the group home community in litigation. Although they serve recovering substance abusers, an unpopular group, they continue to maintain exceptionally high success rates. The program boasts an 80-percent recovery rate for all participants[92]—even though approximately 76 percent of the residents have relapsed in previous programs.[93]

Oxford House's demand for placing six to eight (and often ten to twelve) residents in each home has been a source of contention for the municipalities in which they choose to locate. Officials argue that if Oxford House would simply reduce the number of residents per house to comply with local occupancy restrictions, the claims against them would be dropped. However, Oxford House argues that having at least six to eight residents in each house is a crucial component of the program's success. It is not simply an issue of cost-reduction; with fewer residents, the quality of care could be jeopardized. Joseph Page, of the Missouri Department of Health, explains that more residents

> helps increase early realization of relapses and new members can more easily find someone to relate to. It also increases the chances of recovery and provides more opportunities for people to find a role model.[94]

Oxford House's need to locate their homes in "good neighborhoods" adds another important dimension to the group home controversy. Most people do not have a problem with locating drug treatment or sober living centers in multi-family or commercial zoned areas. Some have even argued that because the group homes are a business, they ought to locate in commercially zoned areas. But Oxford House is unyielding on this issue. As Molloy argues, "the rental homes must be located in 'good residential neighborhoods' to put distance between the participants and commercial zones with liquor stores and areas associated with alcohol and drug abuse."[95]

Finally, the most controversial aspect of Oxford House's mission is their commitment to establishing homes without prior zoning approval, a practice that was criticized by the Seventh Circuit in 1994.[96] Oxford House's "move in first, ask questions later" approach, explained one advocate, "is in keeping with their notion that they are a family. When a family moves in they don't have to ask for permission."[97] Oxford House is widely regarded as the first group home to use "family" as a legal frame—prompting others to follow suit.[98]

Oxford House argues that the process of applying for a zoning variance is discriminatory in and of itself. Residents are subjected to ridicule, facilities may become unavailable, and there is a high likelihood that the variance will not be granted. As Steve Polin, attorney for Oxford House, explains,

> public hearings before zoning boards has [*sic*] a very deleterious and detrimental effect upon the recovery of the residents. It's been our experience that neighbors who object to the presence of a group of unrelated recovering addicts and alcoholics come and forcibly object their—voice their objections to this. The residents are then singled out for I think what would be unfair public scrutiny. Many times if they are required to testify they must identify themselves. . . . And it has been our experience that when having to apply for a special use permit it creates a great deal of uncertainty and anxiety about what the future of their home will be, and the relapse rate increases as a result of those . . . .[99]

Despite judicial rulings requiring group homes to apply for zoning variances before bringing the matter to court, many group homes, including Oxford House, continue to delay zoning applications and notification until after they move in, feeling that it offers the best chance to obtain housing for their clients.

Visibility and Housing Stability

What are the benefits of remaining below the radar for group home operators? Collaborative providers and supporters of early notification would argue that this approach only fans the flames of dissent among future neighbors. Those who employ low-visibility tactics and attempt to minimize public awareness until after housing is secured argue that early notification and transparency increases housing vulnerability for group home residents. Research suggests that providers employing a below-the-radar approach—exemplified by stealth and to a lesser extent cooperative group homes—may face less opposition and experience a higher rate of stable housing. A 1990 study of opposition to group homes for the mentally ill in Maryland revealed the benefits of these low-visibility strategies. Providers employing a "low-profile" approach, which the authors defined as "the advance purchase or rental of housing" prior to notifying neighbors, experienced less opposition compared to providers who focused on public education and community organizing.[100] A study of outreach strategies used by group home operators in Massachusetts concludes that

> Most of the agencies interviewed had abandoned their use of large neighborhood gatherings in favor of small meetings and one-to-one contact. But even those more limited exchanges generated significantly more opposition than non-notification.[101]

A more recent study of a random sample of group homes in several states reveals similar patterns. Roughly half of the sample utilized either collaborative or stealth approaches when siting their group homes. However, 59 percent of operators who notified prior to obtaining their property experienced opposition, whereas only 35 percent of non-notifiers encountered backlash.[102]

I supplement these findings by tracking the outcomes of the siting instances referenced above, where strategies were indicated.[103] The benefit of this approach is that, rather than contacting or surveying already established group homes about their siting tactics, we can track the degree to which collaborative, cooperative, or stealth group homes achieved housing stability.

Of the total number of incidents reviewed between 1996 and 2006, 353 had reportable outcomes. Group homes with positive outcomes resolved any problems they experienced with neighbors or municipalities and were able to keep their home. A negative outcome is one in which the group home operator was unable to keep their house as a result of community or municipal opposition. During the study time period, more than two hundred group home operators were able to keep their homes. Low-profile tactics are highly correlated with successful outcomes. Group home operators who notified neighbors first had a lower success rate than group homes that delayed notification until after the property was procured.[104] Just over half of early notifying operators held onto their homes, while more than three-quarters of those who delayed notification kept their homes. Similarly, group homes that chose to secure their property prior to seeking zoning approval had more positive outcomes, with 87 percent keeping their homes, compared to 50 percent of those who first sought zoning approval (see Table 6.1).

Analyzing housing outcomes by operator type reveals similar patterns. Collaborative organizations kept their group homes in 42 percent of the incidents for which there was a reported outcome. Cooperative group homes held onto their homes 68 percent of the time, and stealth organizations—those maintaining the lowest profile—had an 85-percent success rate (see Table 6.2).

Table 6.1. Percentage of Group Home Operators Who
Secured Housing by Visibility Tactic

	Notification		Zoning	
	Early	**Late**	**Early**	**Late**
Kept House	58	77	50	87
Lost House	34	18	43	11

Source: LexisNexis local newspapers in US, 1996–2006. Search included
"group home" and (court! or oppos!).

Table 6.2. Collaborative, Cooperative, or Stealth Operators
and Housing Success Rates

	Collaborative	Cooperative	Stealth
Kept House	42	68	85
Lost House	46	23	13

Source: LexisNexis local newspapers in US, 1996–2006. Search included
"group home" and (court! or oppos!).

Conclusion

In the end, explained one group home advocate, the question of notification
and outreach comes down to this: "Do you pay now or do you pay later?"[105]
The low-visibility, housing-first approach permits group home residents to
obtain housing immediately and allows providers and advocates to engage
in drawn-out zoning proceedings and court battles while holding onto their
homes. Even if collaborative organizations are able to obtain city approval for
their group home, they may, in the end, as this advocate explained, lose the
property to other prospective buyers or renters.

> For people who go through the zoning process first, it takes them longer
> to find stable housing. If you have already found a house and you are in it
> and they find out about you—you are there and you have the housing.[106]

While court decisions such as *Palatine* have ruled that providers must exhaust
all preliminary siting procedures before litigating their claims, judges may be
indifferent about whether providers pursue these avenues *before* moving into
the property.

The drawback to this approach is heightened community opposition. In addition to harboring negative feelings toward the group home because of the populations they serve, community members may feel more inclined to fight the home if the group proceeds without first asking for community input. Neighbors will respond to triggering events (increased traffic in the neighborhood, the presence of racial minorities or low-income individuals in an affluent white neighborhood) by investigating the home and, ultimately, filing a complaint with the city. This may set off a volatile and contentious debate about the group home and its tactics.

If minimizing opposition is an option or a high priority for group home operators, the decision to go stealth may be too risky. If, however, as one housing expert asserts, opposition toward group homes is "global"—if it is indeed the "process that creates obstacles"—then the question of notification is not about minimizing opposition but rather maximizing housing stability in the face of opposition.

Similar to advocacy for gay and lesbian family rights, the decision of whether or when to employ high-visibility approaches—in this case conducting outreach and notifying neighbors or officials early in the process—may come down to an individual provider's assessment of, or aversion to, the risks associated with backlash. Individuals who feel that opposition can deal the harshest blow while the group home waits to secure housing will elect to minimize any engagement with potential opponents during this period. Those who fear that opposition will be ongoing if they disregard "good neighbor" norms will often engage early with neighbors and zoning officials. However, unlike same-sex parenting advocates whose subterranean advocacy efforts center on venues and legal frames, group home advocates focus on timing. Where same-sex parenting advocates opt for low-profile institutional venues (family or lower courts) or rely on technical or bland legal and popular narratives, group home operators can only control when and in what capacity they will interact with community members and public officials.

It is likely that collaboration works best when there is low potential for opposition. In other words, where the climate is already favorable toward group homes, operators and advocates can afford to be collaborative. As one attorney explained:

My experience has been that where you already have strong political support you can be collaborative. But the collaborative approach generally just gives neighbors a head start. Politically savvy groups like Pine Street Inn in Boston went door-knocking and invited people into their homes one or two at a time—no big groups. They also found a neighbor to champion their cause. But most groups who have used collaborative efforts would not do it again.[107]

Added another,

Notification only works if there is a shared understanding. What do you do when you know you are facing bias or discrimination? The approach differs, especially if the level is high.[108]

However, it is often difficult to predict the likelihood of backlash. Even if a provider has had past success in placing group homes—or a neighborhood has previously hosted group homes—opposition may still ensue. As the above advocate explained:

The dynamic in one neighborhood may be totally different. Having one group home in one area may not help or hurt your chances of getting a group home in another neighborhood. People may acquiesce in their own neighborhood to one group home but that doesn't mean that they will acquiesce to the next. Nor does it mean that the next neighborhood will.[109]

In the end, explained this advocate, "the more sophisticated the group is, the more likely they want to fly under the radar and be less transparent. Almost unanimously the people who try the open-approach opt later for less transparency."[110]

In reality, operators who pursue low-visibility strategies would argue that they are just as committed as their high-visibility counterparts to being perceived as "good neighbors." Just as opposition is inevitable in the eyes of these providers, so, too, is the need for good communication. The only difference is when during the siting process these trust-building strategies occur. As one advocate explained of Oxford House, providers "can do this before they find housing or they try to do what Oxford House does and try to negotiate" after they move in.[111] Anecdotal evidence suggests that once group homes move into neighborhoods, residents typically learn to accept their presence.

Generally what happens is that people who do live close to (group homes) get to the point where they become friends with the people who live there or they don't even notice that they're there.[112]

While there may be an initial increase in opposition to the group home that employs the stealth approach (particularly if they go to court), it is likely that their presence in the community will help to promote collegiality between residents and opponents. Stealth organizations often employ the same community-building tactics used by collaborative organizations—one-on-one meetings, open-houses, citizen committees—but simply pursue them after the dust has settled and housing has been secured. For instance, Oxford House encourages its residents to meet their neighbors and to communicate openly about their time in recovery. They also maintain a significant public presence on community boards and in presentations on sobriety. Despite their more adversarial approach, studies of Oxford House indicate that community members regard Oxford House residents as "good neighbors." They receive high approval ratings relative to other neighbors.[113]

As stated above, it may be experience, rather than early communication, that makes all the difference. "You can't just tell people that things will be okay," counsels one group home operator. "They just need to live through it and find out that we are decent neighbors."[114]

7

Revisiting Visibility

Incrementalism may not get much press, but it does work.
CONGRESSMAN HENRY WAXMAN

VISIBILITY HAS COME to define our understanding of modern civil rights battles. It is difficult to conceive of minority groups being able to effectively debunk long-held societal misperceptions and dismantle institutional barriers without engaging in very public and hotly contested campaigns. After all, in order to alter a status quo in which the majority reaps substantial benefits at the expense of minority rights, those on the losing end must convince an otherwise disinterested public to question or challenge the foundations of a power structure that consistently work to the public's advantage. Through images, narratives, and protests, the "haves" can be shaken from a stupor of complacency and become so moved by these injustices that they are willing to give up their privileged status and be catalyzed into action.

In many ways, rights and public protest go hand in hand. The dawning of the modern civil rights era, for instance, coincides with the birth of the information age. The Civil Rights Movement was launched during the Golden Age of television, which marked the beginning of our insatiable appetite for bite-sized information. And more than most, Martin Luther King, Jr. recognized the importance of visibility as a strategy for promoting civil rights. He and other civil rights activists saw the potential for reaching a captive audience of white middle-class television-owning households through televised broadcasts of civil rights protests and, more importantly, white southern responses. Widespread media attention revealed the ugliness of the southern racial apartheid that existed just below the surface of the seemingly "neutral" doctrine of "separate but equal." In the absence of vivid photographs and video footage of white police officers using billy clubs, fire hoses, and attack dogs against young student protesters, Jim Crow would have likely persisted.

That said, although high-profile tactics clearly play a pivotal role in many civil rights battles, these struggles also rely on below-the-radar strategies. For instance, as Taylor Branch documents, in addition to championing transparency and exposure, King and other civil rights leaders recognized that black civil rights advancement also required a more subterranean approach to complement its high visibility—especially where public officials were concerned.[1] In the months leading up to the Democratic National Convention during the 1960 presidential election, King engaged in clandestine strategies to convince Democratic Party elites to promote civil rights. King's goals were twofold—to obtain explicit national party support and to claim a national candidate ally. King enlisted the help of Congressman Chester Bowles and Harris Wofford to draft a secret platform for the Democratic Party that would embrace civil rights. Where segregationist allies maintained a high-profile campaign, lavishing candidates with public praise for upholding white American values, King operated in the shadows, traveling all over the country to shore up support, court candidates, attend strategy sessions, and secure funds. Ultimately, King's stealth tactics prevailed. John F. Kennedy embraced civil rights as a prong of his candidacy and recommended that his delegates approve the platform in its entirety.

Although most candidates, regardless of partisan affiliation, expressed an eagerness to reach out to black voters, their claims fell short. Only Kennedy made any deliberate or concerted effort to market his candidacy to black voters. Furthermore, like King, Kennedy did so by employing below-the-radar strategies. JFK and Robert Kennedy remained cautious about publicizing Kennedy's sympathies for civil rights out of fear that it would marginalize moderate white voters who were the bread and butter of the Democratic coalition. To keep his base while attracting black voters, he had to maintain two personas: a public profile that pandered to white voters and a far less publicized image as a civil rights supporter. To bolster the latter he dedicated staff to work exclusively on his civil rights agenda, but he moved them off-site to avoid being perceived as a traitor to the Democratic base. He also took the extra step of naming their office the "Democratic National Conference on Constitutional Rights" rather than the more apt (and staff-preferred) "Office of Civil Rights."

In fact, most of Kennedy's key civil rights campaign strategies were made in secret. His now famous phone call to Coretta Scott King upon her husband's arrest and detention in Atlanta was devised in secret by Kennedy's civil rights staff without even Robert Kennedy's knowledge or approval. Upon learning of his brother's conversation with Mrs. King, RFK placed a gag order on any discussion of the phone call. When he, too, eventually felt compelled to call on King's behalf, this time to the judge presiding over King's arrest, secrecy prevailed. Robert Kennedy remained cagey about his involvement even, initially, to staff.

When they ultimately decided to publicize the calls—realizing that it could inspire black voter turnout—they did so through back channels. While the mainstream press ran vague and unsubstantiated stories about the Kennedys' work on King's behalf, the candidate's civil rights staff focused on advertizing them in detail only to black voters. Kennedy's staff printed a pamphlet detailing reactions to the phone call by King's family and black leaders and established a "dummy committee" of religious leaders to sponsor the publication. Then, relying on the very apartheid they were hoping to dismantle, the pamphlets were distributed to African American churches—with very little chance of being picked up by white mainstream media. As Branch describes,

> beneath the notice of campaign professionals, the Kennedy campaign's "blue bomb" was spreading . . . by means of the most effective private communications since the Underground Railroad—the church. Nearly two million copies were being shipped by bus, train, and airplane . . . The confines of race made it easy for the civil rights office to keep the operation secret within their own organization.[2]

More recently, President Obama took advantage of low-visibility mechanisms to advance the civil rights efforts of gays and lesbians. Well before publicly declaring his support for same-sex marriage, and unbeknownst to most, President Obama had been actively working on behalf of same-sex couples who were attempting to overturn DOMA in federal court.[3] Recall from Chapter 3 that LGBT couples residing in marriage equality states successfully argued, in several federal judicial circuits, that DOMA's federal ban on same-sex marriage should be overturned. Initially, during First Circuit proceedings, the Obama administration defended DOMA and argued that Section 3 could survive the lowest rung of judicial review, the standard established in that circuit for cases concerning sexual orientation. However, early in 2011, the Department of Justice did an about face and decided not to defend DOMA in federal court. Litigation had spread to circuits that did not constrain review to this minimal standard, requiring the Obama Administration to determine whether DOMA could survive a higher level of judicial scrutiny. In the end, they concluded not only that DOMA would not survive a more exacting level of judicial analysis, but, because it classified individuals by their sexual orientation for the purposes of designating marital status and disseminating benefits, that DOMA *should* be examined at a higher standard.

Not surprisingly, this attracted some attention. Speaker John Boehner chastised President Obama for "stir[ring] up a controversial issue that sharply divides the nation."[4] Many pondered whether or not Obama had the authority to refuse to defend a law that had the backing of a majority of voters and had been passed through legitimate and time-honored means. "The president swore an oath on the Bible to ensure that the laws be faithfully executed, not to decide which laws are and which are not constitutional." said former House Speaker Newt Gingrich, and described the president as "replacing the rule of law with the rule of Obama."[5]

In a far less publicized, and arguably even more consequential, move, however, the Obama administration articulated its arguments about the need for a more demanding review of marriage bans in a brief filed with the Ninth Circuit.[6] Although his administration continued to be perceived as defendants in the case—because they were still enforcing DOMA—Obama's brief detailed the long history of government-approved degradation and discrimination against gays and lesbians and called for courts to use a more stringent level of inquiry in cases involving sexual orientation. Instead of avoiding litigation (as they had since drafting their letter to Boehner), Obama's DOJ jumped into the fray on behalf of same-sex couples.

Pundits and gay rights advocates have described the brief as "the single most persuasive legal argument ever advanced by the United States government in support of equality for lesbian, gay and bisexual people."[7] What's more, Obama officials drafted the brief while contending with pressures from gay rights groups to "come out" in support of same-sex marriage. Despite the push to publicly support the marital rights of same-sex couples, Obama administration officials remained secretive about their efforts—choosing, instead, to publicize the president's support for marriage equality a full year later, after DOMA had been ruled unconstitutional in federal court.

Elements of low-visibility advocacy are also apparent in early welfare litigation. Melnick describes the "complex, technical, and (let's face it) often boring" tactics used by welfare advocates that, ultimately, transformed the scope and breadth of social welfare programs.[8] For instance, judicial expansion of Aid to Families with Dependent Children (AFDC) relied on interpretation of eligibility rules rather than constitutional doctrine in order to forestall accusations of judicial activism by members of Congress.

Through equally subterranean measures, housing advocates in New York were able to significantly expand the take-up rate of the state's AFDC shelter grants. In one case, advocates convinced a trial court judge to issue a preliminary injunction requiring the state to pay plaintiffs both back rent and monthly assistance. With the help of an "ad hoc bureaucracy" of Legal Aid attorneys and support staff to process claims and add names to the list, the number of plaintiffs receiving assistance increased from 135 to more than 26,000 over a period of six years.

More generally, argues Melnick, welfare litigation made use of heart-wrenching narratives designed to sway sympathetic judges and to "embarrass" administrators and politicians into settlement. As he explains,

> One reason that many cases settle before a ruling by a judge is that politicians and administrators do not relish the type of attention such cases attract. They will be willing to make modest adjustments to make the problem and the attendant publicity go away as soon as possible.[9]

In these cases, low-visibility mediation emerged as a more palatable outcome for public officials and bureaucrats when faced with the threat of negative publicity.

These examples of low-visibility advocacy suggest that our perception that civil rights and visibility go hand in fist is predicated on incomplete information and inaccurate assumptions. Low-visibility advocacy is not new, nor is its primary use to further disenfranchise the "have-nots." Rather, it is a significant and (in some ways by design) overlooked mechanism of social reform.

The case studies highlighted in this book explore the promises and pitfalls of low- visibility policy development in the context of civil rights legal advocacy. Studies of visibility in politics often tout the benefits of transparency. Public debate is the hallmark of deliberative policymaking, and broad-based consensus is the goal. Covert strategies are the tools of the powerful and are often used to divert resources from those in need to line the pockets of the "1 percent." This project tells a different story. Here, low-visibility tactics are used to safeguard the rights of the "have-nots." Rather than fostering goodwill or promoting compromise, visibility and transparency threaten to dismantle any gains made by disenfranchised minority groups through the courts. To minimize the incidence and influence of opposition or backlash, advocates use a range of low-visibility tactics to circumvent or delay public deliberation. Parenting advocates limited, at least initially, legal inquiries to lower courts and framed their arguments in the technicalities of family law and children's welfare doctrines—resisting more polarizing gay rights or constitution-based claims. In so doing they managed to make significant legal gains without provoking widespread backlash. Buttressed by court precedent validating housing rights for individuals with disabilities, some group home operators and advocates elected to sidestep long-practiced norms of public notification and, instead, delay public involvement until after they secured their property. By omitting instances of low-visibility advocacy from studies of civil rights, we both underestimate how activists control public awareness in order to advance civil rights claims and overemphasize the potential for public opposition to hinder these goals.

Visibility and Opposition

As these case studies highlight, visibility is not simply a by-product of civil rights activism. Instead, it can be shaped and molded to further the efforts of advocates. The below-the-radar advocates interviewed for this project perceived public awareness as constraining their ability to implement court victories and believed that social reform could be achieved without engaging in a visible and public debate.

Although the legal structures supporting advocacy for same-sex parenting and housing for the disabled provide opportunities for low-visibility strategies, advocates deliberately harnessed these characteristics in order to minimize the frequency and fury of backlash. Fully cognizant of the destabilizing and disruptive effects of backlash on their clients, the parenting and housing advocates showcased here surveyed their options and chose to pursue strategies that would produce minimal political, legal, or administrative upheaval. Attorneys working on behalf of gay and lesbian parents counseled against appealing cases to higher courts or pursuing constitutional claims out of fear that backlash would ensue. High-profile gay and lesbian advocacy organizations that assisted with parenting litigation wrote anonymous briefs or provided behind-the-scenes support to limit the focus on gay and lesbian rights. And when opposition forces prevailed in their attempts to limit marriage recognition, parenting advocates did their best to distinguish their claims from those advanced on the marriage front, arguing that the only relationship that mattered in their cases was that of parent and child.

These tactics helped diminish the incidence of backlash against parenting advancements and allowed legal precedent to spread and flourish. The autonomy and discretion invested in family court judges, codes of confidentiality governing custody and adoption hearings, the technical quality of family court precedent, and a universal focus on children's welfare rather than parental rights—each of these provided parenting advocates with ample space to advance the claims of gay and lesbian parents without promoting same-sex marriage-like opposition. Despite the public witch hunt against lesbian and gay parents to protect traditional marriage, by 2006 parenting advocates were victorious in half of the states with minimal dissent (at least relative to the tsunami of opposition against *Baehr* and its progeny).

In some ways visibility is even more central to the efforts of group home operators. All group home operators, regardless of strategy, ultimately must decide whether, when, or how to communicate their intentions to property owners or zoning boards. Once they have identified a neighborhood or property to suit their purposes, visibility management is the most important decision that a group home operator will grapple with during the siting process. It is not surprising, then, that visibility is a subject of significant debate and divisiveness among group home providers. As one "collaborative" group home operator described of Oxford House's stealth approach, "they are too aggressive and litigation-happy."[10] Those devoted to the virtues of transparency are convinced that inhibiting public awareness will limit housing progress for all group home residents. Conversely, those who champion secrecy do so because they believe early public involvement will threaten their housing options and their residents' well-being.

In this case low-visibility tactics helped limit the *influence* of backlash. Although group home operators and residents of all varieties typically contend with backlash when they attempt to locate in single-family neighborhoods, those who employ low-visibility tactics are better able to hold on to their homes. By postponing notification to neighborhood associations and zoning boards until after their housing is secured, low-visibility group home operators reduce the likelihood that opposition will result in housing instability for their clients. Where transparent housing operators had limited leverage for protecting their housing security when combating NIMBY forces, those who obtained housing before alerting neighbors and officials of their housing intentions were able to pursue their legal claims from the safety of their home—reducing the influence of backlash.

The Perils of Low-Visibility Advocacy

As with many instances of policy progress, low-visibility wins come at a cost. Reducing visibility and shielding issues and arguments from the prying eye of the public, as some of the advocates in these case studies did, may produce unintended consequences. We know that visibility has its benefits. A system of government that often privileges majority opinion requires advocates at some point to take their issue to the people. The more people that come to recognize, for instance, that the children of gay parents require the same legal protections as the children of straight parents, the less likely that laws barring gays or lesbians from adopting or co-parenting will continue to pose a threat. Similarly, as more property owners become aware of the value of group homes—and experience them as good neighbors—there will be fewer NIMBY struggles. The goal is for group homes and lesbian- or gay-headed households to be accepted and welcomed. *In*visibility only delays these longer-term goals.

Consider this hypothetical: what would American race relations be like today had *Brown v. Board of Education*, or, more importantly, the protests of the Civil Rights Movement, been shielded from public view? Perhaps blacks in the South would have secured some localized victories, but as a society we would have been deprived of the opportunity to learn from and respond to the atrocities of Jim Crow. Journalist George B. Leonard describes the national awakening that occurred through televised coverage of movement protests and brutality as "the senses of an entire nation becoming suddenly sharper, when pain pours in and the resulting outrage turns to action."[11] Many who joined the movement were catalyzed by television footage. Recalls Ruth Morris,

> We watched the news and then we went in and sat down and were eating dinner . . . Our dining room is warm and gay and we were sitting down to a very good dinner. We felt sort of guilty about being there enjoying ourselves after what we had just seen on TV. We both said it at the same time, it just seemed to come out of the blue: Why are we sitting here? Then I said, "I'll pack," and Bull said, "I'll call for reservations."[12]

In the absence of a national dialogue on *Brown* and the highly publicized protests demonstrating the depravity of Jim Crow, coalition building across blacks and whites would have been, at best, delayed and the movement itself discarded as just one of scores of moments of American civil unrest. The national grief that turned Martin Luther King's death into the passage of the 1968 Civil Rights Act may have, instead, been relegated to a sad side note of American history. Visibility promoted action; action leads to change.

Visibility also helped to humanize abstract concepts such as lynching and Jim Crow—realities unfamiliar to most individuals outside of the South. It was this awareness that prompted Mamie Till Bradley to allow *Jet Magazine* to run a post-mortem photograph of her grossly disfigured son, Emmett Till, after his brutal murder at the hands of southern lynchers while he was visiting family in Mississippi.[13] This photograph served as a rallying point for early movement support. As Harold and Deluca argue,

> The widely disseminated image of Emmett Till's mutilated corpse rhetorically transformed the lynched black body from a symbol of unmitigated white power to one illustrating the ugliness of racial violence and the aggregate power of the black community. This reconfiguration was, in part, an effect of the black community's embracing and foregrounding of Till's object body as a collective "souvenir" rather than allowing it to be safely exiled from public life.[14]

Publicity can dispel stereotypes and misperceptions that often accompany calls for civil rights reform. Shapiro, for example, argues that the "stealth" approach used by disability advocates during the passage of the ADA may have created a perfect storm of backlash against the landmark legislation. While members of Congress were able to hear first-hand how discrimination against the disabled exacerbates their physical or psychiatric challenges, ordinary American citizens (many of whom would be subject to the law's provisions as employers, retail owners, and landlords) had little understanding of the legislation or the reason for its passage.[15]

In the realm of same-sex marriage, images of gay nuptials and stories of same-sex couples planning their weddings helped demystify these relationships. Extensive media coverage forced straight individuals to *see* lesbians and gays and no longer turn a blind eye towards gay relationships. Images of middle-aged and middle-class lesbians and gays donned in classic wedding attire contradicted long-held stereotypes of gays and lesbians as promiscuous and sexually deviant. Perhaps this is why the opposition, although volatile and effective, proved short-lived.

For gay rights in particular, the idea of minimizing public awareness may, in the extreme, be viewed as another step back into the closet. Visibility was, in fact, a crucial component of the early LGBT rights movement. Harvey Milk, the first elected gay public official, viewed the decision to come out as critical to both the private health of individual gays and lesbians and the public standing of the community as a whole.

> Gay people, we will not win our rights by staying silently in our closets
> ... We are coming out. We are coming out to fight the lies, the myths,

the distortions. We are coming out to tell the truths about gays, for I
am tired of the conspiracy of silence, so I'm going to talk about it. And
I want you to talk about it. You must come out. Come out to your
parents, your relatives.[16]

Invisibility, for gays and lesbians, may mean acquiescing to those whose tolerance hinges on ignorance. Visibility has encouraged gay individuals and
couples to demand access to benefits that heterosexuals take for granted.
Discontent to have their visibility defined through movies and sitcoms,
gay individuals have come out to demand relationship recognition through
domestic registries and civil unions, seek equality in employment, and push
for hate crimes legislation. For gay youth, the collective visibility of the gay
movement means increased safety, support, and acceptance. Gay youth are
coming out earlier than in previous generations, and are demanding recognition and protection in their schools and communities. This has prompted
gay rights organizations to develop initiatives that deal specifically with the
needs of gay youth (a concept unheard of among previous generations, where
coming out occurred in adulthood).[17]

Despite these advances, however, misperceptions about gay families persist,
particularly regarding the raising of children. School administrators, teachers and doctors all play an integral role in helping usher children safely into
adulthood and, yet, in many regions and communities they remain ignorant
of, or hostile to, LGBT-headed households and their legal standing as families.[18] While low-visibility legal tactics help these families access significant
legal benefits, such as health-care coverage for their children, custody rights
for non-biological parents, and hospital visitation rights, in the long run they
may stall public acceptance of or comfort with gay parents and their children.

Furthermore, relying primarily on judicial discretion can backfire.
Occasionally a judge will buck a legal trend and rule against same-sex couples, as a family court judge in Texas did when she denied two gay dads the
right to appear on their sons' birth certificates. The two-dad family relied on
a surrogate to carry their sons, and each father has a biological connection
to one of the children. Somewhat inexplicably, the family court judge not
only denied the two dads the right to second-parent adopt the children, but
also refused to allow them to appear on any birth certificate, including that
of their biological offspring. The surrogate mother—who shares no genetic
relationship with either child—is currently listed as the sole parent on each
child's birth certificate.[19] In the absence of a national debate about lesbian

and gay parenting rights, these lapses in legal judgment can go unnoticed and unaddressed and can leave parents in the dark about the risks.

Will the low-profile, one-step-at-a-time same-sex parenting struggle inspire an equally slow-dripping but nonetheless devastating backlash, as evidenced by recent litigation-driven birth mother campaigns spearheaded by the conservative Liberty Counsel? Not likely, at least not in areas of the country that have benefited from the tides of tolerance that have overwhelmed conservative efforts. But neither will these efforts seriously challenge the public to reevaluate their perceptions of gay parenting—reconceptions that could lead to consensus and more standardized treatment of lesbian and gay families. Because the public has been largely left out of the parenting movement, LGBT-headed families frequently encounter discriminatory and dismissive behaviors when attempting to enroll their children in school, seek medical treatment for their children, or engage with other parents.[20] Gay parents cannot parent without the acceptance and support of their communities. Public acceptance hinges on public awareness.

For those with mental, intellectual, and physical disabilities, although the decision to covertly move into single-family neighborhoods may help improve short-term housing stability, it may come at the expense of community acceptance. As with gay and lesbian parents, group homes cannot fully enjoy the benefits of single-family living—the sense of community and belongingness—without becoming active and open participants in their homes and neighborhoods. Particularly for individuals in recovery and those with mental illness, the decision to avoid public awareness may only prolong tensions and perpetuate stereotypes.

Implications

These misgivings aside, the case studies provide clear evidence that below-the-radar strategies are a fixture of civil rights legal advocacy and have the potential to be an effective source of policy progress for groups who contend with ongoing social or political isolation. Gay and lesbian parenting advocates employed child-centered frames, invoked technical (rather than principled) legal arguments, and avoided higher court judgments (at least initially) in order to quietly accumulate court validation in a range of states—many of which were otherwise unsupportive of same-sex relationships. Group home operators avoided notifying neighbors and officials of their housing plans until after their housing had been procured.

Low-profile advocacy is also not unique to same-sex family rights or group home advocacy, as explained above. This suggests one clear avenue for future research: Under what conditions are low-visibility tactics deployed or effective? Are there certain policies that invite these tactics? Is their success contingent upon certain policy attributes? It could be that the issues or cases illustrated here have characteristics that not only support low-visibility approaches, but also allow them to flourish. For one thing, each of the case studies explored in this project is fighting on behalf of families. Gay and lesbian parents are seeking legal validation of their relationships and families. Group home operators and residents are similarly asking to be given the same housing options as other—more traditional—families. In these cases advocates are asking that courts provide the same benefits given to traditional or more widely accepted families—housing choice, parental stability, social safety nets—to their clients.

Advocates fighting for non-traditional families may have pragmatic reasons to remain below the radar. It may be that, compared to other issues, those who attempt to expand or redefine family are more vulnerable to the frequency and costs of backlash. For these communities, losses could result in immediate and tangible hardships—housing instability, loss of custody. Visibility may prove too onerous.

There may also be something about the politics of family that requires low-visibility tactics. On the one hand we have a constitutional history of affording individuals considerable autonomy on issues of family formation and governance. Despite efforts to increase government regulation of families beginning in the early 1900s, constitutional doctrine suggests that the "family" should be free from government intrusion. Couples have the authority to decide whether or when to have kids and parents have autonomy over what to teach their kids or where to send them to school. We give family court judges considerable discretion over adoption and custody proceedings in part because we recognize that families are not cookie-cutter or formulaic. Although each family may share certain general similarities, legal decisions are typically based on unique characteristics. It is for this reason that categorical decisions are discouraged in family law. Judges must consider the context of each family who comes to their court before rendering their decision. In other words, families—their relationships, their practices, their choices—are the province of *private* citizens.

On the other hand, families are increasingly the object of significant *public* contestation. They are perceived as a critical tool for raising good citizens and maintaining public order. We believe that individuals who commit to each other will need less and contribute more to society. We believe that children raised in stable families will become happier and more productive adults. And despite precedent that families and family formation are ensconced within a constitutionally protected zone of privacy, we have specific notions of what families should look like and how they should function. Those within the fold of family recognition are given legal legitimacy, social status, and access to a range of financial and social benefits. Those who dare to challenge societal and governmental proscriptions that define how families should look are swiftly chastised as deviants and cast as a threat to individual and societal well-being. So high is the topic of family policy on the public agenda that conservatives have branded an entire movement to protect this cherished institution. For those attempting to both assert their rights to be recognized and validated as a family while also protecting the privacy and autonomy of their dependents, it may be that low-visibility advocacy provides the only acceptable option.

Revisiting Courts and Social Change

The evidence featured in this book also enhances our understanding of the role of litigation in promoting social reforms. While the swift and sweeping success of the court-dominated marriage equality movement clearly undercuts any argument that questions the capacity for courts to produce significant social reform, the low-visibility case studies included in the preceding chapters challenge presumptions about the nature of legal advocacy and its relationship with backlash.

Courts are insufficient agents of social change, so the narrative goes, because they will have to contend with a hostile public. Research on the relationship between courts and social change is, generally, pessimistic about the ability of court-precedent to meaningfully alter the landscape of opportunity for disenfranchised groups. Their reputation as both countermajoritarian and sympathetic to minority rights claims makes courts perhaps even more vulnerable to backlash than other policymaking venues, and may limit their ability to significantly influence civil rights debates. Our collective impression of both the character and promise of using courts to advance minority rights has been formed by *Brown v. Board of Education*, *Roe v. Wade*, and (more recently) *Goodridge v. Dept. of Public Health*. Consequently, we have come to regard court-centered efforts as breeding grounds for backlash and opposition politics.[21]

These assumptions suffer from several shortcomings, highlighted by the parenting and group home case studies. First, by treating litigation as a single strategy (rather than a collection of strategies linked by institutional setting), we ignore the options that are available to legal advocates as they pursue claims on behalf of their clients. Consequently, we miss an opportunity to understand how legal advocates behave strategically; why they pursue specific policymaking mechanisms; and the implications of these choices on policy outcomes. The advocates featured in this project who adopted a below-the-radar approach had a choice of strategy to pursue and elected to employ tactics designed to minimize backlash in order to advance their clients' interests. As Epp argues, the story of civil rights advocacy in the United States is not about court decisions, but about the individuals and groups who pursue them.

> Rights advocacy organizations . . . establish the conditions for sustained judicial attention to civil liberties and civil rights and for channeling judicial power toward egalitarian ends.[22]

Advocacy groups, regardless of whether they use the courts, the legislature, or administrative avenues for promoting their claims may choose to invite attention or shield their issue from the public, advance their arguments through adversarial or collaborative means, or alter the frame depending on the audience.

Even where scholarship on legal advocacy does acknowledge the strategic aspects of litigation, it typically focuses on court victories as the end game, rather than a step toward policy change. In these accounts, legal advocates are portrayed as concerned only with optimizing their chances for positive precedent, perceiving beyond-the-courtroom activity as extraneous or irrelevant. By employing a dispute-centered view[23]—where court verdicts provide one important voice in a chorus of policy elites—I demonstrate that legal advocates play at least two important roles in shaping the influence of court decisions. First, at the front end, advocates choose strategies to maximize the reach of court victories. As they were developing legal strategies to secure court support, for instance, same-sex parenting advocates also chose arguments and venues that would minimize public awareness and appeal to children's rights groups. Post-victory, legal advocates devise strategies to help individuals and groups successfully carry out court edicts. With judicial support in hand, stealth group home advocates chose to delay informing zoning officials or community members of their intention to purchase or rent properties in single-family neighborhoods until after the housing had been procured. Legislative and legal backing opened up opportunities for group homes to employ more assertive (and less transparent) housing strategies.

While the findings presented here do not counter accepted accounts of backlash to the landmark decisions mentioned above they do provide symmetry to a literature that, as Post and Siegel suggest, is soaked in "excessive despair."[24] In a sea of scholarship that attempts to dismiss the potential for the courts to place the rights of the few over the whimsy of the many, it is refreshing to talk about the wins—the court victories that are not simply symbolic but actually enhance the lives of disadvantaged individuals. The children of gay or lesbian parents in many states carry the protections of two legally recognized parents because a few entrepreneurial lawyers and a smattering of courageous family court (and later higher court) judges decided to read gay- and lesbian-headed families into the long-standing traditions of family law. In the words of one advocate:

> To me it is huge social change that when I go to court in some rural place the judges will use language like the word "partner." Maybe that sounds stupid but it is a huge change from treating someone like a pariah. A lot of our judges accept gay couples. That we are doing second-parent adoptions here, yeah quietly, but we are doing them—or administrative stuff like getting both parents' names on birth certificates—to me that is huge.[25]

Individuals with mental and physical challenges are able to enjoy the security, stability, and quietude (save the occasional angry protester) of living in a single-family neighborhood because advocates placed the protection of their clients' court-granted housing rights over the demands of property owners, zoning boards, and public officials to determine group housing prospects.

Did these groups encounter opposition? Of course. As long as homophobia exists there will always be attempts to limit the rights of gay- or lesbian-headed families to live with the same comforts as heterosexual families—just as there will always be property owners who fall prey to the call of NIMBYism. But in these cases, backlash played a far different, and in many ways less consequential or decisive, role than one would expect given the subject and substance of the claims.

One implication from this research is that courts can be effective allies in the struggle for civil rights and social change without engaging in high-impact (and high-cost) litigation. The highly decentralized nature of the American judiciary provides judges with ample authority to interpret facts and precedent according to their own values and in ways that often go both unchallenged and unnoticed by higher authorities. Judicial discretion, then, provides one key ingredient to low-visibility legal advocacy—particularly in the case of same-sex parenting. Would gains in the parenting front be possible in an institutional environment that constrained judicial autonomy? Likely not. Even judges presiding over parenting cases in states with same-sex marriage bans were able to validate second-parent or co-parent arrangements between two individuals of the same gender. Although, by their own admission in interviews, gay rights opponents assumed that barring same-sex marriage would also effectively limit opportunities for gays and lesbians to parent, family court (and eventually higher court) judges were willing to separate the two. Judges had the space to consider and accept advocate arguments that parenting doctrine did not center on the relationship between the parents but rather on the "best interests of the child." Judges could use their discretion to uphold laws barring same-sex couples from marrying while also permitting them to co-parent.

From a practical perspective these accounts suggest that courts are a potent source of policy change and that legal advocates are far more strategic and political than previous studies would suggest. A litigation-focused strategy that spanned decades and encompassed more than half of the nation's states produced significant rights for gay parents—rights that had been denied to many gay and lesbian couples in countries where same-sex marriage was legal. And, for the most part, those rights have endured. Relying on courts and legal doctrine to secure single-family housing helped untold numbers of mentally and physically disabled individuals to secure housing despite the growing epidemic of NIMBYism. How? By coupling these court-focused strategies with tactics designed to reduce public awareness.

It is important to remember, however, that, by constitutional design, no single policymaking venue or strategy is an effective producer of civil rights law (or any law, for that matter). In the institutionally fragmented American political structure, policymaking is meant to be difficult. No group or interest will consistently prevail in the battle for government protection or validation.[26] Our system of checks and balances invites opposition and welcomes dissent. The potential for backlash, therefore, is lurking behind every policy initiative regardless of strategy or venue. Every minority rights advocate, whether legislative, grassroots, or litigation-focused, will have to confront the specter of backlash in their quest for the holy grail of stronger civil rights policy. And in most cases—regardless of venue—the fight will continue, morph, and shift well past any single policy decision as movements grow and circumstances change.

A Visibility Hybrid

In order to establish the contours and consequences of below-the-radar advocacy, this project explores policy arenas in which both high-profile and low-visibility tactics were used. By comparing the progression of low-profile approaches to their more conspicuous counterparts, we can identify the differences in these approaches and their relative benefits and drawbacks. In reality, however, this "comparison" between high- and low-visibility instances of civil rights advocacy creates a false dichotomy. These efforts actually work, either deliberately or unintentionally, in tandem to safeguard the rights of minority groups. Take same-sex family rights, for instance. It is quite possible that same-sex parenting advocates were able to shield their issue from the public eye by capitalizing on the high-profile nature of same-sex marriage. Public distraction over the possibility of marriage equality rendered family court rulings over custody battles irrelevant and insignificant. By the time more visible state supreme courts had begun to legitimize gay and lesbian parenting, same-sex couples in some states had been enjoying co-parenting rights for more than a decade, and the conservative movement had placed all of their faith in an expanding anti-same-sex marriage campaign. As the nation struggled over *Goodridge*, landmark parenting decisions such as *K.M. v. E.G.* (2005) went unnoticed.

The same can be said for group home advocacy. Although group home advocates differ in their approaches to informing or engaging public officials and neighbors, court precedent governing group homes applies to all providers. By risking housing insecurity, collaborative providers can demonstrate the harsh consequences of NIMBYism and provide a compelling narrative about the need for increased procedural protections for group home operators and residents as they establish their homes. A group home that has made a good-faith attempt to reach out to neighbors and has, nevertheless, lost their home to a hostile opposition makes a far more sympathetic plaintiff than a provider who has practiced less above-board tactics.

Even more importantly for the purposes of this project, low-visibility strategies can promote progress in high-visibility campaigns by establishing invaluable facts on the ground that can be marshaled in high-visibility campaigns. For instance, parenting gains have both politically and legally facilitated marriage equality efforts. Politically, arguments that disparage gay and lesbian parents in order to safeguard traditional marriage suffer from the proliferation of gay- or lesbian-headed families. Not only does the average American voter have a much higher chance of knowing or even befriending a lesbian mom or gay dad, but studies can now base their findings on a more statistically robust sample of children raised in same-sex-headed households and over a longer time horizon. In 2014 a federal district court overturned Michigan's ban on same-sex marriage by relying primarily on testimony from parenting experts in order to assess state allegations that children fare better when they are raised by married heterosexual parents. These experts marshaled evidence from scores of studies conducted over the past thirty years that demonstrated conclusively that children do not suffer any adverse consequences when they are raised by gay or lesbian parents.[27]

Of course, legally, same-sex marriage bans from states with progressive parenting laws stand on even thinner ground. It is nearly impossible for a state to validate its marriage ban by citing an interest in preserving heterosexual two-parent families (as almost all states with bans have done) if the state simultaneously provides legal assistance and support to lesbian and gay parents. As the Ninth Circuit pointed out in *Perry v. Brown* (2012):

> California's "current policies and conduct . . . recognize that gay individuals are fully capable of . . . responsibly caring for and raising children." And California law actually prefers a non-biological parent who has a parental relationship with a child to a biological parent who does not; in California, the parentage statutes place a premium on the "social relationship," not the "biological relationship," between a parent and a child.

The same goes for group home advocacy. Much of the precedent on group housing law was established because of the efforts of stealth advocates, in particular Oxford House. They were in a better position to litigate specifically because they had ownership of their property prior to encountering backlash. Furthermore, because these houses move in without first informing their neighbors, they often have the benefit of proving to neighbors that their presence in a neighborhood is of little consequence. Frequently, the only giveaway that alerts neighbors to the presence of a stealth group home is a change in the configuration of cars on the property or the residents themselves conducting outreach. More often than not these homes go unnoticed. Collaborative providers can reference both the precedent and the facts on the ground established by stealth providers in their early appeals to neighbors and zoning boards.

Ultimately, these stories highlight how advocate choices are shaped, constrained, and leveraged not only by a policy's substantive or procedural features, but also through strategic and institutional pluralism. The decision to litigate, for instance, is typically reached within an environment marked by institutional diversity. Rarely does one venue offer the exclusive and final word on a particular policy position. Advocates develop their legal strategies knowing full well that legal action will likely prompt a legislative, regulatory, or popular response. Likewise, from a bird's eye view, low-visibility and high-profile advocacy strategies combine—doctrinally, temporally, geographically, or institutionally—to produce a range of policy possibilities. Advocates may be able to pursue low-profile strategies and achieve meaningful gains because of public preoccupation with other policy debates. And high-profile wins may be scored on the shoulders of hidden, but no less significant, advocate battles.

Interviews

Forty interviews were conducted in the course of this project between 2007 and 2012. These interviews consisted of two-to-three hour conversations (sometimes over the phone but mostly in-person) with lawyers and policy advocates working for lesbian or gay parents and group home residents or their opponents. I also interviewed consultants and scholars. I used snowball sampling to identify the pool of potential interviewees. Through this technique a small sample of participants were identified through content analysis of salient legal cases or news stories. Each of these interviewees was asked to provide a list of additional interviewees. This process was repeated until the lists provided began to overlap. At the point of overlap, the moment at which most of the individuals mentioned had been contacted and had either agreed to participate or were unable to sit for an interview, I ceased the interview process.

The marriage advocates I spoke with represent both national and local organizations. Most often the individuals I interviewed were either the executive directors or the legal directors of their organizations. The parenting advocates I interviewed were similarly dispersed. I interviewed executive, legal, and programmatic directors of national organizations dedicated to LGBT family issues and a range of local (often solo) attorneys working on behalf of lesbian and gay parents. I went to great lengths to interview individuals working on behalf of clients in states with marriage equality and those in states with restrictive marriage and parenting laws. I was very lucky to have spoken to a number of advocates working in states with deeply draconian parenting laws.

The group home community is far more decentralized and scattered than the LGBT advocacy community. I was able to identify, through snowball sampling, the key legal advocates and pioneers—some of whom have a local presence and others who work for elite national organizations or government agencies. I attempted to vary the population of group home advocate interviewees based on their commitment to low or high visibility advocacy. Included in the sample are scholars and advocates who are considered leaders of the collaborative approach and others who have led the charge for secrecy. There are also quite a few who will consider either approach depending on the context for their siting. I also varied the interviewees based on the demographics of their clients. Included in the mix were advocates who worked on behalf of individuals with substance addiction, those with developmental disabilities and individuals with a physical or mental disability.

Federal law concerning the use of "human subjects" in social science research stipulates that the names and identifying features of the individuals who participated in this project remain anonymous. Given the sensitive nature of the topic, many of the advocates interviewed would not have been so candid about their strategies or perspectives without the guarantee of privacy. Below is a list of the general characteristics of those who were included.

Interview 1	Same-sex parenting advocate and scholar	March 2007
Interview 2	High ranking staff in state gay rights organization	March 2007
Interview 3	High ranking staff national anti-gay rights organization	March 2007
Interview 4	Former staff at national gay rights organization; gay rights attorney	April 2007
Interview 5	High ranking staff at national adoption advocacy organization	April 2007
Interview 6	Republican political consultant	March 2007
Interview 7	Gay rights scholar	May 2007
Interview 8	High ranking staff at national gay rights organization	June 2011
Interview 9	High ranking staff at national gay rights/family rights organization	June 2007
Interview 10	Former staff at national gay rights organization	May 2011
Interview 11	East coast same-sex parenting activist	May 2011
Interview 12	East coast same-sex parenting attorney	May 2011
Interview 13	East coast same-sex parenting attorney	May 2011
Interview 14	East coast same-sex parenting scholar and activist	May 2011
Interview 15	Southern same-sex parenting attorney	July 2011
Interview 16	High ranking staff at national gay rights/family rights organization	July 2011
Interview 17	Gay rights scholar	May 2011
Interview 18	West coast parenting attorney	June 2011
Interview 19	Midwest parenting attorney	July 2011
Interview 20	Gay rights scholar	September 2012

Interview 21	Midwest gay rights opponent	May 2012
Interview 22	West coast gay rights opponent	May 2012
Interview 23	Midwest gay rights opponent	May 2012
Interview 24	West coast gay rights opponent	May 2012
Interview 25	Gay rights scholar	September 2012
Interview 26	West coast gay rights opponent	May 2012
Interview 27	West coast gay rights opponent	May 2012
Interview 28	East coast gay rights opponent	May 2012
Interview 29	Staff at national anti-gay rights organization	May 2012
Interview 30	Southern gay rights opponent	June 2012
Interview 31	Department of justice attorney	March 2010
Interview 32	Fair housing attorney	May 2010
Interview 33	Group home scholar	April 2010
Interview 34	Group home operator	March 2010
Interview 35	Disability rights attorney	March 2010
Interview 36	Group home attorney	June 2010
Interview 37	Group home attorney	June 2010
Interview 38	Group home attorney	May 2010
Interview 39	Disability rights attorney	June 2010
Interview 40	Fair housing attorney	March 2010

Group Home Opposition Multivariate Analysis

	Probit Coefficients
Alcoholism Prompt	-0.27^{*}
	(0.11)
Depression Prompt	-0.11
	(0.11)
Schizophrenia Prompt	-0.18
	(0.11)
Homeowner	-0.38^{***}
	(0.09)
Income	-0.03^{**}
	(0.01)
Democrat	0.07
	(0.10)
Republican	.02
	(.10)
Race	0.03
	(0.10)
Ideology	0.41^{***}
	(0.11)
Gender	0.06
	(0.08)
Religious Attendance	0.13
	(0.12)
N	778

* $p<.05$; ** $p<.01$; *** $p<.001$ two-tailed.

Notes

CHAPTER I

1. Carey Goldberg, "Couple Who Stirred Issue of Same-Sex Marriage Still Hopeful," *The New York Times*, July 28, 1996.

2. "New Hawaiian Law Bans Gay Marriages," *The New York Times*, June 24, 1993.

3. David W. Dunlap, "Some States Trying to Stop Gay Marriages Before They Start," *The New York Times*, March 15, 1995.

4. DOMA Hearings, Committee on the Judiciary, July 11, 1996.

5. DOMA Hearings, July 11, 1996.

6. Two additional states, Maryland and Wyoming, had bans in place prior to the Hawaii decision. Missouri had also passed a statutory ban that was later overturned by the state supreme court. They followed up with different legislation barring marriage equality in 2001. (Gay and Lesbian Taskforce, "State Laws Prohibiting Recognition of Same-Sex Relationships," June 30, 2009.)

7. *In re B.L.V.B. and E.L.V.B.* (1993).

8. *Bottoms v. Bottoms*, (1997)

9. *In re the Marriage of Wiarda*, (1993).

10. *In The Interest of Angel Lace M. v. Terry M.* (1994).

11. Sheryl Gay Stolberg, "After Fall of 'Don't Ask,' Pushing for 'I Do,'" *The New York Times*, December 20, 2010.

12. Jeffrey Rosen, "Justice Is Blind, Politically," *Politico*, January 28, 2012.

13. Eric J. Segall, "Beware a Gay Rights Backlash," *Los Angeles Times*, May 15, 2012.

14. Laurence H. Tribe, *Abortion: The Clash of Absolutes* (New York: W.W. Norton & Company), 1992.

15. David Brooks, "Roe's Birth and Death," *The New York Times*, April 21, 2005.

16. Frank Reeves, "A War Cry: Not in My Back Yard," *The Philadelphia Inquirer*, March 19, 1989.

17. Please see Appendix A for details on the interview selection process and the characteristics of those who were interviewed.

18. As of December 2013, sixteen states and the District of Columbia had issued (or were slated to issue) marriage licenses to same-sex couples. Nevada and Colorado provided full-scale "marriage-like" benefits to same-sex couples through civil unions or domestic partnerships. (Gay and Lesbian Taskforce, "Relationship Recognition for Same-Sex Couples in the U.S.," May 24, 2014.) As of July 15, 2014, federal courts overturned bans in Pennsylvania and Oregon, and Illinois had passed legislation permitting same-sex couples to marry. On October 6, 2014 the Supreme Court announced that it would not review appellate decisions from three circuits that overturned bans in five states. The decision prompted the five states and others within the three circuits with similar bans to permit same-sex couples to marry. One month later the Sixth Circuit in *Deboer et. al. v. Snyder et al.* interrupted this trend and upheld state bans in four states, increasing the likelihood of Court intervention. Gay and lesbian couples in Louisiana have filed a similar petition to fast-track supreme court review of a 5th Circuit district court ruling upholding Louisiana's ban. (*Robicheaux et al v. George* 2014).

19. Daily Kos, "The LGBT Civil Rights Backlash," September 30, 2012.

20. Steven A. Boutcher, "Same Sex, Different Politics: Success and Failure in the Struggles over Gay Rights," *Social Forces* 88.3 (2010): 1503–04.

21. This figure includes states where individual counties permit second-parent adoption.

22. Kathleen Hull, "Courting Change: Queer Parents, Judges, and the Transformation of American Family Law (review)," *American Journal of Sociology* 115.4 (2008): 1330–32, at 1332.

23. Emily Previti, "Galloway Township Residents Oppose Plan for Arc Group Homes," *Press of Atlantic City*, February 15, 2010.

24. Final Report of The President's New Freedom Commission on Mental Health, July 22, 2003, 31.

25. Interview 28. Please see Appendix A for a full description of how interviews were selected and basic characteristics of each interview participant.

CHAPTER 2

1. Marshall Ganz, *Why David Sometimes Wins: Leadership, Organization, and Strategy in the California Farm Worker Movement* (New York: Oxford University Press, 2009), 8.

2. Ian Shapiro, "Optimal Deliberation?" *Journal of Political Philosophy* 10.2 (2002): 196–211, 199.

3. Clinton Rossiter and Charles R. Kesler, *The Federalist Papers* (New American Library, 1999).

4. Joseph Bessette asks "whether making [institutions] more deliberative also made them less democratic. At one level," he postulates," the answer is undoubtedly yes." Joseph Bessette, *The Mild Voice of Reason: Deliberative Democracy and American National Government* (Chicago: University of Chicago Press, 1994), 33.

5. Iris Marion Young, "Activist Challenges to Deliberative Democracy," *Political Theory* 29.5 (2001): Benhabib argues that "legitimacy in complex modern democratic societies must be thought to result from the free and unconstrained public deliberation of all about matters of common concern." Seyla Benhabib, "Deliberative Rationality and Models of Democratic Legitimacy," *Constellations* 1.1 (1994): 26–52, 26; Amy Gutmann and Dennis Thompson, *Why Deliberative Democracy?* (Princeton, NJ: Princeton University Press, 2009), 670–90; Archon Fung, "Deliberation Before the Revolution: Toward an Ethics of Deliberative Democracy in an Unjust World," *Political Theory* 33.3 (2005): 397–419; John S. Dryzek, *Deliberative Democracy and Beyond: Liberals, Critics, Contestations* (New York: Oxford University Press, 2002).

6. Dryzek, *Deliberative Democracy and Beyond*.

7. James Madison to W. T. Barry, August 4, 1822. *Writings* 9: 103–09.

8. David Croteau and William Hoynes, *Media Society: Industries, Images, and Audiences* (London: Sage Publications, 2003); Gene Roberts and Hank Klibanoff, *The Race Beat: The Press, the Civil Rights Struggle, and the Awakening of a Nation* (New York: Alfred A. Knopf, 2006).

9. Claude Lewis, "The Whole World Was Watching: Claude Lewis Remembers the 1968 Chicago Police Riot," *The Philadelphia Inquirer*, November 12, 2008. www. philly.com. Accessed on February 10, 2012.

10. Matthew McCombs, "The Agenda-Setting Function of the Press," in *The Press*, ed. Geneva Olverholser and Kathleen Hall Jamieson (New York: Oxford University Press, 2006), 156–68; David Meyer and Suzanne Staggenborg, "Movements, Countermovements, and the Structure of Political Opportunity," *The American Journal of Sociology* 101.6 (1996): 1628–60; Mayer N. Zald and Bert Unseem, "Movement and Countermovement Interaction: Mobilization, Tactics, and State Involvement," in *Social Movements and Organizational Society*, ed. Mayer N. Zald and John David McCarthy (New Brunswick, NJ: Transaction Publishers, 1987), 247–71.

11. Carlos Ball, "Legal Rights in Historical Perspective: From the Margins to the Mainstream: The Backlash Thesis and Same-Sex Marriage: Learning from *Brown v. Board of Education* and Its Aftermath," *William & Mary Bill of Rights Journal* 14 (2006): 1493, 1533.

12. Mettler finds that the "submerged state" has benefited "wealthy Americans and privileged industries" with lucrative benefits while weakening low and middle-class safety nets, all the while circumventing public input. Suzanne Mettler, *The Submerged State: How Invisible Government Policies Undermine American Democracy* (Chicago: University of Chicago Press, 2011), 7. Similarly, Hacker finds that, through subterranean modifications to the tax code, policy elites were able to dismantle many benefits that had been previously reserved for middle- and working-class families. Jacob Hacker, "Privatizing Risk without Privatizing the Welfare State: The Hidden Politics of Social Policy Retrenchment in the United States," *American Political Science Review*, 98.2 (2004): 243–60.

13. Schattschneider argues that the "scope of conflict" refers to the "size of a political organization and the extent of political competition." E. E. Schattschneider, *The Semi-Sovereign People* (New York: Holt, Rinehart, Winston, 1960), 20. Advocates may expand or restrict the scope of conflict depending on their specific needs. Visibility offers one way to alter the scope of conflict.

14. Soss and Schram argue that policy visibility, in conjunction with proximity, can determine the degree to which policy advocates must contend with opposition. Joe Soss and Sanford Schram, "A Public Transformed: Welfare Reform as Policy Feedback," *American Political Science Review*, 101.1 (2007): 111–27. Shapiro argues "deliberation can bring differences to the surface, widening divisions rather than narrowing them." Ian Shapiro, *The State of Democratic Theory* (Princeton, NJ: Princeton University Press, 2003), 27.

15. Fung, "Deliberation Before the Revolution"; Young, "Activist Challenges to Deliberative Democracy."

16. Christian F. Rostbøll, "Dissent, Criticism, and Transformative Political Action in Deliberative Democracy," *Critical Review of International Social and Political Philosophy* 12.1 (2009): 19–36.

17. Fung, "Deliberation Before the Revolution."

18. Jacob Hacker, "Privatizing Risk Without Privatizing the Welfare State: The Hidden Politics of Social Policy Retrenchment in the United States," *American Political Science Review*, 2 (2004): 243–60.

19. As Beland argues, low-visibility incremental change "is not always conservative." Daniel Beland, "Ideas and Institutional Change in Social Security: Conversion, Layering, and Policy Drift," *Social Science Quarterly* 88.1 (2007): 20–38, at 23.

20. A growing literature in sociology, political science, and public law has referred to the context for advocacy and reform as its political, or legal, opportunity structure. For a review of the political opportunity structure, see David S. Meyer and Suzanne Staggenborg, "Movements, Countermovements, and the Structure of Political Opportunity," *American Journal of Sociology* 55 (1996): 1628–60; and David S. Meyer, "Protest and Political Opportunities," *Annual Review of Sociology* 30 (2004): 125–45. Also see Ellen Andersen for a detailed exploration of a policy's legal opportunity structure in *Out of the Closet and into the Courts* (Ann Arbor: University of Michigan Press, 2006).

21. Brian Balogh, *A Government Out of Sight: The Mystery of National Authority in Nineteenth-Century America* (Cambridge: Cambridge University Press, 2009), 314. See also R. Shep Melnick, *Regulation and the Courts: The Case of the Clean Air Act* (Washington, DC: The Brookings Institution, 1983).

22. In his review of the social change literature, Pierceson argues that the "unique position of judges, insulated from political pressure, provides them with a certain distance from the normal political process. Judges, unlike legislators, do not need to take multiple interests and value into account. They make their decisions on the basis of the adversarial legal process—a process that limits the parties to two and often narrows the question involved. Jason Pierceson, *Courts,*

Liberalism, and Rights: Gay Law and Politics in the United States and Canada (Philadelphia: Temple University Press, 2005), 2.

23. Judges may be increasingly responsible to public concerns. Recent Supreme Court elections in Iowa may indicate a shift on the part of the public to hold judges more accountable to majoritarian policy interests. In this instance, three justices on the Iowa Supreme Court were voted off the bench during a retention election because of their votes to grant marriage rights to same-sex couples in the state. In 2012, however, a judge with a similar record was able to retain his position.

24. Pierceson, *Courts, Liberalism, and Rights*, 4.

25. As one study indicates, whether a policy is initiated by a court, through the legislature, or by the voters through the ballot process may influence the degree to which one is willing to work against the policy. In this study participants were more willing to work against a policy when they learned that it was state court devised. Alison Gash and Michael H. Murakami, "Courts, Legislatures, and Ballot Initiatives: How Policy Venues Affect Public Acceptance," paper presented at the Annual Meeting of the American Political Science Association, 2008.

26. Mary Ann Glendon, *Rights Talk: The Impoverishment of Political Discourse* (New York: Simon and Schuster, 1991); Stuart Scheingold, *The Politics of Rights*, 2nd ed. (Ann Arbor: The University of Michigan Press, 2004); Gerald Rosenberg, *The Hollow Hope* (Chicago: University of Chicago Press, 2008).

27. As Mather argues, "a conclusion that courts cannot produce significant social reform cannot be based only on the U.S. Supreme Court. Political scientists accustomed to looking single-mindedly at the nation's highest court may see nothing wrong with such a narrow focus, but clearly any theory of court impact must be based upon a broader range of courts." Lynn Mather, "Theorizing about Trial Courts: Lawyers, Policymaking, and Tobacco Litigation," *Law & Social Inquiry* 23.4 (1998): 897–940, at 900.

28. This book joins the ranks of scholars, such as Barnes and Burke (2015), who study courts and legal battles through a broader policy development/dispute lens. Jeb Barnes and Thomas F. Burke, *How Policy Shapes Politics: Rights, Courts, Litigation and the Struggle Over Injury Compensation.* (New York: Oxford University Press, 2015.)

29. Laura Beth Nielsen, "Social Movements, Social Process: A Response to Gerald Rosenberg," *John Marshall Law Review* 42 (2008): 679.

30. Ghaziani argues that increased visibility of gays and lesbians spawned an incensed opposition to gay rights and LGBT policy advancements.

31. For a good summary of the literature on opposition to court intervention, see Matthew E. K. Hall, *The Nature of Supreme Court Power* (Cambridge: Cambridge University Press, 2010).

32. Jack M. Balkin, ed., *What Brown v. Board of Education Should Have Said: The Nation's Top Legal Experts Rewrite America's Landmark Civil Rights Decision* (New York: NYU Press, 2002), 3.

33. Michael J. Klarman, "How *Brown* Changed Race Relations: The Backlash Thesis," *The Journal of American History* 81.1 (June 1994): 81–118, 118.

34. Ibid.

35. Balkin, *What Brown v. Board of Education Should Have Said*, 22. See generally Gerald Rosenberg, *The Hollow Hope*.

36. William N. Eskridge, "Gay Rights After Lawrence v. Texas: Lawrence's Jurisprudence of Tolerance," *Minnesota Law Review* 88 (2004): 1021; Gerald Rosenberg, *The Hollow Hope*; Cass Sunstein, *One Case at a Time: Judicial Minimalism on the Supreme Court* (Cambridge: Harvard University Press, 2001).

37. R. Shep Melnick, *Regulation and the Court*.

38. Amy L. Stone, *Gay Rights at the Ballot Box* (Minneapolis: University of Minnesota Press, 2012).

39. A. G. Sulzberger, "Ouster of Judges Sends Signal to Bench," *The New York Times*, November 3, 2010. See also Douglas S. Reed, "Popular Constitutionalism: Towards a Theory of State Constitutional Meanings," *Rutgers LJ* 30 (1998): 871; Barbara Gamble, "Putting Civil Rights to a Popular Vote," *American Journal of Political Science* 41.1 (1997): 245–69.

40. Grant Schulte, "Iowans Dismiss Three Justices," *Des Moines Register*, November 8, 2010.

41. See generally Amy Stone, *Gay Rights at the Ballot Box* (Minneapolis: University of Minnesota Press, 2012); Pierceson, *Courts, Liberalism, and Rights*.

42. Reed, "Popular Constitutionalism," 929.

43. Sam Favate, "ACLU Tells Public Schools It's Monitoring School Prayer Complaints," *Wall Street Journal*, August 21, 2012; Associated Press, "Bible Classes in Public Schools?" *CBS News*, February 11, 2009, http://www.cbsnews.com/2100-250_162-1613868.html. For a general review of bureaucratic responses to the early school prayer decisions, see William Ker Muir, *Prayer in the Public Schools: Law and Attitude Change* (Chicago: University of Chicago Press, 1967), as well as Kenneth M. Dolbeare and Phillip E. Hammond, *The School Prayer Decisions from Court Policy to Local Practice* (Chicago: University of Chicago Press, 1971).

44. *Adar v. Smith*, 639 F.3d. 146, 2011. The Supreme Court denied the gay couple's petition for review.

45. Scott Neuman, "Iowa Court: List Both Same-Sex Parents on Birth Certificate," www.npr.org. Accessed on May 20, 2013; "Judge Rules on Couple's Death Certificate Battle," *KCCI News*, www.KCCI.com. Accessed on May 10, 2014.

46. Walter F. Murphy, *Elements of Judicial Strategy* (Chicago: University of Chicago Press, 1964).

47. Kathleen M. Sullivan, "City of Richmond v. JA Croson Co.: The Backlash Against Affirmative Action," *Tulane Law Review* 64 (1989): 1609.

48. In establishing a woman's right to choose, the *Roe* court asserts that during the first trimester a woman should be unconstrained by state regulation to exercise her rights. The Casey Court, conversely, dismantles the logic of the trimester

system and instead establishes that state policies should not pose an undue burden on women in their attempt to get an abortion. States are now free to establish regulations that affect women during their first trimester.

49. Elizabeth Nash et. al., "Laws Affecting Reproductive Health and Rights: 2013 State Policy Review." The Guttmacher Institute, January 2014. www.guttmacher.org. Accessed on November 30.2014.

50. Ibid.

51. Mary Ann Glendon, *Abortion and Divorce in Western Law* (Cambridge: Harvard University Press, 1987); Scheingold, *The Politics of Rights*; also see Pierceson, *Courts, Liberalism, and Rights* for a review of the backlash literature.

52. Michael Klarman, "How *Brown* Changed Race Relations: The Backlash Thesis," *The Journal of American History* 81.1 (1994): 81–118; Carlos Ball, "Legal Rights in Historical Perspective: From the Margins to the Mainstream: The Backlash Thesis and Same-Sex Marriage: Learning from *Brown v. Board of Education* and Its Aftermath." *William & Mary Bill of Rights Journal* 14 (2006), 1493.

53. See Mary Ann Glendon, *Rights Talk*; Kenneth Andrews, "Movement-Countermovement Dynamics and the Emergence of New Institutions: The Case of 'White Flight' Schools in Mississippi," *Social Forces* 80 (2002): 911–36; David J. Garrow, *Liberty and Sexuality* (Berkeley: University of California Press, 1994); Gerald Rosenberg, *The Hollow Hope*.

54. Greenhouse and Siegel offer a good review of these arguments, but counter these claims by arguing that the events leading up to *Roe v. Wade* do not support contentions that the decision sparked the movement. They suggest that a court-centered account of post-*Roe* politics ignores the conflict over abortion rights that existed prior to the Court's landmark decision. Linda Greenhouse and Reva B. Siegel, "Before (and After) Roe v. Wade: New Questions about Backlash," *Yale Law Journal* 120 (2010): 2028.

55. Quoted in Lee Epstein and Joseph F. Kobylka, *The Supreme Court and Legal Change* (Chapel Hill: The University of North Carolina Press, 1989), 207. The authors describe this quote as an "overstatement," but agree that the decision "catalyzed a strong countermovement" whose goal was to dismantle *Roe*.

56. Stephen Engel explains that gay rights organizations were especially concerned about how litigation on gay rights might prompt activity in other branches. Stephen Engel, "Organizational Identity as a Constraint on Strategic Action: A Comparative Analysis of Gay and Lesbian interest Groups," *Studies in American Political Development*, 21 (Spring 2007): 66-91.

57. Amin Ghaziani, *The Dividends of Dissent: How Conflict and Culture Work in Lesbian and Gay Marches on Washington* (Chicago: University of Chicago Press, 2008); Suzanna Walters, *All the Rage: The Story of Gay Visibility in America* (Chicago: University of Chicago Press; 2001).

58. See Thomas Keck, "Beyond Backlash: Assessing the Impact of Judicial Decisions on Gay Rights," *Law and Society Review* 43.1 (2009): 151–86; Mather, "Theorizing

about Trial Courts"; Michael McCann, "Reform Litigation on Trial," *Law & Social Inquiry* 17.4 (1992): 715–43; Pierceson, *Courts, Liberalism, and Rights.*

59. See for instance, Keck, "Beyond Backlash"; Nielsen, "Social Movements, Social Process."

60. In his review of Muciaronni, Boutcher argues that adoption fared better than marriage because it was decentralized in the courts. Steven A. Boutcher, "Same Sex, Different Politics: Success and Failure in the Struggles Over Gay Rights," *Social Forces* 88.3 (2010): 1503–04.

61. John D'Emilio, "Will the Courts Set Us Free?," in *The Politics of Same-Sex Marriage* ed. Craig Rimmerman and Clyde Wilcox (Chicago: University of Chicago Press, 2007), 39–64.

62. Michael McCann, "Reform Litigation on Trial"; Laura Beth Nielsen adds that "legal decisions that establish equality are meaningful in their minds even if they do not always lead to the kind of structural changes we would like to see." Further, a court decision "provides an authoritative symbolic 'victory' for movement activists that provide legitimacy for a social movement," in "Social Movements," 681–82.

63. Rebecca Mae Salokar, "Beyond Gay Rights Litigation: Using a Systemic Strategy to Affect Political Change in the United States," *GLQ: A Journal of Lesbian and Gay Studies* 3 (1997): 385–415.

64. Ibid.

65. Jacob Hacker, "Privatizing Risk without Privatizing the Welfare State"; Christopher Howard, *The Hidden Welfare State: Tax Expenditures and Social Policy in the United States* (Princeton, NJ: Princeton University Press, 1999). Christine A. Kelleher and Susan Webb Yackee, "Who's Whispering in Your Ear? The Influence of Third Parties over State Agency Decisions," *Political Research Quarterly* 59.4 (2006): 629–43.

66. Balogh, *A Government Out of Sight*, 379.

67. Kelleher and Yackee, "Who's Whispering in Your Ear?"

68. Joseph Shapiro, "Disability Policy and the Media: A Stealth Civil Rights Movement Bypasses the Press and Defies Conventional Wisdom," *Policy Studies Journal* 22.1 (1994): 123–32; Linda Hamilton Krieger, "Forward-Backlash Against the ADA: Interdisciplinary Perspectives and Implications for Social Justice Strategies," *Berkeley Journal of Employment & Labor Law* 21 (2000): 1–18.

69. Holzhacker 2007 argues that policies with moral or religious undertones are more likely to attract public attention. Ronald Holzhacker, "The Europeanization and Transnationalization of Civil Socity Organizations Striving for Equality: Goals and Strategies of Gay and Lesbian Groups in Italy and the Netherlands." EUI Working Paper Series RSCAS 2007/36, Florence: Robert Schuman Centre, 2007.

70. David S. Meyer and Suzanne Staggenborg, "Movements, Countermovements, and the Structure of Political Opportunity," *American Journal of Sociology* 101 (1996): 1628–60.

71. Craig Rimmerman, *From Identity to Politics: The Lesbian and Gay Movements in the United States* (Philadelphia: Temple University Press, 2002).

72. Ikemoto refers to gay and lesbian parents as the "dysfertile." She argues that when lesbians "identify themselves as mothers they may remain invisible, simply because lesbian identity as reflected in the dominant parts of the discourse stands in opposition to, not within, motherhood." Excerpted from Mary Joe Frug's *Women and the Law*, 4th edn., ed. Adler et al. (New York: Foundation Press, 2008), 169.

73. Justice Scalia implied that the jury was still out on gay parenting during oral arguments in *Hollingsworth v. Perry*, where he stated "There's considerable disagreement among sociologists as to what the consequences of raising a child in a single-sex family, whether that is harmful to the child or not."

74. D'Emilio, "Will the Courts Set Us Free?," 50.

75. Ibid.

76. Jacob Hacker, "Privatizing Risk without Privatizing the Welfare State"; Cary R. Covington, "Staying Private: Gaining Congressional Support for Unpublished Presidential Preferences on Roll Call Votes," *The Journal of Politics* 49.3 (1987): 737–55; Howard, *The Hidden Welfare State*, 1999.

77. Colleen Grogan and Eric Patashnik, "Between Welfare Medicine and Mainstream Entitlement: Medicaid at the Political Crossroads," *Journal of Health Politics, Policy and Law* 28.5 (2003): 821–58.

78. Martha Derthick, *Policymaking for Social Security* (Washington, DC: The Brookings Institution, 1979).

79. Jacob Hacker, in "Privatizing Risk without Privatizing the Welfare State," argues that the subterranean state resulted in a massive disinvestment of federal funds to the nation's neediest families. He uses the terms drift, conversion, and layering to describe these incremental policy processes of the subterranean state. Howard finds that the welfare state expanded resources to working-class families through incremental and largely unnoticed changes to complex policies like the tax code.

80. Family courts offer specific protections to limit public access to their proceedings.

81. R. Shep Melnick, *Regulation and the Courts*.

82. Pierceson, *Courts, Liberalism, and Rights*, 136.

83. Ibid.

84. William Eskridge, *Equality Practice: Civil Unions and the Future of Gay Rights* (New York: Routledge, 2002), 877. Similarly, Cass Sunstein encourages judges to reduce the reach of their opinions by sticking to the case at hand, "avoid[ing] clear rules," and leaving room for the democratic process to shape the outcome in *One Case at a Time*, ix. Of course, one criticism of this approach in the context of same-sex marriage is that civil unions are not marriage. This low-visibility alternative, then, produces significant substantive deviations.

85. Pierceson, *Courts, Liberalism, and Rights*, 133.

86. Beland, "Ideas and Institutional Change in Social Security," 26.

87. Beland, "Ideas and Institutional Change in Social Security," 34.

88. Ellen Andersen, *Out of the Closet and into the Courts* (Ann Arbor: University of Michigan Press, 2006).

89. Julie Novkov, "The Miscegenation/Same-Sex Marriage Analogy: What Can We Learn from Legal History?" *Law & Social Inquiry* 33.2 (2008): 345–86, at 363.

90. Amy L. Stone, *Gay Rights at the Ballot Box* (Minneapolis: University of Minnesota Press, 2012).

91. Novkov, "The Miscegenation/Same-Sex Marriage Analogy."

92. Michael Klarman, "Brown and Lawrence (and Goodridge)," *Michigan Law Review* 104 (2005): 431–89; Valerie Hoekstra, "The Supreme Court and Local Public Opinion," *American Political Science Review* 94.1 (2000): 89–100.

93. Pierceson, *Courts, Liberalism, and Rights*, 134.

94. Of course, there are some scholars who devote considerable attention to statutory cases. For instance, both Melnick and Teles accord high significance to *King v. Smith*, a Supreme Court case that interprets (and expands) the Social Security Act. See R. Shep Melnick, *Between the Lines: Interpreting Welfare Rights* (Washington, DC: The Brookings Institution, 1994), and Steven M. Teles, *Whose Welfare?: AFDC and Elite Politics* (Lawrence: University Press of Kansas, 1998).

95. Testimony of Assistant Attorney General Thomas E. Perez Before the Senate Committee on Health, Education, Labor, and Pensions on the ADA and Olmstead Enforcement, June 22, 2010.

96. Robert Balton, *The Crusade for Equality in the Workplace* (Lawrence: University Press of Kansas, 2014).

97. *Singer v. Hara*, 1974.

98. *Conaway v. Deane*, 2006.

99. Frank H. Buckley and Larry E. Ribstein, "Calling a Truce in the Marriage Wars," *University of Illinois Law Review* (2001): 561.

100. R. Shep Melnick, "Federalism and the New Rights," in Symposium Issue: Constructing a New Federalism: Jurisdictional Competence and Competition, *Yale Law and Policy Review* 14.2 (1996): 325–54, at 327.

101. Melnick, *Between the Lines*.

102. Melnick, "Federalism and the New Rights"; Barnes finds that Congress is often able to implement legislative overrides of judicial decisions. However, when these decisions involve the rights of minority groups, overrides are less effective at diminishing judicial discretion. See Jeb Barnes, *Overruled? Legislative Overrides, Pluralism, and Contemporary Court-Congress Relations* (Stanford, CA: Stanford University Press, 2004).

103. William A. Gamson, David Croteau, William Hoynes, and Theodore Sasson, "Media Images and the Social Construction of Reality," *Annual Review of Sociology* 18 (1992): 373–93, at 384. Dennis Chong and James N. Druckman, "Framing Theory," *Annual Review of Political Science* 10 (2007): 103–26.

104. Shanto Iyengar, "Speaking of Values: The Framing of American Values," *The Forum* 3.3, Article 7 (2005). In this project I am primarily concerned with

deliberate use of specific frames by advocates as a strategy to reduce issue salience and public opposition. However, judges and courts play a critical role in the framing of judicial decisions. They often have a choice of frames presented to them by either party or through amicus curiae briefs. Judges may also use their own frames while explicating legal arguments.

105. Nelson and Kinder refer to a policy's multidimensionality, in Thomas Nelson and Donald Kinder, "Issue Frames and Group-Centrism in American Public Opinion," *The Journal of Politics* 58.4 (1996): 1055–78. See Valerie Jenness and Kendal Broad, "Antiviolence Activism and the (In)Visibility of Gender in the Gay/Lesbian and Women's Movement," *Gender and Society* 8.3 (1994): 402–23; and Baumgartner and Jones ("policy image") for a discussion of the potential dimensions of policy frames. Frank R. Baumgartner and Bryan D. Jones, "Agenda Dynamics and Policy Subsystems," *Journal of Politics* 53.4 (1991): 1044–74. See also Gordon Silverstein, *Law's Allure: How Law Shapes, Constrains, Saves, and Kills Politics,* (New York: Cambridge University Press, 2009) for a discussion of the potential for legal frames to shape and constrain politics.

106. Mary Bernstein, "Celebration and Suppression: The Strategic Uses of Identity by the Lesbian and Gay Movement," *The American Journal of Sociology* 103 (1997): 531–65; Robert Benford and David A. Snow, "Framing Processes and Social Movements: An Overview," *Annual Review of Sociology* 26 (2000): 611–39.

107. Zald, Mayer N. "Culture, Ideology, and Strategic Framing," *Comparative Perspectives on Social Movements: Political Opportunities, Mobilizing Structures, and Cultural Framings* (1996): 261–74; on *Social Movements: Political Opportunities, Mobilizing Structures, and Cultural Framings,* ed. Doug McAdam, John D. McCarthy, and Mayer N. Zald (New York: Cambridge University Press, 1996), 261–74; Deana A. Rohlinger, "Framing the Abortion Debate: Organizational Resources, Media Strategies, and Movement-Countermovement Dynamics," *The Sociological Quarterly* 43.4 (2002): 479–507; Anne W. Esacove, "Dialogic Framing: The Framing/ Counterframing of 'Partial-Birth' Abortion," *Sociological Inquiry* 74.1 (2004): 70–101; Paul R. Brewer, *Value War: Public Opinion and the Politics of Gay Rights* (Lanham, MD: Rowman & Littlefield Publishers, 2007).

108. Bernstein, "Celebration and Suppression."

109. Nelson and Kinder, "Issue Frames and Group-Centrism in American Public Opinion."

110. Brewer, *Value War.*

111. Robert Entman, "Framing: Toward Clarification of a Fractured Paradigm," *Journal of Communication* 43.4 (1993): 51–58; Nelson and Kinder, "Issue Frames and Group-Centrism in American Public Opinion"; James K. Hertog and Douglas McLeod, "A Multiperspectival Approach to Framing Analysis: A Field Guide," in *Framing Public Life*, ed. Stephen Reese, Oscar Gandy Jr., and August Grant (Mahwah, NJ: Lawrence Erlbaum Associates, 2001), 141–62.

112. Andersen, *Out of the Closet and into the Courts,* 24.

113. Charles Epp, *The Rights Revolution* (Chicago: University of Chicago Press, 1998); Stuart Scheingold, *The Politics of Rights*, 2nd ed. (Ann Arbor: The University of Michigan Press, 2004).

114. Robert D. Benford and David A. Snow. "Framing processes and social movements: An overview and assessment." *Annual Review of Sociology* 26.1 (2000): 611–39, 619. Glendon, *Rights Talk*.

115. In 2012 a Kentucky legislature thwarted a bill in committee to protect students from bullying because "lawmakers worried it would give 'special rights' to gay students." "Bullying Bill Rejected Over Special Rights for Gays," www.wlwt. com. Accessed on May 30, 2014.

116. *Romer v. Evans*, (1996).

117. *Civil Rights Cases*, (1883).

118. Novkov argues that in the context of same-sex marriage, opponents not only made substantive assertions, but also devoted attention to "denying the authority of the courts to promote" marriage equality. See "The Miscegenation/Same-Sex Marriage Analogy," 377.

119. Scheingold, *The Politics of Rights*.

120. Robert Kagan, *Adversarial Legalism: The American Way of Law* (Cambridge: Harvard University Press, 2001).

121. Epp, *The Rights Revolution*, 23.

122. Glendon, *Rights Talk*, 171.

123. Chester Hautman, "The Case for a Right to Housing," *Shelterforce*, Issue 148 (Winter 2006), National Housing Institute.

124. Stephen M. Engel, "Frame Spillover: Media Framing and Public Opinion of a Multifaceted LGBT Rights Agenda," *Law & Social Inquiry* 38.2 (2013): 403–41, 414.

125. Grogan and Patashnik, "Between Welfare Medicine and Mainstream Entitlement," 846.

126. Susan Gluck Mezey, *Queers in Court: Gay Rights Law and Public Policy* (Lanham, MD: Rowman & Littlefield, 2007).

127. Brian F. Harrison and Melissa R. Michelson, "Not That There's Anything Wrong with That: The Effect of Personalized Appeals on Marriage Equality Campaigns," *Political Behavior* 34.2 (2012): 325–44.

128. Jonathan Rauch, "Prop 8 Ads' Invisible Gays," *LA Times*, October 26, 2008.

129. Rauch, "Prop 8 Ads' Invisible Gays."

130. Ibid.

131. Novkov, "The Miscegenation/Same-Sex Marriage Analogy," 377.

132. Melnick, "Federalism and the New Rights."

133. Lauren Wilson, "SCOTUS Hears Arguments on Marriage Equality and DOMA," www.NAACP.org. Accessed on May 26, 2013.

134. Ibid.

135. Mark V. Tushnet, *The NAACP's Legal Strategy against Segregated Education, 1925–1950* (Chapel Hill: University of North Carolina Press, 2005); Stephen

L. Wasby, *Race Relations Litigation in an Age of Complexity* (Charlottesville, VA: University of Virginia Press, 1995).

136. Keck argues that "backlash proponents tend to misspecify the actual strategic dilemma that advocates faced." Modern same-sex marriage was not formed by national groups. They were initiated by individual couples. See "Beyond Backlash," 176.

137. Of course, American history is replete with examples of national organizations intervening into local governance in order to protect local minority groups from elites who are silencing their rights. In the early days of group home advocacy, for instance, the Department of Justice played a pivotal role in helping operators and residents secure their housing rights.

138. Similarly, just as locally driven campaigns can have national import, so, too, can national campaigns be particularistic and exclusive. "Astroturf" campaigns—those led by national elites who are hoping to be perceived as bottom-up and grassroots driven—are not representative of the constituencies they claim to serve.

139. Young, "Activist Challenges to Deliberative Democracy," 26.

140. Joshua Cohen, "Procedure and Substance in Deliberative Democracy," *Deliberative Democracy: Essays on Reason and Politics* (1997): 407–37, 413.

141. Young, "Activist Challenges to Deliberative Democracy."

142. Fung, *Deliberation before the Revolution*, 406.

143. Lynn M. Sanders, "Against Deliberation," *Political Theory* 25 (1997): 347–76.

144. Rostbøll, "Dissent, Criticism, and Transformative Political Action in Deliberative Democracy"; Sanders, "Against Deliberation."

145. Fung, *Deliberation before the Revolution*, 401.

146. Gamble, "Putting Civil Rights to a Popular Vote"; Elisabeth R. Gerber, "Legislative Response to the Threat of Popular Initiatives," *American Journal of Political Science* 40.1 (1996): 99–128; Thomas E. Cronin, *Direct Democracy: The Politics of Initiative, Referendum, and Recall* (Cambridge: Harvard University Press, 1989); Daniel C. Lewis, "Direct Democracy and Minority Rights: Same-Sex Marriage Bans in the U.S.," *Social Science Quarterly* 92.2 (2011): 364–83; David B. Magleby, "Chapter 5: Opinion Formation and Opinion Change in Ballot Proposition Campaigns," in *Manipulating Public Opinion*, ed. Michael Margolis and Gary A. Mauser (Pacific Grove, CA: Brooks/Cole, 1989).

147. David Goodman, "Vermont's Happily Ever After," *Mother Jones*, April 8, 2009. okhenderson.com. Accessed on January 31, 2011.

148. Fung, *Deliberation before the Revolution*.

149. E. E. Schattschneider, "Intensity, Visibility, Direction, and Scope," *American Political Science Review* 51.4 (1957): 941.

150. Balogh, *A Government Out of Sight*, 6.

151. Covington, "Staying Private."

152. Meyer and Staggenborg, "Movements, Countermovements, and the Structure of Political Opportunity," 1641.

153. Meyer and Staggenborg, "Movements, Countermovements, and the Structure of Political Opportunity," 1642.

154. Meyer and Staggenborg, "Movements, Countermovements, and the Structure of Political Opportunity," 1641.

155. Keck, "Beyond Backlash."

156. Simone Chambers, "Deliberative Democratic Theory," *Annual Review of Political Science* 6 (2003): 307–26; Michael X. Delli Carpini, Fay Lomax Cook, and Lawrence R. Jacobs, "Public Deliberation, Discursive Participation, and Citizen Engagement: A Review of the Literature," *Annual Review of Political Science* 7 (2004): 315–44.

157. Mucciaroni argues that decentralization helps explain how gay parenting advocates were able to secure statewide victories in ten states and county-wide victories in fifteen additional states.

158. Robert Self, *All in the Family: The Realignment of American Democracy since the 1960s* (New York: Hill and Wang, 2013).

159. See generally Patricia Strach, *All in the Family: The Private Roots of American Public Policy* (Stanford, CA: Stanford University Press, 2007); Patricia Strach and Kathleen S. Sullivan, "The State's Relations: What the Institution of Family Tells Us about Governance," *Political Research Quarterly* 64.1 (2011): 94–106; Priscilla Yamin, *American Marriage: A Political Institution* (Philadelphia: University of Pennsylvania Press, 2012); Linda McClain, *The Place of Families: Fostering Capacity, Equality, and Responsibility* (Cambridge, MA: Harvard University Press, 2006); Naomi Cahn and June Carbone, *Red families v. blue families: Legal Polarization and the Creation of Culture* (New York, NY: Oxford University Press, 2010); Kathleen Sullivan and Carol Nackenoff, "Family Matters as Public Work: Reformers' Dreams for the Progressive Era Juvenile Court," APSA 2013 Annual Meeting Paper.

CHAPTER 3

1. Pat Buchanan, Republican National Convention, August 17, 1992.

2. Christopher Connell, "Quayle Begins Battle for California," *The Associated Press*, September 8, 1992.

3. Ellen Debenport, "Gays Fear They'll Be GOP's New Willie Horton," *Capital Times*, August 19, 1992.

4. Tonja Jacobi, "How Massachusetts Got Gay Marriage: The Intersection of Popular Opinion, Legislative Action, and Judicial Power," 15 *Journal of Contemporary Legal Issues*, 219 (2006).

5. Joe Rollins, "Same Sex Unions and the Spectacle of Recognition," *Law & Society Review* 39, 2 (2005): 457–83, reviewing Jonathan Goldberg-Heller at 463. See Goldberg-Hiller, *The Limits to Union* (Ann Arbor: The University of Michigan Press, 2002).

6. Celestine Bohlen, "Ex-Moral Majority Aide Seeks to Unseat Lynchburg Senator," *The Washington Post*, October 9, 1983, B1.

7. See, for example, Gerald Rosenberg, *The Hollow Hope*; Sunstein, *One Case at a Time*.

8. The Vatican issued a report on Tuesday October 14, 2014 in which it stated that gays and lesbians have "gifts to offer" the church and same-sex unions can offer "precious support" to gays and lesbians. Immediately, the report and its contents were under fire by conservative members of the church. In response the Vatican backtracked and described the report as "a working document" rather than "the final word from Rome." Delia Gallagher and Daniel Burke, "Under Conservative Assault, Vatican backtracks on gay comments," *CNN*, Wednesday, October 15, 2014. http://www.cnn.com/2014/10/14/world/vatican-backtrack-gays/index.html. Accessed on October 15, 2014.

9. Jason Pierceson, *Same-Sex Marriage in the United States* (New York: Rowman and Littlefield, 2013); Julie Novkov, "The Miscegenation/Same-Sex Marriage Analogy; Peggy Pascoe, "Sex, Gender, and Same-Sex Marriage," in *Is Academic Feminism Dead? Theory in Practice*, ed. The Social Justice Group at the Center for Advanced Feminist Studies, The University Of Minnesota (New York: New York University Press, 2000), 86–129.

10. *Baker v. Nelson* (1971).

11. http://special.lib.umn.edu/rare/trettersample.phtml.

12. "The Law: Adopting a Lover," *Time Magazine*, September 6, 1971.

13. *New York Times*, January 5, 1972.

14. Lornet Turnbull, "Gay Man Sees Big Changes Since '72 Laws," *The Seattle Times*, April 4, 2006.

15. *Singer v. Hara* (1974).

16. *New York Times*, April 27, 1975.

17. *Associated Press*, March 15, 1979.

18. *Associated Press*, March 15, 1979.

19. Moni Basu, "Love Wins in Gay Couple's 40-year Immigration Fight," *CNN*, June 28, 2014, www.cnn.com. Accessed on September 18, 2014.

20. Ibid.

21. Ibid.

22. "Behavior: The Homosexual: Newly Visible, Newly Understood," *Time*, October 31, 1969.

23. "The Homosexual in America," *Time*, January 21, 1966.

24. Ibid.

25. Ghaziani, *The Dividends of Dissent*, 33.

26. *Associated Press*, May 31, 1977.

27. Pierceson, *Same-Sex Marriage in the United States*.

28. *Associated Press*, October 22, 1982.

29. *Associated Press*, June 29, 1984.

30. *Associated Press*, November 10, 1982.

31. Philip S. Gutis, "Small Steps Toward Acceptance Renew Debate on Gay Marriage," *The New York Times*, November 5, 1989.

32. Jane Brody, *The New York Times*, November 14, 1978.

33. *United Press International*, October 3, 1980.

34. Interview 13. See Appendix A for a summary of the interview sampling process, interview dates and basic demographic information about the participants.

35. Gutis, "Small Steps Toward Acceptance."

36. Ibid.

37. Michael Klarman, *From the Closet to the Altar: Courts, Backlash, and the Struggle for Same-Sex Marriage* (New York: Oxford University Press, 2012).

38. Gutis, "Small Steps Toward Acceptance."

39. *Associated Press*, October 28, 1986.

40. Nielsen, "Social Movements, Social Process: A Response to Gerald Rosenberg."

41. Steven Vegh, "Marriage Ban Proposal Heading for Legislature," *Post Press Herald Maine Sunday Telegram*, February 8, 1997.

42. Daniel R. Pinello, *America's Struggle for Same-Sex Marriage* (New York: Cambridge University Press, 2006), 2.

43. Michael Klarman, *From the Closet to the Altar*; Thomas M. Keck, "Beyond Backlash: Assessing the Impact of Judicial Decisions on LGBT Rights," *Law & Society Review* 43.1 (2009): 151–86.

44. William Rubenstein, "Divided We Litigate: Addressing Disputes Among Group Members and Lawyers in Civil Rights Campaigns," 106 *Yale Law Journal* 1623 (1996–97).

45. Tarrow and Dorf refer to this as "anticipatory countermobilization." Michael C. Dorf and Sidney Tarrow, "Strange Bedfellows: How an Anticipatory Countermovement Brought Same-Sex Marriage into the Public Arena," *Law and Social Inquiry* 39.2 (Spring 2014): 449–73.

46. Stuart Taylor, Jr. "Supreme Court Hears Case on Homosexual Rights," *The New York Times*, April 1, 1986, A24.

47. Amy Stone, *Gay Rights at the Ballot Box* (Minneapolis, MN: University of Minnesota Press, 2012), 15.

48. P. Gutis, "Small Steps Toward Acceptance Renew Debate on Gay Marriage," *The New York Times* (1989).

49. Craig A. Rimmerman, *From Identity to Politics: The Lesbian and Gay Movements in the United States* (Philadelphia, PA: Temple University Press, 2002).

50. Interview 12.

51. For a comprehensive review of same-sex marriage litigation, see Jason Pierson, *Same-Sex Marriage in the United States: The Road to the Supreme Court* (Plymouth, UK: Rowman and Littlefield, 2013).

52. Catherine Toups, "Judge Rejects Proposal by Gays," *The Washington Times*, January 3, 1992.

53. "Same-Sex Marriage Leads to Court Battle," *The Washington Times*, November 30, 1992.

54. "Gay Marriage Rankles Austin Fundamentalists," *Orlando Sentinel*, July 16, 1992. Accessed on October 15, 2014.

55. Ibid.

56. Christopher Connell, "Quayle: Disagrees with Alternative Lifestyles 'Not Gay-Bashing'," *The Associated Press*, August 21, 1992.

57. Daniel Pinello, *America's Struggle*, 27.

58. Ibid.

59. Stone, *Gay Rights at the Ballot Box*.

60. Daniel Pinello, *America's Struggle*, 26.

61. Priscilla Yamin, *American Marriage: A Political Institution* (Philadelphia, PA: University of Pennsylvania Press, 2012).

62. Interview 21. Please see Appendix A for a detailed discussion of the interviewee selection process and general characteristics about the interview participants.

63. Interview 11.

64. Interview 13.

65. Interview 14.

66. Interview 21.

67. Pierceson, *Same-Sex Marriage in the United States*; Engel 2007; Nielsen, "Social Movements."

68. Interview 15.

69. Michael Klarman, *From the Closet to the Altar*, 110.

70. Michael Klarman, *From the Closet to the Altar*, 111.

71. Douglas S. Reed, "Popular Constitutionalism: Towards a Theory of State Constitutional Meanings," *Rutgers Law Journal* 30 (1998): 871.

72. Daniel Pinello, *America's Struggle*, 27.

73. Interview 11.

74. *Brause and Dugan v. Department of Vital Statistics*, February 27, 1998.

75. Prior to 2004, four states had altered their constitution to either ban same-sex marriage or restrict its consideration to legislative venues: Alaska (1998), Nebraska (2000), Nevada (2002), and Hawaii (1998). See Christine Vestal, "Gay Marriage Ripe for Decision in 3 Courts," Stateline.org, March 1, 2007.

76. Ruth Bader Ginsburg argues that, in *Roe v. Wade* the Court made a mistake in moving ahead of, rather than working with, the legislature. She advocates for a more cautious approach—similar to that used in *Brown v. Board of Education*. Ruth Bader Ginsburg, "Speaking in a Judicial Voice," *New York University Law Review* 67.6 (1992).

77. *Lewis v. Harris*, (2006)

78. Pierceson, *Same-Sex Marriage in the United States*, 113.

79. Ibid.

80. Democratic Party Platform, July 26, 2004. http://www.presidency.ucsb.edu/ws/index.php?pid=29613. Accessed on November 30, 2014.

81. Republican Party Platform 2004, http://www.presidency.ucsb.edu/ws/index.php?pid=25850. Accessed on November 30, 2014.

82. Paul Farhi, "Kerry Again Opposes Same-Sex Marriage," *Washington Post,* May 15, 2004.

83. Epstein and Segal argue that issue salience (specifically in judicial politics) can be measured through mentions in *The New York Times*. Lee Epstein and Jeffrey A. Segal, "Measuring Issue Salience," *American Journal of Political Science* 44.1 (2000): 66–83.

84. Speeches were accessed through the American Presidency Project. http://www. presidency.ucsb.edu. Accessed on July 12, 2014.

85. George W. Bush, "Defending the War," York, PA, July 9, 2004.

86. Same-sex marriage and abortion are equally absent in John Kerry's presidential campaign speeches.

87. Focus on the Family continues to assert—despite studies documenting the contrary—that "children do best on every measure of well-being when raised by their married mother and father" and maintain their efforts to publicly support and push for relationship and parental restrictions on same-sex couples; www. focusonthefamily.com. Accessed on July 21, 2014.

88. A review of Dobson's arguments can be found at www.focusonthefamily.com. Accessed on September 18, 2014.

89. In their analysis of these hearings, Liu and Macedo find that two claims emerge: "traditional heterosexual marriage protects and fosters the well-being of children" and "same sex matrimony would spell the end of marriage itself." Frederick Liu and Stephen Macedo, "The Federal Marriage Amendment and the Strange Evolution of the Conservative Case Against Gay Marriage," *PS: Political Science & Politics* 38 (2005): 211–15, at 211.

90. Congressional Record, Vol. 150, p. S7906, Testimony of Senator Rick Santorum, July 12, 2004, Motion to Proceed on the Federal Marriage Amendment.

91. Federal Marriage Amendment Hearing, May 13, 2004. www.gpo.gov. Accessed on November 30, 2014.

92. Ibid.

93. This argument appears in the arguments in favor section of Oregon's measure 36. However, similar arguments were made to support other state constitutional gay marriage bans.

94. "Why a Marriage Amendment Is Necessary," Republican Policy Committee, March 28, 2006.

95. I created a random sample of a hundred local newspaper articles on same-sex marriage for each year between 1996 and 2006 (except for 2001 and 2002, years in which the population totals did not exceed 100). The sample was derived from the population of local articles, from all states, pulled from LexisNexis through a key term search among headlines and lead paragraphs for the following phrases: "same-sex marriage," "homosexual marriage," "gay marriage," "lesbian marriage." The search also required that the articles mention the term "court" to limit the content analysis to articles that mention court cases or court involvement generally.

96. Liu and Macedo, "The Federal Marriage Amendment."

97. Elisabeth J. Beardsley and Eric Convey, "Bush, O'Malley Back Marriage Amendment," *Boston Herald*, December 17, 2003.

98. Linda Feldmann, "Culture Wars Pose Risks for Both Parties," *The Christian Science Monitor*, November 20, 2003.

99. Interview 21.

100. Gary Bauer Testimony, Senate Judiciary Hearings, Defense of Marriage Act, July 11, 1996.

101. Steven G. Vegh, "Christian Group Fights Law with the Law," *The Philadelphia Inquirer*, November 27, 2003.

102. Scott Lindlaw, "Bush Watching State Court Cases on Gay Marriages," *The Associated Press*, July 31, 2003.

103. Regarding New Jersey, see Ben Nuckols, "Maryland's Highest Court Hears Same-Sex Marriage Arguments," *The Associated Press*, December 5, 2006.

104. Mary Otto, "As Md. Court Weighs Same-Sex Marriage, Plaintiffs Hear Echoes of Previous Fight," *The Washington Post*, December 4, 2006.

105. Mark Sherman, "House to Vote on Stripping Federal Courts of Jurisdiction over Gay Marriage," *The Associated Press*, July 21, 2004.

106. Shaun Sutner, "Use of 1913 Rule Miffs Supporters of Gay Marriage," *Telegram and Gazette*, April 30, 2004, A1.

107. "Courts Take a Look at Gay Amendment; Election Challenge Called Premature," *New Orleans Times-Picayune*, August 24, 2004.

108. Barb Galbincea, "Marriage Ban Effect on Gays Varied; Some Flee, Others Battle in Courts Over Interpretation," *The Plain Dealer*, November 29, 2005.

109. Claudia Rowe, "Matt Foreman, National Gay and Lesbian Task Force," *Seattle-Post Intelligencer*, August 13, 2005.

110. Bill Clinton, "It's Time to Overturn DOMA," *The Washington Post*, March 7, 2013.

111. *The Advocate*, September 25, 2009, http://www.advocate.com/news/daily-news/2009/09/25/clinton-i-was-wrong-about-gay-marriage.

112. Paul Farhi, "Kerry Again Opposes Same-Sex Marriage," *Washington Post*, May 15, 2004. Accessed on October 15, 2014.

113. Reid J. Epstein, "Don't Miss It: John Kerry Backs Gay Marriage," *Politico*, July 22, 2011, Accessed on November 30, 2014.

114. Tim Mak, "Colin Powell Endorses Gay Marriage," *Politico*, May 23, 2012. Accessed on October 15, 2014.

115. "NAACP Backs Same-Sex Marriage," *UPI*, May 19, 2012, http://www.upi.com.

116. Jennifer Preston, "G.O.P Senator Who Backed Gay Unions Won't Run," *The New York Times*, May 9, 2012.

117. Justin Sinker, "Romney Spokesman Says Republican Criticism of Gay Ex-Staffer 'Disappointing,'" *The Hill*, May 3, 2012.

118. Maggie Haberman, "Bush '04 Pollster: Change in Attitudes on Gay Marriage Across the Board," *Politico*, May 11, 2012. http://www.politico.com/blogs/burns-haberman/2012/05/bush-pollster-change-in-attitudes-on-gay-marriage-123235.html. Accessed on November 30, 2014.

119. Nathaniel Frank, "How Gay Marriage Finally Won at the Polls," *Slate Magazine*, November 7, 2012. http://www.slate.com/articles/news_and_politics/politics/2012/11/gay_marriage_in_maryland_and_maine_the_inside_strategy.html. Accessed on November 30, 2014.

120. This approach was particularly prevalent in the 2012 ballot campaigns in Washington and Maine, which legalized marriage for gay and lesbian couples. See, for instance, Sunnivie Brydum, "Win Claimed in Washington: Voters Affirm Marriage Equality," *The Advocate*, November 7, 2012.

121. Carrie Wofford, "Why Equality is Winning: Two Factors Caused Public Opinion on Gay Rights to Shift So Quickly," *U.S. News and World Report*, March 26, 2014, quoting public relations expert Doug Hatt.

122. Interview with Nate Silver, "All Things Considered," National Public Radio, May 10, 2012. www.npr.org. Accessed on November 30, 2014.

123. "Polls on Gay Marriage Not Yet Reflected in Votes," *CBS News*, May 28, 2012. www.cbs.com. Accessed on November 30, 2014.

124. Ibid.

125. Ibid.

126. This group is pursuing a ballot measure to dismantle the amendment in 2014.

127. Interview 16.

128. Lyle Denniston, *DOMA: U.S. Takes Tough Line on Marriage Denial*, SCOTUSblog (February 22, 2013, 8:28 PM), http://www.scotusblog.com/2013/02/doma-u-s-takes-tough-line-on-marriage-denial/. Accessed on April 16, 2014.

129. The Bipartisan Legal Action Group consists of a group of Members of Congress who took on coordinating the legal defense of DOMA after the Obama Administration determined that it could not be constitutionally defended.

130. *US v. Windsor* (2013).

131. Ibid.

132. Bill Moyers Transcript, *PBS*, February 26, 2010.

133. Interview 13.

134. As of October 15, 2014 federal courts had paved the way for same-sex couples to marry in Utah, Oklahoma, Virginia, Indiana, Idaho, Oregon, Pennsylvania, Wisconsin, Colorado, and Nevada. Cases were pending in eight additional states. www.freedomtomarry.org. Accessed on October 15, 2014.

135. Alex Dobuzinskis, "Majority of Americans Support Gay Marriage in Poll," *Reuters*, May 20, 2011.

136. "Leading Gay Marriage Opponent on Losing the Battle: 'I have a lot more freedom now!,'" *The Huffington Post*, March 20, 2014. www.huffingtonpost.com Accessed on May 19, 2014.

137. "Judge Strikes Down Pennsylvania Same-Sex Marriage Ban," *NBC News*, www.nbcnews.com. Accessed on July 21, 2014. A *Washington Post* article estimated that, as of October 7, 2014, approximately 54% of gays and lesbians living in the U.S. resided in states with marriage equality. Philip Bump, "A majority of gay Americans now live in states where gay marriage is legal," *Washington Post*, October 7, 2014. Accessed on October 15, 2014.

138. Brent Griffiths, "Iowa Supreme Court Ruling Expands Birth Certificate Rights for Lesbian Couples," *The Daily Iowan*, May 6, 2013.

139. Trudy Ring, "Iowa Lesbian Couple Win Fight Over Child's Death Certificate," *The Advocate*, December 21, 2012.

140. "Ron Baity, North Carolina Pastor, Suggests Gays Should Be Prosecuted Like They Were Historically," *The Huffington Post*, May 7, 2012. www.huffingtonpost.com. Accessed on June 1, 2013.

141. "Charles L. Worley, North Carolina Pastor: Put Gays and Lesbians in Electrified Pen to Kill them Off," *The Huffington Post*, May 21, 2012. www.huffingtonpost.com. Accessed on September 18, 2014.

142. "Kansas Pastor Curtis Knapp: Government Should Kill Gays but 'They Won't'" *Huffington Post*, May 30, 2012, www.huffingtonpost.com. Accessed on July 21, 2014.

143. www.rightwingwatch.com. Accessed on October 15, 2014.

144. Lorenzo Ferrigno, "Attack after same-sex marriage shines light on Michigan hate crime law," *CNN*, April 7, 2014.

145. Erin Fuchs, "Expert: 'Desperate Anger' Is Driving the Rise in Anti-Gay Hatred," *Business Insider*, May 21, 2013. www.businessinsider.com. Accessed on October 15, 2014.

146. Adam Taylor, "NYPD Say Fatal West Village Shooting A 'Hate Crime,'" *Business Insider*, May 18, 2013. www.businessinsider.com. Accessed on October 15, 2014.

147. "New FBI Data Shows Hate Crimes Based on Sexual Orientation on the Rise," *HRC*, December 10, 2012. See also "Hate Crimes Accounting," The Federal Bureau of Investigation, http://www.fbi.gov/news/stories/2012/december/annual-hate-crimes-report-released/annual-hate-crimes-report-released. Accessed on September 18, 2014.

148. Alexi Tzatzev, "There's a Disturbing Trend Involving Anti-Gay Hate Crime in the U.S.," *Business Insider*, December 12, 2012. www.businessinsider.com Accessed on September 18, 2014.

149. Erin Fuchs, "EXPERT: 'Desperate Anger' Is Driving the Rise in Anti-Gay Hatred," *Business Insider*, May 21, 2013. www.businessinsider.com. Accessed on September 18, 2014.

150. Tracey Kaplan, "Surge in Anti-Gay Hate Crime Cases," *San Jose Mercury News*, March 16, 2009.

151. Kaplan, "Surge in Anti-Gay Hate Crime Cases."

152. Interview 28.

153. Interview 13.

1. Theodore Postel, "Adoption by Lesbian Couple," *Chicago Daily Law Bulletin*, March 22, 1996, 1.

2. Martha Shirk, "Lesbian to Help Raise Boy; 'Equitable Parent' Idea Applied to Relationship of Woman, 2-Yr-Old," *St. Louis Post-Dispatch*, May 9, 1995, 1A.

3. Christopher Wills, "Bisexual Mother Wins Custody Battle in Appellate Court," *Associated Press*, December 18, 1996.

4. This figure includes states that had passed both a statutory and a constitutional ban in the same time period.

5. Andrea Stone, "Drives to Ban Gay Adoption Heat up in 16 States," *USA Today*, February 20, 2006.

6. "Equality from State to State: Gay, Lesbian, Bisexual and Transgender Americans and State Legislation 2004," Human Rights Campaign, www.hrc.org.

7. This figure was calculated from data featured in Human Rights Campaign's Equality State to State Report for 2005 along with that year's newspaper articles on same-sex parenting. Jeffrey Gilbert, "Ban on Gay Foster Parents Heading to Senate," *Houston Chronicle*, April 21, 2005.

8. In 2006 nineteen legislative proposals were introduced in ten states; only Utah's successfully passed in the legislature.

9. Deb Price, "Move to Ban Gay Adoptions Will Hurt Children," *The Detroit News*, January 9, 2006, 9A.

10. Mubarak Dahir, "Anti-Gay Adoption Measures Falter," *PrideSource*, March 2, 2006. www.pridesource.com. Accessed on October 15, 2014.

11. *Associated Press*, "House Leaders Say Banning Gay Adoption is Not a Priority," *Akron Beacon Journal*, February 11, 2006.

12. Stone, "Drives to Ban Gay Adoption Heat up in 16 States."

13. Soni Jacobs, "The 2006 Georgia Legislature: Poll on Priorities," *Atlanta Journal-Constitution*, January 8, 2006, 1F.

14. "ABA Addresses Some Public Policy Issues," *St. Louis Daily Record*, February 2, 2006.

15. Matt Canham, "Legislators Short on Votes Needed to Override Vetoes," *The Salt Lake Tribune*, March 30, 2006.

16. This is likely a gross underestimation of actual same-sex parenting victories. Cases were gathered from bibliographies compiled by the Gay and Lesbian Advocates and Defenders (GLAD). These lists include precedent-setting or landmark cases on same-sex parenting. Cases that followed these precedent-setting cases were not included. According to GLAD there are more than thirty documented precedent-setting victories concerning same-sex adoption. Gay and Lesbian Advocates and Defenders, "Bibliography of Adoption Cases," June 2006. GLAD

has also compiled a list of more than twenty landmark victories focusing on custody and visitation conflicts arising from children born into same-sex relationships. "Selected Bibliography of Recent Co-Parent Cases," October, 2005.

17. Between The Lines, September 23, 2004: "Attorney General: Unmarried Couples Cannot Adopt in Michigan," *PrideSource.* www.pridesource.com. Accessed on November 30, 2014.

18. Jerry Filteau, "Catholic Charities in Boston Archdiocese to end adoption services," *Catholic News Service,* March 13, 2006.

19. *In re Bonfield,* 96 Ohio St. 3d 218, 2002.

20. *Hansen v. McClellan,* 2006.

21. Human Rights Campaign, "Equality from State to State," 2007, 37.

22. The *Cole* court argued that the fundamental right to engage in private consensual sexual activity was impaired by the fostering and adoption ban.

23. *Boseman v. Jarrell,* 2010.

24. *In re: the Adoption of I.M.,* Court of Appeals of Kansas, November 9, 2012.

25. John Leland, "Parenthood Denied by Law—After a Same-Sex Couple's Breakup, a Custody Battle," The New York Times, September 12, 2014.

26. *Adar v. Smith,* 2010.

27. National Center for Lesbian Rights, "Adoption By Lesbian, Gay, and Bisexual Parents: An Overview of Current Law" August 2011, 4.

28. National Center for Lesbian Rights, "Adoption by Lesbian, Gay, and Bisexual Parents: An Overview of Current Law," January 2004.

29. National Center for Lesbian Rights, "Legal Recognition of LGBT Families," December 2013, 3.

30. Interview 16.

31. Dahlia Lithwick, "Kids Need Parents More than Politics," *The Times Union,* March 16, 2006, A15.

32. Interview 16.

33. Commonwealth ex rel and *Bachman v. Bradley,* (1952).

34. *Leonard v. Leonard,* (1953)

35. *Nadler v. Superior Court,* (1967).

36. *Schuster v. Schuster,* (1978).

37. Interview 15.

38. Kimberly Richman, *Courting Change: Queer Parents, Judges, and the Transformation of American Family Law* (New York: New York University Press, 2008), 48.

39. *M.P. v. S.P.,* (1979).

40. Interview 13.

41. *M.P. v. S.P.,*

42. Interview 1.

43. Data in this section were collected from the Gay and Lesbian Advocates and Defenders Bibliography of Adoption Cases, June 21, 2006.

44. *In re Adoption of M.M.S.A.* No. D8503-61930 (Or. Circuit Ct., Multnomah County, September 4, 1985).

45. For a complete review of cases on same-sex parenting rights, see Kimberly Richman, *Courting Change.*

46. *In re Adoption of (Child A and Child B),* (1988); *In re Child 1 and Child 2,* (1989); *In re the Interest of E.B.G.,* (1989).

47. GLAD, Bibliography of Adoption Cases, June, 2006.

48. *In the Interest of Hart,* (2001).

49. *In the Matter of the Petition of L.S. and V.L. for the Adoption of a Minor (T.) and (M.),* (1991); *In re M.M.D. & B.H.M.,* (1995).

50. *In re Petition of K.M. and D.M. to Adopt Olivia M.,* (1995); *In the Matter of the Petition of C.M.A. a/k/a C.M.W. and L.A.W.,* (1999).

51. *In re the Adoption of M.M.G.C., H.H.C., & K.E.A.C.,* (2003); *In re Adoption of K.S.P.,* (2004); *In the Matter of Infant Girl, et al. v. Morgan Co. Fam. & Ch.,* (2005)

52. *In re Petition of D.L.G. & M.A.H.,* (1996).

53. *In the Matter of the Adoption of Two Children by H.N.R.,* (1995).

54. *In the Matter of the Adoption of Evan,* 153 Misc. (1992); *In re Jacob, In the Matter of Dana,* (1995); *In re Adoption of Carolyn B.,* (2004).

55. *In re Adoption of R.B.F. and R.C.F.,* (2002).

56. *In re B.L.V.B. and E.L.V.B.* (1993).

57. GLAD, Bibliography of Adoption Cases, June 2006.

58. *Russell v. Bridgens,* (2002).

59. *K.M. v. E.G.,* (2005), time for grant or denial of rehearing extended to 11-10-05 (September 6, 2005); *Elisa B. v. Superior Court,* (2005).

60. *In the Interest of E.L.M.C.,* (2004), *cert. denied,* 2004.

61. *Chambers v. Chambers,* (2002).

62. *In re Parentage of A.B.,* (2004).

63. *E.N.O. v. L.M.M.,* (1999); *T.F. v. B.L.,* (2004).

64. *V.C. v. M.J.B.,* (2000).

65. *L.S.K. v. H.A.N.,* (2002); *T.B. v L.R.M.,* (2001).

66. *Rubano v. DiCenzo,* (2000).

67. *State of Washington on behalf of D.R.M. v. Wood,* (2001); *In re the Parentage of L.B.,* (2004).

68. *Downey v. Muffley,* (2002).

69. *In re Marriage of Dorworth,* (2001).

70. Justin Stoner, "Gay Parents," *City News Services,* June 17, 1998.

71. Wayne Parry, "Lesbian Wins Full Co-parenting Rights to Partner's Newborn Daughter," *Associated Press,* May 26, 2005.

72. Alan Cooper, "Court: Give Birth Certificate to Gay Parents," *Richmond Times Dispatch,* April 23, 2005.

73. In 2002 the American Academy of Pediatrics weighed in with a mega-study, arguing that children who are raised in same-sex households fare no better or

worse than those in heterosexual households. American Academy of Pediatrics, Policy Statement, *Pediatrics* 109.2 (2002): 339–40.

74. *In re Adoption of Baby Z.,* (1999).

75. *In re Adoption of Luke,* (2002); *In re: Adoption of Jane Doe,* (1998).

76. Lester Graham, "How judges were stopped from granting two-parent adoptions to gay and lesbian parents," *Michigan Radio,* June 11, 2013. www.michiganradio. org. Accessed on October 16, 2014.

77. In 2012 an appellate court refused to overturn a second-parent adoption issued by a probate court judge in 2005 in *Usitalo v. Landon.* However, the primary issue in this case was whether the probate court lacked subject matter jurisdiction over the adoption request. The appellate court found that the probate judge did have subject matter jurisdiction and that "if the parties disagreed with its interpretation of the statute, they would have had to appeal within 21 days of its original ruling of the adoption in 2005." *Usitalo v. Landon* (Mich. Ct. App. 2012).

78. It should be noted that on several occasions the Supreme Court also refused to hear arguments that would overturn state rulings supporting adoption and parental rights for gay parents. It is likely that their refusal is less a statement about their position on the issue and more a reflection of their position on federalism and state police powers.

79. The figures here represent opinions of individuals who were asked questions about *both* marriage equality and adoption rights. Individuals who refused to answer the question or who responded "I don't know" were not included in the calculations. Roughly 9 percent of participants who were asked about marriage equality did not answer the question. Six percent of those asked about adoption did not respond.

80. Human Rights Campaign, *Equality from State to State* 2006, www.hrc.org.

81. A slightly (but significantly) smaller majority opposes same-sex marriage or adoption in states that did not ban same-sex marriage through the initiative process (57 and 53 percent, respectively).

82. Strongly opposing same-sex marriage increases the probability of strongly opposing adoption by 52 percentage points.

83. Stacey Winakur, *The Daily Record,* Morris County, N.J., July 8, 2000, p. 1.

84. Interview 16.

85. Interview 13.

86. Interview 16.

87. Interview 1.

88. Interview 17.

89. See Engel (2007) for a discussion of venue spillover.

90. Interview 15.

91. Interview 2.

92. Interview 3.

93. Interview 21.

94. Interview 22.

95. Interview 23.

96. Interview 24.

97. Interview 23.

98. Interview 24.

99. Interview 13.

100. Interview 18.

101. Interview 16.

102. Interview 15.

103. Eleanor Michael, "Approaching Same-Sex Marriage: How Second Parent Adoption Cases Can Help Courts Achieve the 'Best Interests of Same-Sex Family,'" 36 *Connecticut Law Review*, 1439, 2004.

104. Christopher Colorada, "Tying the Braid of Second-Parent Adoptions: Where Due Process Meets Equal Protection," 74 *Fordham Law Review* 1425, 2005.

105. Colorada, "Tying the Braid."

106. Amanda C. Pustilnik, "Private Ordering, Legal Ordering and the Getting of Children: A Counterhistory of Adoption Law," 20 *Yale Law & Policy Review* 263, 2002.

107. Richman, *Courting Change.*

108. Interview 1.

109. Richman, *Courting Change.*

110. Jane S. Schacter, "Constructing Families in a Democracy: Courts, Legislatures and Second-Parent Adoption," 75 *Chicago-Kent Law Review* (2000): 933.

111. The U.S. Supreme Court ultimately refused to grant cert. and let stand the appellate court's ruling in favor of the Florida statute.

112. Interview 1.

113. Ibid.

114. Ibid.

115. Ibid.

116. Interview 4.

117. Ibid.

118. Interview 15.

119. Interview 14.

120. Interview 9.

121. Interview 24.

122. Interview 11.

123. Interview 12.

124. Interview 11.

125. Interview 15.

126. Interview 7.

127. Interview 12.

128. Interview 1.

129. Interview 5.

130. The case-by-case nature of family law cases, as well as the "best interest of the child" standard, grants judges wide latitude in considering the character of each individual claimant. This gives judges the opportunity to minimize the importance of the claimant's sexual orientation.

131. Richman, *Courting Change*, at 161.

132. Interview 9.

133. Interview 1.

134. Ibid.

135. Bob Egelko, "Court to Set Rules for Parental Disputes Between Gays," *San Francisco Chronicle*, September 2, 2004, B3.

136. Geoffrey Fattah and Deborah Bulkeley, "Custody Ruling May Affect Other Cases," *Deseret Morning News*, December 10, 2004.

137. Interview 6.

138. See for instance Andrea Stone, "Both Sides on Gay Adoption Cite Concern for Children," *USA Today*, February 20, 2006.

139. Interview 12.

140. Interview 3.

141. Interview 26.

142. Jim Rutenberg, "Mary Cheney's Pregnancy Is Just Fine, Bush Tells Magazine," *The New York Times*, December 15, 2006.

143. "This Week with George Stephanopolous," July 27, 2008.

144. Interview 8.

145. Interview 5.

146. Richman, *Courting Change*, 161.

147. Interview 16.

148. Interview 4.

149. Brian Tashman, "FRC's Peter Sprigg Suggests Kidnapping Laws Shouldn't Protect Gay Parents," *Right Wing Watch*, March 8, 2013.

150. Liberty Counsel website: http://www.lc.org/index.cfm?PID=14102&AlertID=897, May 20, 2014.

151. "Divorce Case Exposes Minors to Homosexual Environment," *One News Now*, June 17, 2009.

152. 129 Ohio St. 3d. 417 (2011).

153. Interview 29.

154. Bob Unruh, "Lesbian Demands Custody of Christian Mom's 6-Year Old," *World Net Daily*, April 18, 2008. Similar arguments were presented in *Embry v. Ryan*—a case involving a lesbian couple who registered as domestic partners and entered into a second-parent adoption of Ryan's biological daughter in Washington. After moving to Florida the couple split up. A Florida appellate court ruled that full faith and credit required the state to recognize the Washington adoption.

155. "Bryan Fischer Defends Call for 'Underground Railroad' Abduction of Children from Gay Parents," *The Huffington Post*, August 9, 2012. www.huffintonpost.com. Accessed on November 18, 2014.

156. In *Stadter v. Siperko* (2008) the Liberty Counsel successfully supported the rights of the biological lesbian mom to prevent visitation by her former partner. The two lesbians had not received a second-parent adoption and had not established a legally binding shared parenting agreement that recognized the role of the non-biological parent. In "Strange Bedfellows: Lesbian Moms and Anti-Gay Legal Groups," Nancy Polikoff describes attempts by gay rights opponents to partner with gay and lesbian parents; http://www.beaconbroadside.com/broadside/2008/06/post.html. Accessed on November 30, 2014.

157. Interview 3.

158. Interview 27.

159. Interview 10.

160. Interview 11.

161. Interview 10.

162. Interview 16.

163. Interview 12.

164. The population of articles on same-sex adoption/parenting available on LexisNexis was compiled using the following terms: "same-sex adopt! or parent!" "gay adopt! or parent!" "homosexual adopt! or parent!" "lesbian adopt! or parent!" This search required the mention of the term "court" and also stipulated that "same-sex marriage," "gay marriage," or "homosexual marriage" not appear in the article in order to avoid repetition among the datasets.

165. Framing was analyzed using the following coding scheme. I noted each time an article mentioned gay rights, discrimination, gay-bashing, children, children's rights/welfare, family, family values, tradition, religion, implications for society, and whether the issue creates a slippery slope. I also took note of each time the article discussed the policy in terms of legal/financial benefits or as a states' rights issue. To analyze how courts and judges were discussed, I noted each mention of the courts or judges, coded whether the statements characterized courts or judges in a negative or positive light, and categorized the specific descriptions. I also noted each time an article mentioned a court case outside of the newspaper's media market. Articles appearing in national sources or the wire services were excluded from this portion of the analysis.

166. This confirms Mucciaroni's aggregate analysis of articles on same-sex parenting between 1994 and 2004. He finds that adoption was hardly ever characterized as a rights issue but most often as a children's welfare issue. Mucciaroni, *Same Sex, Different Politics*.

167. A few same-sex marriage supporters began to lose confidence in the courts and referred to some judges as "wimps."

168. In light of the large number of ballot initiatives resulting from three court victories on same-sex marriage, understanding the degree to which adoption cases are covered beyond their jurisdiction may give us some insight into why backlash was less prominent relative to same-sex marriage.

169. Interview 15.

170. Glennisha Morgan, "Matt Barber of Liberty Counsel Compares Gay Adoption to Having Kids," *Huffington Post*, May 30, 2013, http://www.huffingtonpost.com/2013/05/30/matt-barber-gay-adoption-_n_3354661.html. Accessed on October 15, 2014.

171. Interview 28. This local organization opposed to same-sex marriage is tracking parenting litigation in their state in order to devise a strategy. During Interview 29 one opponent stated that his organization has adopted a "strategic" approach to parenting litigation. They wait for cases to come to them and then intervene where appropriate.

172. Interview 16.

173. Congress has considered legislation that would remove from foster parent and adoption agencies any ability to categorically deny individuals the ability to parent based on their sexual orientation. The Every Child Deserves a Family Act would prohibit all agencies receiving federal funding from discriminating against prospective foster or adoptive parents because of their sexual orientation or gender identity.

CHAPTER 5

1. According to the Departments of Justice (DOJ) and Housing and Urban Development (HUD), group homes are defined as "housing occupied by groups of unrelated individuals with disabilities."

2. "Room for Everyone," *Chapel Hill Herald,* December 24, 1996.

3. Tom Held, "Group Homes Get Few Warm Welcomes," *Milwaukee Journal Sentinel*, September 2, 1996.

4. Carol Marbin Miller, "Neighborhoods Resist Homes for Retarded," *St. Petersburg Times*, August 19, 1996, 1B.

5. Ibid.

6. Kimberly Pohl, "Neighbors Oppose Possible Group Home in Quiet Palatine Neighborhood," *[Chicago] Daily Herald*, February 5, 2012. Palatine has been the location of several contentious group home battles.

7. Joseph Fried, "Three Seized in Arson of Foster Home," *The New York Times*, May 1, 1987.

8. Michael Winerip, "Fire at Home for Mentally Ill on L.I. is Ruled Arson," *The New York Times*, December 31, 1987.

9. Michael Winerip, "L.I. Suspect Arson in Blaze at Site of a Proposed Group Home," *The New York Times*, February 22, 1989.

10. Stone, *Gay Rights at the Ballot Box.*

11. There have been instances where group home opponents have attempted to limit both state and federal protections for particular group homes. However, the vast majority of their attempts to block group homes comes in the form of pointed attacks against specific group home siting plans.

12. Michael Winerip, *9 Highland Road: Sane Living for the Mentally Ill* (New York: Pantheon Books, 1994), 29–30.

13. Richard Hogan, "It Can't Happen Here: Community Opposition to Group Homes," *Sociological focus* (1986): 361–74, at 365.

14. David Mechanic and David A. Rochefort, "Deinstitutionalization: An Appraisal of Reform," *Annual Review of Sociology* 16 (1990): 301–27, at 302.

15. Leonard A. Jason, David R. Groh, Megan Durocher, Josefina Alvarez, Darrin M. Aase, and Joseph R. Ferrari, "Counteracting 'Not in My Backyard': The Positive Effects of Greater Occupancy within Mutual-Help Recovery Homes," *Journal of Community Psychology* 36 (2008): 947–58.

16. Phil Sutin, "Neighbors Oppose Plan for Group Home in St. Louis County, Mo.," *St. Louis Dispatch*, November 1, 2004.

17. Alice Gomstyn, "Neighbors Hostile to Group Home Proposal," *The Providence Journal*, October 13, 2004.

18. Alia Beard Rau and Chris Fiscus, "Some Neighbors Unhappy with Influx of Group Homes," *Associated Press*, July 10, 2004.

19. Kenneth Baar, "The National Movement to Halt the Spread of Multifamily Housing, 1890–1926," *Journal of the American Planning Association* 58 (1992): 39–48, at 41.

20. Dolores Hayden, *Redesigning the American Dream: The Future of Housing, Work, and Family Life* (New York: W.W. Norton & Company, 2002), 25.

21. Hayden, *Redesigning the American Dream.*

22. Ibid.

23. Jill Replogle, "Study: Single Family Homes May be History," KPBS, December 14, 2011. www.kpbs.org. Accessed on October 15, 2014.

24. Many cities and states have drafted legislation to limit the proximity of group homes to each other in order to avoid saturation. Many courts have argued that a denial of an exemption constitutes a violation of the reasonable accommodations doctrine under the FHA.

25. "Public Understanding of Mentally Ill Lags," *The Daily News*, August 18, 1978, 3, quoting an excerpt from the President's Commission on Mental Health final report of April 1978.

26. Testimony of Leslie Scallot, "Hearings on S. 506," Subcommittee on the Constitution of the Committee on the Judiciary, United States Senate, March 21, 22, May 2, June 5, 11, and September 17, 1979.

27. Testimony of Leslie Scallot, "Hearings on S. 506." See also Kanter, Arlene S. "Home of One's Own: The Fair Housing Amendments Act of 1988 and Housing

Discrimination against People with Mental Disabilities, A," *American University Law Review* 43 (1993): 925.

28. Mental Health Law Project, "A Summary of Activities, July 1979–June 1981," July 7, 1981, p. 4. The Rockefeller Archive Center, storage.rockarch.org. Accessed on May 30, 2014.

29. Ann Marie Rizzo, Anthony M. Zipple, James Pisciotta, and Sheldon Bycoff, "Strategies for Responding to Community Opposition in an Existing Group Home," *Psychosocial Rehabilitation Journal* 15.3 (1992): 85.

30. *Halderman v. Pennhurst*, (1985).

31. Ibid.

32. *Halderman v. Pennhurst*, (1981).

33. *Halderman v. Pennhurst*, (1983).

34. 416 U.S. 1 (1974).

35. In the mid-1980s, the city of Yonkers, NY, was enjoined from continuing to use zoning to intentionally create racially segregated communities and schools *(United States v. Yonkers Board of Education*, SDNY 1985).

36. *Moore v. East Cleveland*, (1977).

37. *City of Cleburne v. Cleburne Living Center*, (1985). Although the court refused to classify individuals with intellectual disabilities (mental retardation) as a quasi-suspect class requiring heightened review, the court invalidated the ordinance using the rational basis test.

38. Harold A. Ellis, "Neighborhood Opposition and the Permissible Purposes of Zoning," *Journal of Land Use & Environmental Law* 7 (1991): 275. Ellis argues that this presumption of validity hamstrung a range of group home arguments (280).

39. The Fair Housing Act of 1968 bars discrimination in housing on the basis of race, religion, or national origin.

40. *Luger v. City of Burnsville*, (1980).

41. Testimony of Drew S. Days III, "Hearings on S. 506."

42. Testimony of Days, "Hearings on S. 506."

43. There were some who wanted to block all drug and alcohol addicts from protection. However, they ultimately decided to follow the definition of handicap articulated in the Rehabilitation Act (as amended in 1978).

44. "Markup on S. 2222 and H. R. 5200 Fair Housing Amendments Act of 1979," U.S. House of Representatives, Committee on the Judiciary, March 5, 1980.

45. Interview 32.

46. Title 42 Section 3604 (f)(2).

47. Title 42 Section 3604 (f)(3)(B).

48. The Anti-Drug Abuse Act of 1988 stipulates that in exchange for receiving federal funding, states must "establish, directly or through the provision of a grant or contract to a nonprofit private entity, a revolving fund to make loans for the costs of establishing programs for the provision of housing in which individuals

recovering from alcohol or drug abuse may reside in groups of not less than 4 individuals."

49. The 1990 language stated that a disabled individual includes anyone who "has successfully completed a supervised drug rehabilitation program and is no longer engaging in the illegal use of drugs or has otherwise been rehabilitated successfully and is no longer engaging in such use"; and anyone who is "participating in a supervised rehabilitation program and is no longer engaging in such use."

50. *Baxter v. City of Belleville*, 720 F. Supp. 720 (S.D. Ill. 1989).

51. *US v. Southern Management Corp.*, (1992)

52. Interview 31.

53. It should be noted that the standards of proof or level of review for FHAA cases on the whole is mixed across the circuits. Although many apply strict scrutiny to these cases, some circuits still apply the rational basis standard for FHAA violations. Although rational basis still provides some protection for group homes, when used in the context of group home siting cases, courts typically grant great deference to local governments and group home opponents. More recently, courts have applied more stringent standards in determining what constitutes housing opportunities. In some circuits, courts argue that equal housing opportunities require extensive housing choice for disabled individuals. Others have crafted a more limiting doctrine implying that disabled individuals are entitled to access to group homes, but not necessarily to housing in communities or residences of their choice. In these cases courts have denied a group home provider's requests for a zoning variance when there is space in other nearby group homes. Finally, although most courts employ the typical burden-shifting analysis employed in civil rights cases—requiring plaintiffs to demonstrate that the accommodation is necessary and then requiring defendants to demonstrate that the policy is unreasonable—some courts (the 4th and 5th Circuits) place most of the burden of proof on plaintiffs.

54. Laurie C. Malkin, "Troubles at the Doorstep: The Fair Housing Amendments Act of 1988 and Group Homes for Recovering Substance Abusers," 144 *University of Pennsylvania. Law Review* 757 (1995–96): 783.

55. Jonathon Rothwell and Douglas S. Massey, "The Effect of Density Zoning on Racial Segregation in U.S. Urban Areas," *Urban Affairs Review* 44 (2009): 779–806.

56. Interview 32.

57. *Community Housing Trust v. Dept. of Consumer and Reg. Affairs* (2003).

58. *Elliott v. City of Athens*, (1992).

59. The buildings were on the same lot.

60. "Ibid."

61. *City of Edmonds v. Washington State Building Code Council*, (1995).

62. *City of Edmonds v. Oxford House Inc.*, et al. (1995)

63. Ibid.

64. *Dr. Gertrude A. Barber Center, Inc. v. Peters Township*, (2003).

65. Allison Zippay, "Psychiatric Residences: Notification, NIMBY, and Neighborhood Relations," *Psychiatric Services* 58 (2007): 109–13.

66. Miranda S. Spivack, "Neighbors Oppose Effort to House Needy Near Bethesda Park," *The Washington Post*, March 23, 2008.

67. Kenneth Todd Ruiz, "Group Home, City at Odds," *Pasadena-Star News*, August 17, 2007.

68. For example, Carissa Schively, "Understanding the NIMBY and LULU Phenomena: Reassessing our Knowledge Base and Informing Future Research," *Journal of Planning Literature* 21.3 (2007): 255–66; Michael B. Gerrard, "The Victims of Nimby," *Fordham Urban Law Journal* 21 (1993): 495; Tim Iglesias, "Managing Local Opposition to Affordable Housing: A New Approach to NIMBY," *Journal of Affordable Housing*, 12 (2002): 78–121.

69. See *Combating NIMBYism[:] What a Difference a Community Makes*, The Department of Health and Human Services, http://www.promoteacceptance.samhsa.gov/publications/combatingNIMBY.aspx. Accessed on November 30, 2014.

70. Michael Dear, "Understanding and Overcoming the NIMBY Syndrome," *Journal of the American Planning Association* 58 (2007): 288–300. Accessed on October 16, 2014.

71. Frank Reeves, "A War Cry: Not in my Back Yard," *The Philadelphia Inquirer*, March 19, 1989.

72. National Law Center, "Access Delayed, Access Denied." This study found that 58 percent of opponents contacted their locally elected officials, 30 percent went to the media, 21 percent initiated a petition, and 6 percent went to court.

73. *Associated Press*, "Lawsuit Filed Over Refusal to Permit Group Home," January 23, 2004.

74. Lauren Markoe, "Good Neighbors; Group Home Finds Peace in Braintree," *The Patriot Ledger*, June 28, 1996, 11c.

75. Michael Davis, "Village Won't Try to Prevent Group Home," *Albuquerque Journal*, June 13, 2002, 1.

76. John Christoffersen, "Proposed Home for Mentally Ill Sparks Long Legal Battle," *Associated Press*, March 16, 2002.

77. "Good Shepherd Manor Sues City of Momence for Discrimination against Disabled," *PR Newswire*, May 4, 2001.

78. Zachary Mider, "Group Home Wins Temporary Court Order on Trash Pickup," *Providence Journal-Bulletin*, September 23, 2003.

79. "Ramsey Group Home Opposed; Would Aid Elderly with Alzheimer's," *The Record*, June 21, 1996.

80. Donald Bertrand, "Group Home Plan Thwarted," *Daily News*, May 15, 1996, 1.

81. Dianne Williamson, "West Side Neighbors Live in Fear; Group Home for Girls Looks at Highland St.," *Sunday Telegram*, April 24, 2005.

82. Interview 37.

83. Stanley Ziemba, "Nuns Get Preliminary OK to Occupy House in Joliet," *The Chicago Tribune*, October 6, 1998.

84. Anne Schneider and Helen Ingram, "Social Construction of Target Populations: Implications for Politics and Policy," *American Political Science Review* 87.2 (1993): 334–47.

85. Robert Wilton, "Grounding Hierarchies of Acceptance: The Social Construction of Disability in NIMBY Conflict," *Urban Geography* 21 (2000): 586–608, at 587.

86. Wilton, "Grounding Hierarchies of Acceptance," 589.

87. Cameron Whitman and Susan Parnas, *Fair Housing: The Siting of Group Homes for the Disabled and Children* (Washington DC: National League of Cities, 1999), iii.

88. Wilton, "Grounding Hierarchies of Acceptance," 591.

89. Wilton, "Grounding Hierarchies of Acceptance," 604.

90. It should be noted that between 2004 and 2006, incidences of opposition toward group homes serving emotionally disturbed youth and the developmentally disabled have decreased while opposition toward group homes for recovering drug addicts or the mentally ill has increased.

91. This does not include cases that were filed but were resolved through consent decrees or mediation, or where the suit was subsequently dropped.

92. Interview 35.

93. Letter to the Editor, *Riverfront Times*, February 2, 2000.

94. Peter Simon, "Proposal for Group Home Draws Mixed Reviews," *Buffalo News*, March 15, 1996, 5B.

95. Dear, "Understanding and Overcoming the NIMBY Syndrome," 294.

96. Ibid.

97. Laurie C. Malkin, "Troubles at the Doorstep: The Fair Housing Amendments Act of 1988 and Group Homes for Recovering Substance Abusers," 144 *University of Pennsylvania. Law Review* 757 (1995–96): 291.

98. Dear, "Understanding and Overcoming the NIMBY Syndrome," 294. Dear argues that "a major impetus for 'aggressive autonomy' was the passage of the Fair Housing Amendments Act."

99. Sarah Talalay, "Palatine's Win Based on Process," *The Chicago Tribune*, October 13, 1994.

CHAPTER 6

1. Toshiana Baker, "Planning Board OKs Group Home," *The Post-Standard*, March 26, 1997, C3.

2. Mike Todd and Karen Warren, "Not in My Back Yard," *Austin American-Statesman*, January 6, 1995.

3. Mike Ivey, "City Plan Panel Cool to Proposal for Group Home," *The Capital Times*, July 7, 1998, 2a.

4. Colbert King, "Zeke's House: The Fight Goes On," *The Washington Post*, August 18, 2001, A21.

5. Ibid.

6. Los Angeles County, Department of Mental Health, "A Guide to Successful Siting Strategies," November 2004.

7. Michael Pena, "Neighbors Shut Out Disabled," *The San Francisco Chronicle*, September 27, 2000, A19.

8. Jake Thompson and Stephen Buttry, "Opponents in D. C. Call Boys Town Bad Neighbor," *Omaha World Herald*, September 3, 2001, 1a.

9. Carolina Gonzalez, "Anger in Bay Ridge," *Daily News*, January 15, 1998, p. 2.

10. Mark Lisherson, "Fighting Barriers to Acceptance," *Milwaukee Journal Sentinel*, September 19, 1999.

11. Thompson and Buttry, "Opponents in D. C. Call Boys Town Bad Neighbor."

12. Tom Haydon, "Neighbors to Meet with Group about Home for Mentally Ill," *The Star Ledger*, August 30, 2001, 60.

13. Todd and Warren, "Not in My Back Yard."

14. Mark Brunswick, "As Group Homes Move to New Communities, a New Wave of Concern Arises," *Star Tribune*, July 14, 1997, 1a.

15. Marie Leech, "Residents Resist Proposed Group Home," *Pasadena Star-News*, February 25, 2002.

16. Tucker McQueen, "Calvary Home's Image Problem," *The Atlanta Journal and Constitution*, September 27, 1997, 5C.

17. Marie Leech, "Residents Vow to Fight Group Home in San Gabriel," *Pasadena Star-News*, February 26, 2002.

18. Clare Marie Celano, "Freehold Resident Irked at Lack of Presentation about Group Home," *News Transcript*, October 3, 2012.

19. Todd and Warren, "Not in My Back Yard."

20. Richie Rathsack, "Group Home Communicates with Wary Neighborhood," *Record-Journal*, February 7, 2011.

21. Michael Allen, "Getting Beyond NIMBY," in *The NIMBY Report* 1 (2003), 16.

22. Ann T. Fathy, "Fair Housing Law: Zoning and Land Use Issues," 14.

23. Dear, "Understanding and Overcoming the NIMBY Syndrome," 291.

24. Carissa Schively, "Understanding the NIMBY and LULU Phenomenon," *Journal of Planning Literature* 21.3 (2007): 255–66, at 257.

25. Arielle Levin Becker and Jacqueline Rabe, "Hearings on Group Home Locations Debated in Legislature," *CT Mirror*, February 7, 2011.

26. Fathy, "Fair Housing Law."

27. Mark Shanahan, "City Drops Scrutiny of Group Homes," *Portland Press Herald*, June 8, 2001, 1B.

28. Becker and Rabe, "Hearings on Group Home Locations."

29. Beth Kaiman, "Coming Home," *Portland Press Herald*, November 6, 1997, P. 4E.

30. Lisherson, "Fighting Barriers to Acceptance."

31. Fathy, "Fair Housing Law."

32. LA County, "A Guide to Successful Siting Strategies," 118.

33. LA County, "A Guide to Successful Siting Strategies," 18.

34. Interview 37.

35. Kaiman, "Coming Home."

36. Kelly B. Casey, "Group Homes Clustered in County," *Tribune Review*, February 5, 1995, 1.

37. Banducci, "Neighbors of Group Home to Take Objections to Council."

38. Interview 36, June 2010.

39. "City Council Abandons Policy of Special Meetings for Group Homes," *Associated Press*, June 8, 2001.

40. Felicia Thomas-Lynn, "Group Home Zoning Change Backed," *Milwaukee Journal Sentinel*, February 23, 2006, 3.

41. Banducci, "Neighbors of Group Home to Take Objections to Council."

42. Becker and Rabe, "Hearings on Group Home Locations."

43. Ibid.

44. Cameron Whitman and Susan Parnass, *Fair Housing: The Siting of Group Homes for the Disabled and Children* (Washington DC: National League of Cities, 1999).

45. Interview 39.

46. *Association for Advancement of Mentally Handicapped v. City of Elizabeth* (1994); *Larkin v. State of Michigan Department of Social Services* (1996); *Arc of N.J. v. N.J.; Borough of Merchantville v. N.J.* (1996); *Oconomowoc Residential Programs Inc v. City of Milwaukee* (2002); *US. v. Village of Marshall* (1991); *Children's Alliance v. City of Bellevue* (1997).

47. *Borough of Merchantville v. NJ* (1999).

48. *Regional Economic Community Action Program v. City of Middletown* (2002). See also *County of Charleston v. Sleepy Hollow Youth Inc.* (2000) ("the FHA was intended to prohibit discrimination based on false and overprotective assumptions about the needs of the handicapped."); *Tu v. City of Belleville* (1997) (decreased residential property values are not a valid reason to deny a reasonable accommodations request).

49. *Good Shepherd v. City of Momence,* (2003).

50. *Sanghvi v. City of Claremont* (2003).

51. *Cimarron Foothills Community Association v. James and Betty Kippen* (2003).

52. *Michigan Protection and Advocacy Service v. Babin* (1994)

53. *United States v. Hughes* (1994)

54. *United States v. Village of Palatine* (1994)

55. *Oxford House v. Village of Virginia Beach* (1993)

56. See for instance *Oxford House Inc. v. City of Albany.* (1993) or *Oxford House v. City of St. Louis,* (1996)

57. See for instance *United States v. Village of Palatine* (1994)

58. *Larkin v. State of Michigan Dept. of Social Services* (1996).

59. *Sunnyside Manor v. Township of Wall(2005).*

60. Interview 31.

61. Ibid.

62. Ibid.

63. Interview 35.

64. Ibid.

65. Interview 32.

66. See Jim McKeever, "DeWitt Decides Against Legal Challenge Over Group Home," *The Post-Standard*, March 10, 2005, 6; and Scott Sandline, "Limits on Group-Home Populations may be Dismantled," *Albuquerque Journal*, May 25, 1995, C1.

67. Interview 31.

68. Interview 36.

69. Interview 33.

70. Interview 37.

71. Interview 36.

72. Interview 36.

73. Interview 36.

74. Interview 34.

75. Lois M. Takahashi and Michael J. Dear, "The Changing Dynamics of Community Opposition to Human Service Facilities," *Journal of the American Planning Association* 63.1 (1997): 79–93, at 81.

76. Interview 33, May 2010.

77. LA County defines "high-profile outreach" as "collaboration with the community often starting before any formal public hearings," p. 15. See also Michael Dear, "Understanding and Overcoming the NIMBY Syndrome," *Journal of the American Planning Association* 58.3 (1992): 288–300.

78. Michael Allen, "Why Not in Our Back Yard?" *Planning Commissioners Journal* 45 (Winter, 2002): 1.

79. Iglesias, "Managing Local Opposition to Affordable Housing," 79.

80. Malkin, "Troubles at the Doorstep," 799.

81. Iglesias, "Managing Local Opposition to Affordable Housing," 80.

82. Zeke MacCormack, "Group Home Sneaks by Neighbors; Fredericksburg Ignores Zoning Code, Residents in Acquiescing," *San Antonio Express-News* (Texas), January 18, 2003.

83. Interview 33.

84. LA County, "A Guide to Successful Siting Strategies," 14–15.

85. Pat Dawson, "Group Home Residents Ok for Now," *Pittsburgh-Post Gazette*, November 14, 1996, E7.

86. Included in this sample are incidences where strategies about either notification or zoning were reported, but not both. Therefore, the total sample is larger than

the population of articles used to determine whether the group home operator could be classified as collaborative, cooperative, or stealth.

87. This group only includes articles that reported decisions on when to notify neighbors and when to obtain housing approval. Instances where only one or the other was reported are not included in these figures.

88. Any person suspected of substance abuse would be brought before each of the members of the house for a vote. If a majority of the residents believe that substances were used, the person is evicted immediately. www.oxfordhouse.org.

89. The Oxford House Manual, 1–10, www.oxfordhouse.org.

90. Oxford House Website, www.oxfordhouse.org.

91. Interview 35.

92. Ibid.

93. William H. Freivogel, "West Coast Case to Affect Oxford House Havens Here," *St. Louis Post-Dispatch*, March 2, 1995, 5B.

94. Barb DePalma, "Two Groups Urging Change in Occupancy Ordinance," *St. Louis-Post Dispatch*, November 11, 1993, Zone West, 1.

95. H. Jane Lehman, "Supreme Court to Hear Case on Group Home; Oxford House Challenges Limits on Residents as Discriminatory," *The Washington Post*, December 17, 1994, E1.

96. *US v. Village of Palatine*,

97. Interview 36.

98. Interview 40.

99. *United States v. Village of Palatine*,

100. Stanley Wenocur and John R. Belcher, "Strategies for Overcoming Barriers to Community-Based Housing for the Chronically Mentally Ill," *Community Mental Health Journal* 26.4 (1990): 319–33, at 321.

101. Zippay, Allison. "Establishing Group Housing: Community Outreach Methods," *Administration in Social Work* 23.2 (1999): 33–46, 43.

102. Allison Zippay, "Psychiatric Residences: Notification, NIMBY, and Neighborhood Relations," *Psychiatric Services* 58.1 (2007): 109–13.

103. Of course, the drawback to this approach is that only those siting instances that attracted some degree of media attention (and, likely, opposition) are included. This analysis, then, measures the degree to which group home strategy correlates with success when opposition is a factor or potential obstacle.

104. A smaller number of incidences in the sample (281) reported traceable strategies and outcomes.

105. Interview 36.

106. Ibid.

107. Interview 35.

108. Interview 37.

109. Interview 35.

110. Ibid.

111. Interview 36.

112. Quote by Pat Craig, Texas Department of Mental Health and Mental Retardation cited in Mike Todd and Karen Warren, "Not in My Back Yard," *Austin American-Statesman*, January 6, 1995.

113. Joseph Ferrari, Leonard A. Jason, Ron Blake, Margaret Davis, and Bradley Olson, "This is My Neighborhood: Comparing United States and Australian Oxford House Neighborhoods," *Journal of Prevention & Intervention in the Community* 31.1-2 (2006): 39–47.

114. Ellen Dockham, "Tension: Group Home Pits People Vs. Property," *Winston-Salem Journal*, May 1, 2003, 1.

CHAPTER 7

1. Taylor Branch, *Parting the Waters: America in the King Years 1954–63* (New York: Simon and Schuster, 2007).

2. Branch, *Parting the Waters*, 372.

3. Alison Gash, "Obama's Support More than Just Talk," *Politico*, May 11, 2012. www.politico.com. Accessed on June 22, 2013.

4. Brian Montopoli, "Obama Administration will No Longer Defend DOMA," *CBSNEWS*, February 23, 2011, www.cbsnews.com.

5. Devin Dwyer, "Critics Call Obama DOMA Decision an Executive Power Grab," *ABC World News*, February 24, 2011.

6. See *Golinski v. United States Office of Personnel Management et. al* Defendants' Brief in Opposition to Motions to Dismiss

7. Chris Geidner, "DOJ's Admission of the 'Regrettable Role' of the Federal Government in Anti-Gay Discrimination and Criticism of State and Local Discrimination is Historic," *MetroWeekly*, July 5, 2011.

8. Shep R. Melnick, "Entrepreneurial Litigation: Advocacy Coalitions and Strategies in the Fragmented American Welfare State," in *Remaking America: Democracy and Public Policy in an Age of Inequality*," ed. Joe Soss, Jacob Hacker, Suzanne Mettler (New York: Russell Sage Foundation, 2007), 51–74.

9. Melnick, "Entrepreneurial Litigation."

10. Interview 3.

11. Clayborne Carson, David J. Garrow, Gerald Gill, Vincent Harding, and Darlene Clark Hine, *The Eyes on the Prize Civil Rights Reader: Documents, Speeches, and Firsthand Accounts from the Black Freedom Struggle* (New York: Penguin Books, 1991), 213.

12. Carson, et al., *The Eyes on the Prize Civil Rights Reader* 216.

13. Sarah Flynn. *Voices of Freedom: An Oral History of the Civil Rights Movement from the 1950s through the 1980s*, ed. Henry Hampton, and Steve Fayer (New York: Random House, 1991).

14. Christine Harold and Kevin Michael DeLuca, "Behold the Corpse: Violent Images and the Case of Emmett Till," *Rhetoric & Public Affairs* 8.2 (2005): 263–86, at 263.

15. Shapiro, "Disability Policy and the Media."

16. San Francisco Gay Pride Parade, 1978.

17. "Coming Out in Middle School," *National Public Radio*, September 29, 2009.

18. Alison Gash and Judith Raiskin, *Parenting Without Protection*. Paper presented at the Annual Meeting of the Midwest Political Science Association, April 2012.

19. Jorge Rodriguez-Jimenez, "Judge Says Gay Dads Can't Adopt, Be Listed on Birth Certificate," *The Advocate*, June 18, 2014. www.advocate.com. Accessed on November 30, 2014.

20. Gash and Raiskin, *Parenting Without Protection*.

21. Charles Haar, *Suburbs under Siege: Race, Space, and Audacious Judges* (Princeton, NJ: Princeton University Press, 1996); Michael Heise, "State Constitutional Litigation, Educational Finance, and Legal Impact: An Empirical Analysis," 63 *University of Cincinnati Law Review* (1994): 1735; Klarman, "How Brown Changed Race Relations: Brown and Lawrence (and Goodridge)"; Douglas Reed, *On Equal Terms: The Constitutional Politics of Educational Opportunity* (Princeton, NJ: Princeton University Press, 2003); Rosenberg, *The Hollow Hope*.

22. Epp, *The Rights Revolution*, 6.

23. McCann, in "Reform Litigation on Trial," uses this term to critique Rosenberg's argument in *The Hollow Hope*, describing Rosenberg's analysis as court-centered.

24. Robert Post and Reva Siegel, "Roe Rage: Democratic Constitutionalism and Backlash," 42 *Harvard Civil Rights-Civil Liberties Legal Review* (2007): 373–434, at 374.

25. Interview 15.

26. See Grossman's discussion on actor success models. *Matthew Grossman, Artists of the Possible: Governing Networks and American Policy Change Since 1945.* (New York: Oxford University Press, 2014.)

27. The decision was later overturned on appeal by the 6th Circuit in *DeBoer et. al. v. Snyder et. al.* (2014) and, as of this writing, is awaiting Supreme Court review.

Index